Their Determination *to* Remain

Their Determination *to* Remain

A Cherokee Community's Resistance to the Trail of Tears in North Carolina

Lance Greene

THE UNIVERSITY OF ALABAMA PRESS

Tuscaloosa

The University of Alabama Press
Tuscaloosa, Alabama 35487-0380
uapress.ua.edu

A Dan Josselyn Memorial Publication

Inquiries about reproducing material from this work should be
addressed to the University of Alabama Press.

Typeface: Arno Pro

Cover design: Lori Lynch

Cataloging-in-Publication data is available from the Library of Congress.
ISBN: 978-0-8173-2112-3
E-ISBN: 978-0-8173-9385-4

For TJ Holland

Contents

Illustrations

Figures

TABLE

Foreword

As the majority of their nation was forced to Indian Territory in the late 1830s, a small group of about a hundred Cherokees fled to the North Carolina mountains. There, these holdouts pursued a largely overlooked path of resistance. Without tribal sovereignty or US citizenship, they built new homes on ancient homelands. But in the context of a biracial slaveholding society, they were left with no clear geographic or social place.

A community formed around the home of Betty Welch—a white slaveholding woman—her Cherokee husband, and the enslaved men and women who also lived on their modest estate. Welch's Town, as the lands became known, was distinctively of the South and the Native South. Lance Greene reveals how the members of the community retained Cherokee values, their ethos of communalism, their privileging of village autonomy, and their commitment to subsistence farming. In doing so they rejected some of the norms of the white South. Yet their connection to enslavement and other institutionalized forms of oppression shaped their resilience and resistance. Their autonomy, to some degree, relied on Welch's whiteness and the power that it provided her.

In *Their Determination to Remain*, Lance Greene has made an important contribution to the scholarship on southern and Native American history. We are delighted to include it in the Indians and Southern History series and look forward to seeing how it and the series help rewrite the history of the region and its diverse peoples.

Andrew K. Frank
Angela Pulley Hudson
Kristofer Ray

Acknowledgments

This book is the result of an immense amount of support from friends, family, and colleagues.

Paul Webb played a role at the beginning. I had searched for the Welch plantation site for two years when Paul asked whether I had seen the 1860 Valley River Gold Company map, which showed the location of the Welch house. The map was curated in the University of North Carolina (UNC) Southern Historical Collection, but at the time it had not been entered into their digital database. I found the record in the card catalog and within two weeks had located the site. Many thanks to Paul for that tidbit and for countless conversations about Appalachian history and archaeology.

The site is owned by Jim and Jeanette Wilson and farmed by Burke West. They were all very hospitable and welcoming to a group of archaeologists who took over a small plot of their pasture for weeks at a time.

Funding for fieldwork was generously supported by several granting organizations. I would like to thank these organizations for the following awards: the Wenner-Gren Fieldwork Grant, the North Carolina Archaeological Society Grant-in-Aid Program award, the UNC Center for the Study of the American South Summer Research Grant, and the UNC Research Laboratories of Archaeology Timothy P. Mooney Fellowship.

The archivists and librarians at the UNC Southern Historical Collection, the David M. Rubenstein Rare Book and Manuscript Library at Duke University, the National Archives, and the National Anthropological Archives were knowledgeable and obliging. In particular, Daisy Njoku and Barbara Watanabe at the National Anthropological Archives and Lindsay Muha at the National Archives were incredibly helpful in providing information on the locations of historic maps and photographs. A portion of "Welch Plantation, December 1850" was published in Lance Greene, "Community Practice in a Post-Removal Cherokee Town," in *Investigating the Ordinary: Everyday Matters in Southeast Archaeology*, eds. Sarah E. Price and Philip J. Carr (Gainesville: University of Florida Press, 2018): 39–52.

I would like to thank Tom Whyte for his extensive analyses of the Welch site faunal collection. Tom has always been willing to share his extensive knowledge of historic and prehistoric Southern Appalachian foodways. Rob Cuthrell, under the guidance of Margaret Scarry, performed floral analysis that helped me address key questions.

Steve Davis of the Research Laboratories of Archaeology at UNC generously offered to photograph Qualla vessels for me, and Trevor Lovin, the Cherokee County GIS Coordinator, provided digital copies of the Reuben Deaver maps.

I owe a great debt of gratitude to the anonymous reviewers for their detailed and thorough review of my manuscript. In particular, one reviewer provided broad recommendations and line-by-line comments, which significantly improved this book.

Wendi Schnaufer at the University of Alabama Press has tirelessly supported me and this project. I appreciate her willingness to keep gently nudging me and to advocate for me.

My interest in Cherokee removal era archaeology began when I volunteered on excavations of Cherokee farmstead sites directed by Brett Riggs. That experience drew me to historical archaeology and sparked a growing interest in the archaeology of Native American life. Brett introduced me to the story of the Welches and has been key to the project. Brett's insight and knowledge are unparalleled, and his mentorship has been invaluable. We have shared some fascinating, hilarious, and occasionally terrifying moments together in the field. I value his support and friendship.

William (Bill) Jurgelski's excellent research on the Cherokee reservees has been a wonderful resource. Bill and I became good friends on an archaeological project in a part of the world far from southern Appalachia. Years later we realized we had the same research interests. Working with Bill has always been rewarding; he is a first-rate scholar and a hilarious storyteller.

So many anthropology professors have guided and mentored me. I want to acknowledge Gerald Schroedl, who first introduced me to archaeology and then taught me how to do primary research. Vin Steponaitis served as a mentor and advocated for my research. A warm debt of gratitude goes to Silvia Tomaskova, who enabled me to think about archaeology in new ways and nurtured my confidence. Her teaching and mentoring have been incredibly important to me.

A small group of research colleagues was wonderfully supportive. Carie Little Hersh, Mark Plane, Julio Rucabado-Yong, and Mook Kim made my experience more interesting, rewarding, and calm. Discussions with Mark about archaeological method and theory greatly improved my research, while his humor sustained me. Other UNC students, including Amber Vanderwarker, Chris Rodning, and Tony Boudreaux, contributed their time and knowledge during my research. Colleagues Dan Sayers and Jared Wood willingly listened as I worked through problems in the manuscript. I received feedback on several conference presentations from numerous colleagues, including Phil Carr, Hank McKelway, and Todd Ahlman.

I directed excavations at the Welch plantation site in 2004 and 2006. I was lucky enough to have a crack team of archaeologists help me perform the fieldwork. I was even luckier that they were all good friends. Brett Riggs, Scott Shumate, Bill Jurgelski, Mark Plane, Jon Marcoux, Greg Wilson, and Eric Hoover, sometimes paid but usually not, tirelessly worked to carefully excavate and document the site. Their unenviable tasks included bailing out waterlogged features, endless backfilling, and establishing barbed-wire and electric fences to deter curious cows from stepping into our excavation units.

During my fieldwork and archival research I got to know many members of the Eastern Band of Cherokee Indians (EBCI) in Cherokee and Robbinsville, North Carolina. I have enjoyed those interactions, and they taught me a lot about Cherokee history and culture. I would like to thank the staff of the Tribal Historic Preservation Office and the Kituwah Preservation and Education Program. In particular, it has been a pleasure to work with Russ Townsend and Beau Carroll. I have enjoyed working with Tom Belt, the Coordinator of the Cherokee Language Program at Western Carolina University; he has taught me a great deal.

I would like to thank Noeleen McIlvenna for the countless conversations about history and archaeology. She challenges me to keep writing but reminds me that there is more to life than work. Her love and support keep me balanced. Tess Greene, as always, entertains me. Her strength and courage make me strive to be a better person.

I dedicate this book to my close friend TJ Holland. As director of the Junaluska Museum in Robbinsville and as Cultural Resources Supervisor for the EBCI, TJ was always willing to share his expertise. I worked with TJ for fifteen years; he was always a supportive, insightful colleague. Beyond that, his friendship and generosity made my time in western North Carolina a joyful experience. Our long conversations about archaeology, history, fine art, railroads, and gardening enriched my life. Without TJ this book would not have been possible.

Introduction

We continued our course S.W. down the [Valley River] valley on the right bank
of the stream, the valley enlarging to a mile of rich bottom land surrounded
by lofty and picturesque hills covered with fine woods. This was the Paradise
of the Cherokees, their wigwams being built on graceful knolls rising above
the level of the river bottom, each of them having its patch of Indian corn with
indigenous beans climbing to the top of each plant, and squashes and pumpkins
growing on the ground. The valley now contracted as we advanced but contained
a great many thousand acres of the most fertile land. Any thing much more
beautiful than this fine scene can scarcely be imagined; two noble lines of
mountains enclosing a fertile valley with a lovely stream running through it.

—George Featherstonaugh, *A Canoe Voyage up the*
Minnay Sotor (London: R. Bentley, 1847)

On August 27, 1836, George Featherstonaugh, an English geologist who
observed much of the Cherokee removal in North Carolina, rode on
horseback along the banks of the Valley River, admiring the scenic beauty.
Here he paused and witnessed "the Paradise of the Cherokees," known locally
as the Valley Towns, a collection of Cherokee communities spread out along
the upper Valley River in the mountains of western North Carolina.[1] His writing presents an idyllic contrast to the violent ethnic cleansing attempted by the
US Army two years later against those communities he was describing. The
Trail of Tears, carried out in thousands of instances across the southeastern
US, marked a dark turning point in American history when racially motivated
attacks on Native Americans became government policy. Yet some communities subverted this state power. One such community is the subject of this story
(Figure I.1).[2]

In mid-summer 1838, around four hundred Cherokees in the Valley Towns
chose to remain in the area at any cost. They actively resisted the US Army
during the military occupation of their land. They did not use force, as the army
expected, but fled into the mountains. There they evaded the army, all through
the fall until late November. A third succumbed to starvation, disease, and

exposure. Children and elderly died in staggering numbers.[3] But by using these tactics, those who survived remained in their homeland and would be able to rebuild their towns. The postremoval era presented new challenges. They had no home of their own; the state had sold their lands at auction. They were not citizens of North Carolina or the United States and retained no rights provided by these governing bodies. What lay in store for these stateless people?

Their Determination to Remain tells the story of one segment of those Cherokees, roughly a hundred people, whom the army classified as "fugitives," hiding from military forces and avoiding the forced emigration. The central characters are the Welches, a family who risked everything to help the "fugitives." Betty Welch, a white woman, and her husband, John Welch, identified by the army as a "mixed blood" Cherokee, owned a plantation along the Valley River. They held nine African Americans in bondage. The Welches, like the people they helped, paid dearly for their actions against the US Army. John Welch was imprisoned, abused, and permanently disabled by army officers, and his children had to flee the state to avoid arrest. The enslaved African Americans

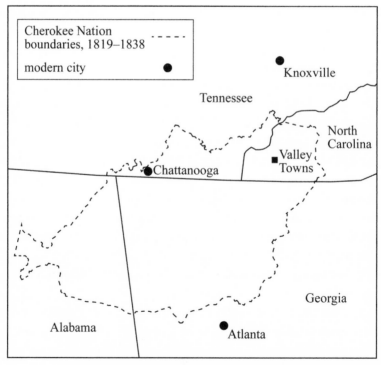

FIGURE I.1. Boundaries of the Cherokee Nation, showing location of the Valley Towns. (Lance Greene)

on the plantation, like the Cherokee "fugitives," saw a third of their group die during the military occupation. After the army left the region, the Welches helped the fugitives build a new community on their plantation, called Welch's Town. Betty became the plantation owner and a forceful spokesperson for the people there. In telling the stories of these people, this book reveals changes in racial and gender violence, and the impacts of these institutionalized forms of oppression. But it also shines a light upon Cherokee resilience in the face of monstrous power.

The story of the Welches, and hundreds of other Cherokees who quietly risked their lives to stay in the mountains, is an important part of American history. Buried in the archives and in countless archaeological sites, their important narrative reveals the gaps and weaknesses in state power and the ways that groups with few resources sidestep or subvert that power. *Their Determination to Remain* investigates the lives of people rarely discussed by historians. Although the sad history of the Trail is widely known, little has been written about the resistance to the forced emigration by "ordinary" Cherokees, those who were not wealthy or directly involved in politics.[4] Their story's significance lies in its focus on a small community's successful subversion of military occupation and subsequent challenge to racial hegemony. It also reveals the complexities of racial and gender stereotypes, and the horrifying impacts of those assumptions on people during the antebellum era.

Their Determination to Remain attempts to answer several related questions: 1) How did the people of Welch's Town reclaim their livelihood and their community? 2) What was the relationship between the Welch family and the members of Welch's Town, and did it include exchange of goods or services? 3) What political, economic, and social power did Betty Welch exert, and were these powers based on her control of a plantation or on the rights of women in traditional Cherokee society? 4) What was life like for the enslaved people, mostly women and children, held captive by the Welches, and how was it different for them compared to those held by white enslavers on Upper South plantations?

The answers to these questions extend beyond the Valley Towns of the 1830s and 1840s. They reveal changes in perceptions of race and gender occurring in the United States and affecting the lives of millions of people. They address significant issues in Native American and African American histories and race and gender studies.

The central challenge and goal of this book is to counter the "archival silences" that have diminished and, in some cases, vilified these people. These archival silences, which refer to the power of the written document, and its writer, to objectify the person or people being written about, were extremely successful tools of oppression. They continue to serve that role in the erasure of individuals and groups from the past. For example, historian Marisa Fuentes argues that the records written about enslaved women in eighteenth-century Barbados portray them as "spectacularly violated, objectified, disposable, hypersexualized, and silenced." Historians and historical archaeologists who attempt to tell these stories have the daunting task of reconstructing the fullness of lives intentionally hidden or misrepresented.[5]

This research is unique in its approach to telling these stories. Historic documents of the removal and postremoval eras of the Valley Towns are intertwined with archaeological data from the site of the Welch plantation. In excavations performed at the Welch plantation site, archaeologists recovered artifact assemblages that document the period from roughly 1820 to 1850.[6] Archaeology challenges archival silences; although archaeological remains never present a complete picture, they escape the political biases that guide the creation of historic documents. Broken and discarded artifacts and other remnants of everyday life were deposited with no intent. Yet our trash reveals who we are.

≈

By the time Featherstonaugh looked across the Valley River, the Revolutionary era "Indian Wars" of the southeastern United States had been over for forty years. Americans were quickly settling throughout the region. Yet tens of thousands of Native Americans still called the region home and controlled millions of acres. The value of land soared as cotton became more profitable; capitalist desires to acquire tribal lands drove violent racism. Although forced emigration had been discussed since George Washington's presidency, the urgency grew throughout the early nineteenth century. Cherokees, like the other tribal groups, understood this growing pressure and fought to withstand it and maintain their land.

Indian removal was tied to other major trends of the 1830s. A cotton boom, an influx of European immigrants, and the expansion of African American enslavement drove westward expansion and capitalist growth. This decade witnessed immense changes in the politics, economy, and demography of the United States. The Cherokees and other southern tribes were not immune to these events or to the effects of Jacksonian "democracy." By the time of the

Cherokee removal in 1838, more commonly known as the Trail of Tears, the Upper South was enmeshed in this quickly expanding market system. In contrast to the popular myth of nineteenth-century Southern Appalachia as a precapitalist, egalitarian society, the region was, by 1840, characterized by the control of land and wealth by a few, by intergenerational poverty, and by an increasing rigidity in racial and gender classifications.[7]

Those Cherokees who refused to leave the region adhered to the concept of town and community autonomy. In the fall and winter of 1838, they thwarted the power of the army. Afterward they faced growing racism, as an influx of white people expected the region to be free of any Native American presence. They were also separated from the bulk of the tribe, now settled almost a thousand miles away in "Indian Territory." The absence of the vast majority of tribal members weakened social networks, created enormous stress, and heightened the fear of the unknown for those few who stayed.

As a plantation mistress, Betty Welch wielded incredible economic and social power beyond the plantation at a time when married women had very limited rights. As recent research shows, plantation mistresses embraced the racial violence of enslavement and profited from it.[8] It is clear that Betty embraced slavery, even though she had spent her entire adult life in Cherokee society, where racial hierarchies were more fluid. The power that Betty exercised was partly due to her marriage to a Cherokee man who had few of the rights white citizens enjoyed. Historic documents reveal strategic timing in changes of property ownership and legal powers. By 1841 Betty owned the plantation and maintained power of attorney for her family. The family understood that whiteness provided unassailable rights.

My research also attempts to recover the lives of those enslaved by the Welches. At the time of removal, the Welches held nine African Americans in bondage. Three—Isaac, Nelly, and Phillis—were adults. Six were children, including Nelly's daughter Jane and Phillis's children, Bill, Claire, and Henderson. A six-year-old boy named Frank, whose parentage is unclear, was also a member of this group. When the US Army began arresting people on the Welch plantation in September 1838, Nelly also had a newborn baby, less than two weeks old. The army marched all nine of the enslaved to Fort Cass, a concentration camp in eastern Tennessee. Three would die there.

Until the last decade, there have been few extensive studies of Cherokee enslavement.[9] Recent research critically investigates the phenomenon. Historians Tiya Miles and Fay Yarbrough tell the stories of two very different Cherokee families and their involvement in African American enslavement.[10] Their combined work begins to reveal Cherokees' changing perceptions of slavery throughout the nineteenth century and how the Cherokee Nation struggled, culturally and legally, with the institution. Tiya Miles's book, *The House on Diamond Hill*, is based on the Diamond Hill plantation operated by James Vann in the early nineteenth century, which held enslaved a Black community of over one hundred people. Although the book focuses on the two-story brick house built by Vann's son Joseph in the early 1820s, Miles successfully discusses the radical changes in Cherokee society during the early decades of the nineteenth century, which included the enslavement of African Americans.[11] In contrast, the enslaved at the Welch plantation before removal had access to no such population. On the farm there were eight or nine people, and there were few other Black individuals, enslaved or free, in the region. How did they view the demographic shift—the emigration of Cherokees and immediate influx of white people—that the removal wrought? Did it eliminate any hope of freedom? In the years following removal, the white population grew, as did the population of enslaved African Americans. Did this expand the community for those held on the Welch plantation?

Racial hierarchies were inseparable from definitions of gender. Eighteenth-century Cherokee society had well-defined gender roles in which both women and men had specific but relatively equal duties and privileges. Years before the removal in 1838, Cherokee women saw their political and economic power diminishing. Although their mothers had enjoyed the full right to speak in town councils, women were now largely excluded from council meetings. Many Cherokee men began to see themselves as rightful property owners, patriarchs, and politicians. Women were acutely aware that this loss of power applied to many aspects of their lives. Within a span of a generation, their rights to own property, to participate in public debate, and to transfer tribal identity to their children were weakened or lost.[12]

While racial classifications were becoming more formalized in the Southeast, gender roles were becoming equally calcified. Classification of white women illustrates the connection between race and gender clearly. White women were becoming the arbiters of whiteness and "purity" within the household, which was being defined as the central place of value creation in the new republic. As the main arbiters of these values, white women had to separate themselves from "degraded" and "inferior" races, both Indian and Black. Whiteness was central to maintaining value, so racial separation was central to being a good American. In white society, expectations of Black, white, and Indian women underpinned racial hierarchies. As white women came to be seen as the arbiters of purity and submission, Black and native women became castigated as lascivious, demanding, and dirty. These perceptions of the latter groups had a long history in colonial conquests but were sharpened and redefined in the early nineteenth century.[13]

The impact of these definitions of racialized gender clearly played out in the removal on Valley River, where numerous women and children of Cherokee and African American parentage died, but Betty Welch remained on her plantation and all of her children survived. In this setting Betty gained her substantial power through different cultural perceptions. In her branch of Cherokee society, most people still understood the role of women as economically and politically powerful. In white society Betty gained her power from her whiteness and her control of the labor of nine enslaved African Americans. Betty's image, from a white perspective, suffered from her marriage to a Cherokee man.[14]

For Cherokees, the Valley Towns region that Featherstonaugh traversed in the summer of 1836 was the core of their tribal land base. Even as leaders ceded enormous tracts of land during the late eighteenth and early nineteenth centuries to the American state in hopes of preventing war or removal, this region always held several communities, partly because the mountainous landscape limited white inroads. The physical landscape was imbued with Cherokee myth. Ancient stories were tied to specific locations, such as Tlanusiyi, a spot at the mouth of Valley River that was the home of a giant leech, and Sehwateyi, a mountaintop at the head of the Cheoah River where a giant hornet had its nest.[15] Historians have often claimed that this attachment to the land was the reason Cherokees resisted persistent attempts to remove them. Indeed, Cherokees in the mountains were very attached to their land, particularly the old towns, including the "mother towns" that held great historic and spiritual significance.[16]

However, they were equally attached to their communities, in ways that were inseparable from the geographic locations in the region. The autonomy of Cherokee towns and the town as a key marker of identity are well documented in the literature on eighteenth-century Cherokees.[17] They struggled to maintain their towns, which served as the foundation for autonomous, local governance, including centuries-old kinship structures. This strict adherence to local autonomy is referred to here as localism. A town was the nexus for cultural interactions. In conjunction with the clan system, it helped define appropriate age, gender, and family roles. Cherokee culture was matrilineal and matrilocal. Children inherited their clan identity from their mother, and when a woman and man married, they lived in the town of the woman's mother. Women in these communities wielded significant political and economic power. This power was threatened by the dissolution of town autonomy and the rapid expansion of Cherokee national laws.[18]

With such a tight allegiance to the local, many Cherokees rejected national governance, whether from the United States or even the newly created Cherokee Nation. The laws of the Cherokee National Council and the newly formed Cherokee National Committee, originally constituted in 1809 to withstand external pressures to sell tribal lands, quickly shifted to internal matters and began converting the Cherokee Nation into a capitalist, patriarchal society. National laws passed in the early decades of the nineteenth century limited the powers of autonomous Cherokee towns and outlawed practices that had been Cherokee tradition for centuries.[19]

Some small Cherokee communities, in rejecting these rapid changes, left the Cherokee Nation beginning in the first decade of the nineteenth century. Groups migrated as far as Arkansas.[20] Others traveled just outside the boundary of the Cherokee Nation. The Calhoun Treaty of 1819 enabled Cherokee families to become "citizen reservees" and to acquire land in the United States, if they were willing to surrender Cherokee citizenship and accept US citizenship. Articles 2 and 3 of the treaty stipulated the rights of the "reservees." Each head of household who accepted a 640-acre (1 square mile) tract accepted United States citizenship and held their "reserve" in fee simple, which could be sold by them or willed to their children. Although American leaders thought none would accept, in fact around seventy-five families accepted the offer. Most of the reservees chose a tract that adjoined several other reservees' tracts, thereby reestablishing their communities and creating a much larger area owned by Cherokees. The Welches accepted the offer. Reservees included the Owls, Axes, and other families who would live at Welch's Town two decades later. They abandoned the Cherokee Nation in 1819 to establish their own communities, constructed on the old villages and mother towns along the Little Tennessee River.[21]

They would make the same choice twenty years later. As the bulk of the tribe was forced west, they opted to separate from the Cherokee Nation in favor of maintaining their local towns. The members of Welch's Town also kept other core elements of Cherokee society. Community ethos, corporate responsibility, and subsistence-level farming were mainstays in the rejection of Western society.[22] Although on the surface it seems unlikely that a group of "traditional" Cherokees would be so closely connected to the Welches, a planter family, their connections make sense in light of decades of interaction. They shared important cultural ties. For the Welches and the members of Welch's Town, as with many other Cherokees at the time, the central factor in being "traditional" was town membership.

Historians have sometimes defined nineteenth-century Cherokee individuals or groups ambiguously as "traditional" or "westernized," with little clarification of what those terms mean. However, cultural change during the era varied by geography and other variables, and different aspects of society changed at different speeds. For Cherokees of the era, "traditional" could refer to participation in cultural practices including community-based clans, matrilineality and matrilocality, subsistence-level farming, and community sharing of labor and goods. These practices maintained the economic and political power of women in Cherokee society. "Traditional" has also been used to refer to fluency in the Cherokee language, a belief in medical/spiritual practitioners such as conjurers, a variety of phenotypic traits, and citizenship.[23]

Historians John Finger and Theda Perdue have argued that, for the eastern Cherokee in the early nineteenth century, "traditionalism" included subsistence-level farming, localism, and adherence to clan laws. This included following clan strictures about marriage as well as the continued practice of "blood vengeance" or "blood law" (see chapter 1 for description of this phenomenon).[24]

In an investigation of the 1835 census, William McLoughlin and Walter Conser Jr. documented different levels of cultural change at the time of the removal. The study focused on geographic variation and found that "the Cherokees of North Carolina were distinctly different from the rest of the nation in 1835. Those Cherokees living in the Great Smokies had less racial mixing, proportionately fewer white skills, proportionately less wealth, and proportionately fewer readers of English." "White skills" referred to the use of spinning wheels, looms, and mills and to plowing with a horse or mule. The study also documented a much lower per capita number of enslaved African Americans. This region, the mountainous section of the Cherokee Nation and roughly coinciding with the westernmost portion of North Carolina, was long considered by visitors a "traditionalist" stronghold.[25]

Finger makes an important observation. Although Cherokees in the mountains were considered more "traditional" than most Cherokees in other parts of the Cherokee Nation, they were quite different from their parents' or grandparents' generations. Communities were composed of "nuclear families in log homes" and "practiced a primitive agriculture, supplemented by hunting, fishing, and gathering." Finger writes that these traits were similar to those of white farmers in the region. He also shows that for most of these Cherokee families, men had started doing much of the agricultural work and saw themselves as head of household. These "headmen" of towns led meetings at townhouses, which were considered physical symbols of a localist approach and a rejection of national governance. They also continued playing stickball and performing all-night dances. Finger shows that even in the mountains substantial changes were occurring in local Cherokee society. He argues that many Cherokees in the region accepted a "nominal kind of Christianity" in which Cherokees participated in both traditional belief and Christian worship.[26]

Here, I argue that the aspect of "traditionalism" most significant to the members of Welch's Town was localism, which, of course, incorporated other aspects of Cherokee culture, including an adherence to the role of the clan system. Instead of using the term "traditional," I attempt to be more specific and use descriptions such as "eighteenth-century" or "clan-based," depending on the context. For example, the intrusion of Cherokee national governance, such as outlawing "blood vengeance," was a usurpation specifically of clan law, and not a broad attack on "traditional" Cherokee life.

While the Welch family embraced certain aspects of Western society, they also adhered to some facets of Cherokee communal society, as illustrated by their giving aid during and after removal to many of the Cherokees who fled into the mountains. Welch's Town was a Cherokee enclave that existed for more than fifteen years (1839–55), during which these two communities, the Welch plantation and nearby Welch's Town, functioned separately. The former, a southern plantation, was public and disguised the latter, a small Cherokee community, from public view. Low visibility was important in the years after removal. Widespread white resentment was projected onto Cherokees who still lived in the area. The associations forged between the Welches and the members of Welch's Town were a classic patron-client relationship, which allowed this and other Cherokee communities to remain in North Carolina.

Patron-client relationships, or clientelism, generally include reciprocity, an unequal balance of power, a dyadic structure, and face-to-face interaction. Within this reciprocal relationship, however, there is a wide range of inequality between patron and client, based on the ability of the patron to supply protection, goods, land, or other necessities that the client has difficulty acquiring. The client, in accepting the terms of the relationship, in return supplies labor, defense, or other skills needed by the patron. Alternatively, the client can "vote with his feet" and abandon the relationship altogether. Clientelism usually involves face-to-face interactions between patron and clients and is a central aspect of how the relationship is formed and evolves. The economic aspect of the relationship is only one of many. The relationship is often based in trust and affection between the groups. A patron and client may be associated by kinship, locality, a series of exchanges over a long period of time, and intergenerational patronage.[27]

Clientelism can also serve to form bonds between members of the groups as they deal with outside pressures from the state or from colonial powers. This may be the case with the Welch family and other reservees; they lost significant holdings under the 1819 Calhoun Treaty. The displacement of so many Cherokees from their 640-acre reservations shortly after the treaty increased distrust of the US government among many Cherokees in the region.[28]

This relationship did not form overnight as a response to removal. The Welches and many of the members of Welch's Town had known each other for decades; community ties with other Cherokee families living along Valley River between 1820 and 1838 probably played a significant role in the Welches' decision to direct and supply large-scale resistance to forced removal.

The Welches ultimately retained control of their plantation on Valley River. Much of their property was stolen during removal, but their land was safely held by Capt. John Powell, a white ally. More importantly, their land would constitute a safe haven for numerous Cherokee families, many of whom had nowhere else to go. The Cherokees who remained in the area were traumatized by loss but had achieved their goal of enduring in their homeland, away from the Cherokee Nation and, at least for a time, from the federal government. In the aftermath of the removal, for those who had hidden in the mountains and watched their children die from starvation and disease, being "Cherokee" took on new meaning.

For the Welches and those living in Welch's Town, town membership overruled other classifications, including race, ethnicity, and citizenship. The exception on the plantation was African American enslavement by the Welches, which illustrates the changing perception by at least a portion of Cherokees regarding race and slavery. This was the third community living on Welch land—nine enslaved African American men, women, and children. During the removal, their arrest and imprisonment in eastern Tennessee resulted in the deaths of a third of the group. This mortality rate was similar to those of many families of Welch's Town during the removal. This may have drawn those two communities together in the following years. Close social interactions between Cherokees and African Americans during this era have been documented in other parts of the old Cherokee Nation.[29] In the case of the Welches it is unclear if their enslavement of African Americans affected their relationship with the members of Welch's Town. Although little is recorded about how most Cherokees felt about enslavement during the early nineteenth century, it was still uncommon, especially in the mountainous regions of the Cherokee Nation. A small number of free Black individuals lived in the region at the time, as well as a small number of people of African Cherokee descent.[30]

The figure of Betty Welch provides some insight into the violent and unpredictable world of racial and gender violence in the antebellum South. Up to the time of the removal, Betty is almost invisible in the historic record. Illiterate, she left no personal papers. However, the unusual circumstances of the removal and its aftermath propelled her into a position of power. As the only white head-of-household, the real estate and property of their plantation were transferred into her name. She forcefully maintained the farm and publicly fought for the disbursement of Cherokee funds and for the right of Cherokees to stay in North Carolina in the face of a secondary removal effort in the 1840s. Her ability to achieve this power and status resided in her marriage to a Cherokee man and her acceptance of Cherokee tradition. Documents reveal she exercised considerable influence both with the army during removal and with white businessmen afterward. For them, her power derived from her ownership of a plantation. While most accepted her influence, they certainly did not enjoy it. In 1844, Betty foiled the plans of lawyer J. W. King, who was trying to swindle claims funds from a Cherokee family. In correspondence to his partner he referred to her as "that Demon in Human shape."[31] For Cherokees, her influence was less controversial. As noted, women in eighteenth-century Cherokee society had held a great deal of economic and political power.

Cultural Hybridity

In untangling these strands of cultural adaptations in a triracial household during the mid-nineteenth century, a theoretical approach that focuses on how and why people make choices in multicultural encounters is useful. Interpretation of the material culture left behind by the people on the Welch plantation and the choices they made is guided by theories of hybridity. Hybrid cultures display a mix of social and cultural traits that derive from the interactions of different cultures. Hybridity theory reveals an ambivalence experienced by people in these situations, in which some aspects of a new culture, often particularly material culture, are welcomed, even as other aspects, such as social, political, or military control begin to erode their sovereignty. Theories of cultural hybridity enable the study of encounters between different cultures, beginning with the first European colonial endeavors, and continuing to the present. Anthropological studies of cultural encounters have been widespread for decades, focusing on similar phenomena, such as acculturation, assimilation, creolization, and syncretism.[32] Studies of acculturation and assimilation have been criticized for focusing too much on the loss of indigenous practices and material culture in the wake of European colonialism, and have largely been abandoned.[33] Creolization and syncretism are still in use, but most anthropologists see these phenomena as representing different kinds of interactions or results than hybridity.[34]

The concept of hybridity has been used in anthropology to understand a variety of colonial encounters.[35] In these studies, hybridity can be briefly defined as "the new cultural forms produced through colonization that cannot be neatly classified into a single cultural or ethnic category."[36] This definition applies to novel combinations of material culture as well as novel artifact forms. It also includes nonmaterial aspects of culture, such as language. As anthropologist Matthew Liebmann clearly describes, the definition and use of hybridity differs from the other forms of cultural interaction in other ways. Liebmann writes that hybridity "shines a light on the subversive, counterhegemonic discourses inherent in mixed forms."[37] It allows one to look at these hybrid forms and cultures as challenging the power and authority of the dominant culture. Certainly, wealthy Cherokee planters such as James Vann and Major Ridge challenged the hegemonic southern white culture by publicly displaying, through their wealth, education, architecture, dress, and language, that they could achieve an elite status that rivaled southern white planters".[38] Their attempts were not completely successful, as the expanding ideology of "whiteness" excluded people of color from permanently or fully enjoying this status. If wealthy Cherokees such as the Vanns and Ridges did use their wealth to challenge the hegemony of elite white culture, we must also consider their actions within the Cherokee Nation. For much of the tribe, their actions created consternation and resentment. Many considered their motives to be centered on their own personal wealth, not on maintaining a tribal land base.

This attempt by a small minority of Cherokees, however, brings to light another aspect of hybridity: the "profound ambivalence generated in colonized peoples, the simultaneous appeal of and aversion to colonialism."[39] A discussion of this ambivalence is significant in that it shows that there was not a singular reaction by Cherokees or other groups to colonization or the on-slaught of Western people and ideologies. Within the Cherokee Nation, a con-tinuous and nonlinear tug-of-war persisted regarding non-Cherokee people, behaviors, and material culture. As historical archaeologist Kathleen Deagan points out, an artifact introduced from outside the group at some point may become normalized and seen as "traditional" by its users within the group.[40] This is certainly the case with some of the imported artifacts that appear on mid-nineteenth-century Cherokee sites. Some items, such as brass kettles, were accepted by most very early and became "traditional" artifacts relatively quickly. Other materials, such as Western styles of architecture (brick houses) and men's dress (silk coat and vest), continued to be rejected by the majority well into the nineteenth century. By 1830 Cherokees had been in contact with white traders for over a century, and much of the material that traders sold them—brass and cast-iron kettles, firearms, and iron tools such as axes and hoes—was not necessarily considered "foreign." The same is true for livestock such as hogs, cattle, and chickens, and plants such as apples and peaches. Many of these items became so incorporated into Cherokee life that they were seen as normal or "traditional," even though the materials had a recent introduc-tion into Cherokee life. Most Cherokees understood the advantages of some Western goods and, while simultaneously resenting Western inroads into their country, desired some of these materials. This ambivalence makes the mean-ings of artifacts from archaeological contexts more difficult to interpret but reflects the complexity of personal and social ties and behaviors.

Part of the varied nature of acceptance of Western traits was the issue of cultural grammar.[41] Sometimes the transition from one artifact or material as-semblage to another was easy, because the cultural grammar was similar. For example, cast-iron kettles were similar in form to the large open-mouthed ce-ramic vessels produced for centuries by Cherokee women. However, in the case of many of the artifacts discussed here, this was not the case. Handmade Cherokee ceramics reflected the cultural grammar tied to food production, consumption, and sharing. Cherokees consumed much of their food from communal bowls and pots, and did not sit down together to eat meals at pre-scribed times. The ceramic vessel assemblages (as well as utensils) associated with Western modes of consumption—matching sets of plates, cups, and sau-cers—were ill fitted for these practices. Therefore, the presence of large num-bers of sherds associated with these ceramic wares indicates a transition in those households to Western dining practices.

While much hybridity theory focuses on two groups—the colonizer and the colonized—we must consider the three groups on the Welch plantation, and within the Cherokee Nation as a whole. The diversity of people on the Welch farm after removal included several ethnic and racial backgrounds. Trying to understand the function and meaning of imported (Western) goods on the plantation is a useful endeavor, but we must also consider the effects of the African American population. We have no record of the backgrounds of the enslaved people held by the Welches. At the Vann plantation, some of the enslaved in the 1820s were from central or western Africa. If this was the case on the Welch plantation, a hybrid culture on the farm might have included material culture, foods, language, and other cultural practices from not only Cherokee life and Western culture but African influences as well.

Archaeologists have stressed the importance of local context in understanding hybridity.[42] Archaeologically, it is the collection of materials—the ceramic sherds, glass fragments, the architectural and food remains—that lets us tease out how a family or community lived. In addition to the artifacts, the context of the kinds of deposits these material assemblages were recovered from is important. For example, were the artifacts recovered from a cellar pit, a privy, or a midden deposit? Were they all present in a single soil zone, or scattered throughout several depositional events? Were they thrown into the cellar pit, or did they wash in after the house was gone? An acute focus on these questions as a basic methodology in archaeology has enabled archaeologists to gain more knowledge of past cultures than was earlier considered possible.

A focus on the social, cultural, and economic context of a group is also important in archaeological research. In this case an appropriate scale and question might be: "What were the main cultural, economic, and political concerns for Cherokees in the mid-nineteenth century, and how did their material culture reflect these concerns?" In this approach, time and space have a major impact on how a group conceives of and uses certain kinds of material culture. For example, when blue shell-edged pearlwares were introduced into the market in the 1820s, elite families acquired them as status symbols, as a means to display wealth and luxury. By 1840 the popularity of the ware had declined, and they were seen as everyday dishes for most people. The context can be made even more specific. For Cherokees, blue shell-edged pearlware had additional layers of meaning, including an acceptance of Western styles of dining wares and adherence to patterns of individualized servings and regularly timed meals.

The more we know of the historical context of the group we are studying, the more the material culture helps us interpret the cultural beliefs of that group. Archaeologists Ian Hodder and Scott Hutson clarify this: "The subjective internal meanings which archaeologists can infer are not 'ideas in people's heads,' in the sense that they are not the conscious thoughts of individuals. Rather, they are public and social concepts which are reproduced in the practices of daily life."[43]

≈

The archaeology of the Welch plantation, then, can help us see how they conceived of their place in the social environment roughly a decade after removal, how they fit themselves into a society that included small enclaves of Cherokees and ever-growing numbers of white and Black people.

This contextual approach in archaeology has some similarities with what has been termed microhistory by historians. Methodologically, study begins at the micro-level, generally a particular site or person. As the investigation continues, the scale is expanded to a regional or national level and incorporates a discussion of larger-scale economic and political issues of the period. In this way, the study of a single site can inform large-scale events. Much of the research done in historical archaeology, whether stated explicitly or not, incorporates a microhistory approach, in which an archaeological site is used, ultimately, to make broader statements about the political history of the period. This is also often the case in history, including Cherokee history; Miles's *The House on Diamond Hill* uses this approach.

Research in archaeology and social history has intensified its focus on embodiment: the physical lives that people lived and the sensory experiences of their existence.[44] In *Contested Bodies*, Sasha Turner discusses the struggle between abolitionists and planters to control enslaved women's reproductive lives in Jamaica in the early nineteenth century. Turner argues that "thinking of enslaved people as having bodies that could be adorned, experience pain and pleasure, reproduce, and express desire, for example, allows us to access alternative experiences of slavery."[45] In *Their Determination to Remain*, I attempt to investigate those "alternative experiences" for all who survived along the Valley River after the removal. Archaeology is a powerful tool in the study of embodiment. It focuses on the quotidian, the unremarkable aspects of daily life. In investigating past lives, archaeologists look at sites and material culture. Landscape, architecture, clothing, adornment, dining, tasks, games, and leisure activities are revealed by careful excavation and analysis.

METHODS

The chapters in this book are organized to counter the archival silences using a variety of approaches. The first involves the use of primary documents to establish a historical narrative. A wealth of primary documents allows us to track some aspects of the Welches from 1835 to 1855. Most of these documents are tied to the removal or its aftermath. The military project of forced emigration required the creation of several kinds of census, property, and real estate data that otherwise would not exist for the Cherokees of the 1830s and 1840s. Many of these data include racial and gender stereotypes of Native Americans as perceived by officers and by white civilians hired to aid in data collection. Other sources derive from federal census records, local correspondence, and storekeepers such as William Holland Thomas, who was closely involved with the North Carolina Cherokees during and after removal and who was an obsessive record keeper.[46]

Second, archaeological evidence is intertwined with historical narrative and provides a unique insight into the choices that people made in the past and how they viewed themselves socially and culturally. Archaeological excavations at the Welch plantation focused on three subsurface cellar pits that had been beneath the floor of the first house, a small cabin, the Welches built on the property in 1822. During excavations archaeologists recovered hundreds of artifacts dating from 1820 to 1850. The wide variety of artifacts include mass-produced items such as ceramics, glasswares, utensils, buttons, brass pins, gunflints, and cut nails. A smaller number of hand-carved stone items like smoking pipes, gaming disks, and talc pencils reflect the continuation of some local Cherokee crafts. Hundreds of bone fragments tell us what the Welches consumed, and how they processed and prepared their foods, and help answer the question about the relationship between the family and the members of Welch's Town.[47]

The material assemblage reveals information about the lives of the Welch family roughly a decade after the removal. Excavations at the Welch house site enable us to see into the world of the Welch family in an intimate way that historic documents alone cannot. The materials from the three cellar pits reflect the activities of a wealthy family that outwardly presented themselves as westernized plantation owners, with a substantial house filled with imported dining wares to host officers, agents, and businessmen. The artifacts also reveal the continued production and use of hand-carved items that Cherokee men had been making for centuries. The lack of certain artifacts, such as handmade

Cherokee ceramics, illustrates that not all local crafts were practiced on the plantation.

Just as historic documents were created through a variety of biases, archaeologists are challenged by the biases of deposition and preservation in the archaeological record. It is a different problem than in archival research; there is very little intentional human bias. People unconsciously lose small artifacts and throw away broken ones. The bias is created through preservation and deposition factors. Organic materials such as food remains (often with the exception of bone), wood, leather, and fabric rarely survive in the ground; bacteria consume these materials quickly except under specific environmental conditions. Differences in deposition, how and when an artifact is deposited on a site, affect what can be recovered by archaeologists. Is it buried quickly or left on the ground surface? Is it in an area that will be disturbed by erosion, or is it in a protected soil layer? These factors create a bias of absence and misrepresentation of certain kinds of artifacts. It is the task of the archaeologist to identify the effects of these factors and account for them. As historians deal with human bias, archaeologists are challenged by the biases created through natural phenomena.

In historical archaeology those gaps are often addressed through the historic record. For example, the 1850 federal agricultural census describes the Welch farm production in detail. We know how much corn and oats they grew, the number of livestock they raised, and how much wool they produced. In contrast, the faunal data tell us that the Welches also ate wild game such as deer, rabbit, turkey, raccoon, largemouth bass, and snapping turtle, none of which are documented in the historic record. The combination of these data helps us address some of the research questions posed here. The Welch plantation output barely increased through the 1840s, although they had an increased labor force of seventy-five to one hundred people (the people of Welch's Town) living on their land.[48] Both archaeological and documentary data suggest the members of Welch's Town did not provide substantial or sustained labor on the Welch plantation. An investigation of federal census records reveals the labor provided by the Welch family and the people they enslaved was adequate to manage annual crop and livestock production. The Cherokees of Welch's Town did provide labor, by tending Welch livestock in the mountains and providing the Welches with wild game and plant foods, a practice documented both through historic records and faunal remains. But it was seasonal and relatively insignificant within a plantation economy. The Welches could have fared quite well with the labor provided by themselves and the people they held in bondage. In addition, Betty proved she was not interested in the legal fees stemming from the Cherokee claims that so many lawyers clamored for in the years following removal.

The combination of data also enables us to reconstruct the plantation architecture in more detail. The removal era property valuations describe the Welch's first house on Valley River, built in 1822, as a single-room log cabin with a stone chimney base and stick-and-clay chimney. Archaeologists excavating the cellar pits beneath that structure found fragments of window glass, revealing the presence of at least one window, a rare element in most Cherokee houses of the period. The lack of foundation stones and post features suggests the house was built on sill logs.

A wealth of historic documents and the remnants of the material world at the site, spanning from roughly 1820 to 1850, helps interpret the Welches' views on some of the issues that underpinned their lives: the racial, ethnic, class, and gender prejudices of the antebellum era. They also help us understand how the Welches viewed themselves and their "place" within the various communities along the Valley River. This combination of historic and archaeological data enables historical archaeologists to expand our knowledge of foodways, architecture, clothing and personal adornment, and personal behaviors that often reflect aspects of identity, such as smoking; the smoking pipes archaeologists recovered from the site were handmade from local pipestone, even though store-bought molded clay pipes could be purchased at local stores for pennies.

A third kind of evidence is presented here. "Welch Plantation, December 1850" presents a fictional narrative of the Welch plantation roughly a decade after removal. Evidence for the events in the narrative comes from both archaeological excavations at the Welch house site and the primary documents written about the Welch family during and after removal. Such fictional accounts have been used previously in archaeological research and have served at least two purposes.[49] First, this form of writing can bring historic characters to life more than standard academic approaches, by creating an intimate view of their lives. Second, these stories can generate questions the researcher had not considered and therefore can serve as a form of research. In *Black Feminist Archaeology*, Battle-Baptiste writes that her exposure to classic works of African American fiction enabled her to "see outside of the archaeological toolbox" and allowed her to fill gaps in the discussion of research at archaeological sites.[50] How did the Welches negotiate the three worlds in which they participated: small Cherokee towns, the enslaved African American community on their plantation, and the expanding white settlements around them? Why did they support the Cherokees hiding in the mountains during removal? How did they maintain their strong support for Cherokee sovereignty and yet hold African Americans in chattel slavery?

Historians have also embraced alternative genres of writing. Marisa Fuentes, discussed earlier, uses fictional narratives to counter archival silences. Tiya Miles's novel *Cherokee Rose* tells the story of Jinx Micco, a Cherokee woman in the present day who travels to the site of the Cherokee Rose Plantation in northern Georgia to research a girl who disappeared from tribal records. There she meets Cheyenne Cotterell, an African American woman who has just purchased the plantation. In telling the story of these two women and their recounting of the difficult history of their families, Miles tells the story of Cherokee enslavement of African Americans prior to removal.[51]

Their Determination to Remain is largely organized chronologically. Chapter 1 provides a broad description of the Cherokee Nation at the time of removal. During the 1830s the members of the Cherokee Nation were struggling with the questions of how to stave off demands for more land cessions and how to adapt to Western society. A small percentage of Cherokees openly embraced the tenets of capitalism and began to practice large-scale agriculture and other business ventures. Perceptions of race and gender were shifting within the nation as well, and some Cherokees accepted the enslavement of African Americans as part of the capitalist enterprise. Chapter 1 also describes some of the major Cherokee land cessions of the early nineteenth century and the responses by Welches and the people who would become members of Welch's Town.

Chapter 2 discusses the nearly three-year military occupation of the Cherokee Nation from 1836 through 1838 and how military operations and resistance to forced emigration were carried out in the Valley Towns. The removal was a full-scale military occupation of a sovereign nation, and the commander, General Winfield Scott, called it a war. The Cherokees who fled his advancing armies and the enslaved African Americans on the Welch plantation suffered great loss.

Chapter 3 describes the immediate aftermath of the removal. Cherokee families struggled to find a place to live. Welch's Town formed quickly, and the Welch plantation itself underwent major changes. The enslaved people on the Welch farm who survived removal endeavored to recover from the deaths of so many in their community but otherwise found their world little changed as their forced labor continued. The chapter also investigates how racial and gender roles and expectations affected members of the different communities on Welch land.

Chapter 4 describes the daily and seasonal tasks carried out on the plantation and in Welch's Town and how the different communities there adapted to the postremoval environment. Chapter 5 focuses on the legal challenges faced by the Cherokees along the Valley River after the removal. Constant solicitations by lawyers, ready to swindle them out of the funds owed them by the government for lost property, troubled the community. Throughout the 1840s, as federal agents attempted to coerce the Cherokees in North Carolina to agree to a "voluntary removal," Betty Welch repeatedly appears in the historic record as a staunch defender of Cherokees' rights to remain in the state and to receive all of the funds owed them.

~

In the 1830s much of America saw Cherokees and other Native Americans as symbols of a past age in a rapidly industrializing nation. The federal government used military force to carry out the goals of the state, what would a few years later proudly be called Manifest Destiny. Yet many Cherokees and others resisted these violent changes. Some, such as the Seminoles in Florida, fought back through armed combat; others, such as several Cherokee national leaders, through petitions. The Cherokees of the Valley Towns resisted by fleeing and hiding in the steep mountainous areas they had known for generations, and that the army was ill prepared to traverse. During and after removal, however, they needed assistance. Wealthy landowners such as the Welches and William Holland Thomas provided resources and, after removal, places to rebuild. These patrons were necessary for other reasons; their whiteness protected them from attack and arrest. They enjoyed additional power through their wealth, much of it dependent on enslaved labor. Ironically, those African Americans held in bondage enabled a small number of Cherokee families to challenge white hegemony; Cherokees like the Welch, Ridge, and Vann families defied the ideology of white supremacy by establishing plantation estates.

The relationships between "full-blood" Chinoque Owl, "mixed-blood" John Welch, and African American Isaac in the summer of 1838, as with all the relationships on Welch land, existed within the context of southern gendered racial hierarchies. Power struggles, attempts at control, obedience, tradition, and resistance occurred on the ground and face-to-face. The story of the Welches during the mid-nineteenth century illustrates the complexities of race and gender in the antebellum South and reveals a story of coordinated resistance to state power.

Their Determination to Remain attempts to explain how those complexities affected the lives of three intertwined communities during the antebellum era. It uses primary documents as well as archaeologically derived material culture to describe the lives of these people. Telling the stories of the people within these three communities equitably is a challenge and reflects what Fuentes calls the "conditions under which our subjects lived."[52] The oppression and demonization of individuals and groups in the 1830s and 1840s create difficulties in retelling their lives now; historians' and archaeologists' subjects are often largely absent in the historic record. Presenting the people who lived on Welch land as complex actors making practical choices within this context is the goal of this book.

Welch Plantation, December 1850

John Welch rested on a rough handmade chair placed near the front door of the log house. The winter sun was setting, and harsh, oblique shadows spread across the brown fields below him, to the narrow strip of trees that lined the Valley River. The plantation he and Betty had built was thriving. Behind the house, out of sight, numerous buildings, other cabins built for his nine slaves, stables, workshops, and a blacksmith shop, attested to the wealth of the family. This was in spite of all that had happened. John could barely make out the trees in the distance, even the large sycamores with their grayish-white trunks and peeling bark. He even needed help walking these days. Not that long ago he had been in the prime of his life, but that was before.[1]

John turned his attention to a log cabin that stood no more than fifty feet from where he sat. It looked old and decrepit and small. It had no windows, only a small front door. The rough board roof sagged, and the old stick and clay chimney was beyond repair. The large sill logs resting on the ground were beginning to rot, and the three cellar pits beneath the rough puncheon floor, used for decades to store fruits and vegetables, soured. This was the house he had built with Betty thirty years ago, when they first came to the Valley River. That was the first time white men had tried to run them off their property, back in 1819, and that time they had been successful. Even though Betty was white, John thought, she wasn't like most white people. She had lived most of her life with Cherokees. She had learned to speak Cherokee early on, mainly because John and most others didn't speak English and saw no reason to learn it. By the 1830s their family was growing fast, and they had built their new house, with the help of Isaac, a slave they had owned for years. This new house was big, forty feet long, with two rooms. It was more comfortable than their first house and had modern furnishings—plank floors, shuttered windows, and a heavy stone chimney base. They had kept the old house and turned it into a kitchen. There the women of the plantation, family members and slaves, cooked and performed other tasks, too. They mended clothes and sewed new clothes for farm use and for sale at William Holland Thomas's store nearby. The kitchen was the domain of women, and John rarely entered.

Finally, Betty came out of the house and urged John to come back in. The sun had set, and the chill was settling fast. She took his arm and helped him slowly back into the house, and into a chair near the large fireplace. The cold bothered him so much more than it had before his imprisonment.

It was December, and the morning frosts were getting heavier. The Welches had put up the last of the crops, and now they turned to cold-weather jobs of farm maintenance and indoor activities. Betty had discussed with John construction of a new kitchen for a couple of years, and they now agreed the job needed to be done. It would require a lot of labor, for it involved not only building a new kitchen but tearing down the old one. Everyone would be involved in the construction. John had requested the help of the *gadugi*, the communal work party, from nearby Welch's Town. He knew they would help, but he still followed the proper procedure of approaching the town leaders, Chinoque, whom some called John Owl, and The Axe. They immediately agreed to help. It would be difficult for the Welches to do the job alone, given John's ill health, a reminder to Welch's Town that, years ago, he had suffered along with them.[2]

A few days later, most of Welch's Town came to the farmhouse. Chinoque and Liddy Owl led the largest group from the small cluster of cabins on Townhouse Branch. The Axe and Aqualla walked with their children—Salkana, Nelly, Ihuhy, Eteganah, and George—and their families, some of whom lived close by, on Welch's Mill Creek. Others came from other directions to the plantation on Valley River. In all, over fifty people gathered, young and old, from the scattered cabins of Welch's Town, clustered along Welch's Mill Creek and Townhouse Branch, Hanging Dog Creek, and Vengeance Creek. They had lived here for just over a decade on Welch land, and the small community was growing. They brought with them food collected in the mountains. Betty had prepared for their arrival. The area behind the old kitchen was set up for cooking on a large scale, with massive cast-iron pots and kettles hung over cooking fires. Piles of firewood bordered the area, and tools had been set out around the kitchen. Betty had her slaves working on it. She depended on Phillis, whom they had owned almost as long as Isaac. Phillis had been preparing nonstop, cleaning out every item from the old kitchen, and bringing up plenty of food from the new, large cellar under the main house. Phillis's baby was not a year old and required more care than most her age. She had Jane helping her, mostly by keeping the baby while she cleaned or hauled food. Phillis loved Jane like she loved her own daughters; she was the only thing left to remind Phillis of

Nelly. Jane couldn't remember her mother, and Phillis often described Nelly's funny ways that had always made Phillis laugh.

Just cleaning out the old kitchen had taken most of the previous day. Most numerous were the items used in cooking for the three dozen or so people on the plantation. The dishes—including blue-rimmed plates; delicate red, green, and blue hand-painted bowls and cups; and sponge-patterned saucers—were stacked and moved carefully to the main house. Phillis had strained under the weight of the heavy stoneware crocks used to store fruit through the winter, and the stoneware butter churns she carried to the barn or into the house. Untold hours had been spent by women churning the fresh buttermilk into cream and butter. Betty made good money selling butter in Murphy, although not nearly as much profit as from selling homemade clothing. Countless other items for cooking and serving food, the glassware and utensils, tinware cups and bowls, and a large tin coffee pot, were all moved to the main house until the new kitchen could be stocked. Several rough chairs scattered around the dark kitchen had provided a space for women to sit and sew. Not that the fireplace and a candle in a brass stand that sat on a small table had ever provided much light. They talked as they worked, and the small items they worked with in the dark and smoky room often slipped from their fingers. Brass pins, bone buttons for rough work clothes and brass buttons for jackets, tiny brass hooks for clasping handmade dresses, all fell onto the uneven puncheon floor. The split-log floorboards were old and sagging, and gaps had opened up between them. Hooks and pins fell through the large cracks, could not be recovered, and were forgotten. In this old kitchen, all of the women living on the plantation worked at tasks as long as there was daylight. Mostly they spoke English. Neither Phillis nor the younger slaves spoke Cherokee very well, and the Welch women spoke English as easily as they spoke Cherokee. After dinner the Welches would return to the main house. Phillis and her daughters would continue their toil into the evening. At one time she had had Nelly to keep her company, but that was before the army marched them all across the mountains to the prison camp.

Shortly after daybreak the men gathered at the kitchen. Ned Welch and John Powell were in charge of the work. Ned, John and Betty's oldest son, now a capable farmer himself, lived nearby with his family. John Powell was the only other white person on the plantation, and it had taken the community a long time to accept him. After all, he had come to the Valley River as a militia officer during the occupation. Even after he had married Mary, John and Betty's oldest daughter, many in the community hesitated to trust him, but that was in the past. Ned's brothers were there to lend a hand as well. Isaac, who had helped the Welches build their first house, was gone, but Frank, whom they had also owned for years, was now eighteen and was assigned many of the same tasks. The other men had come from Welch's Town. Old Axe couldn't do much, but his strong sons would do their part. John Owl, Toonahnaluh, and Locust were there, as were Feather, Teesuttaskih, and Wayuhahtillih. Nearly two dozen men in all began tearing down the kitchen shortly after daybreak. They would reuse many parts of the old building, although dismantling was more time consuming than razing. The board roof, composed of rough-sawn lumber from a sawmill on Valley River, was old and rotted. The boards were taken off and stacked near the cook fires to be burned by the women. The men saved many of the cut-iron nails, but the rusted and bent ones were dumped unceremoniously on the ground.

The women built and maintained the fires in the yard behind the house and prepared an astonishing variety of foods. Betty was in charge of organizing the food preparation, but she, like everyone, deferred to Aqualla, who gave orders to the younger women. Betty's daughters Mary and Martha, and the women from Welch's Town—Liddy and Winnih Owl, Aqualla's daughters Salkana and Nelly, and Ahnewakih, Nancy Feather, Cunnooweelih, and Nahyuhhoola—worked steadily. They would keep the fires burning and the pots cooking for the next two days. The other women from Welch's Town—Jinnih, Nicy, Ihyohstuh, and Ollie—all had children under five years old. These young mothers took turns watching the children inside the Welch house. Although nothing seemed unusual to these younger people, for the older people of Welch's Town, men and women, it was a beautiful wonder to have so many small children in the community.

People huddled around the smoky fires, thinking about the job ahead of them. The women roasted and boiled several kinds of meat: beef, pork, chicken, turkey, and domesticated rabbit. During the fall the people in Welch's Town had been tending the Welch cattle and hogs in the mountains, where they fattened on mast, thick beds of acorns and chestnuts. A cow had been butchered for the occasion, and the beef was boiled. Chinoque chopped the limbs into pieces with an axe, and then broke open the dense long bones with a hammer. Chinoque had learned this method from his parents and grandparents. This way they got all of the marrow, with its fat needed to survive harsh winters. They had done it with deer. Chinoque, like others his age, had found it worked just as well with cows and pigs, although people outside Cherokee communities who saw the practice refused to try it.[3]

Betty had selected several chickens and turkeys from their fowl yard, and rabbits from the hutch. She preferred the domesticated European rabbits, which grew larger, to the wild cottontail rabbits that were native to the region. She had Phillis bring out corn from the crib and beans, apples, and peaches from the cellars. Betty had bought rice from Thomas's store. It couldn't be grown in the mountains and was a regular import from the lowcountry. She also purchased coffee beans, and a large tin coffee pot was kept full all day. Betty had made sure her own children were hard at work. Rebecca was now fifteen, and Betty charged her with making sure the roasting ears of corn, still in their husks, did not burn. Rebecca wanted to be in the house, where it was warm and where she could play with all of the children. The women of Welch's Town prepared more fires to cook other kinds of foods. They had brought white-tailed deer, wild rabbit, raccoon and squirrel, wild greens, and nuts.

As the wind carried the heavy smell of wood smoke mixed with the scents of numerous dishes being prepared, the men faced the heaviest part of the job: dismantling and moving the large hewn logs that made up the walls of the structure. The logs had been set in place thirty years before and had settled and been sealed together with years of chinking—clay used to fill the gaps between the logs, hardened by long exposure to sunlight. Many of the logs were still in good shape and would be reused. John and Isaac had originally hewn and notched them by hand to fit one on top of the other, and Ned carefully marked them with a thick pencil carved out of talc. The old puncheon floor was discarded, though. It was worn and rotted in places, and a plank floor would be built in the new kitchen.

The new kitchen would be a single room, the same dimensions as the old one, built onto the back of the main house. There would be no interior door, no access through to the main house. A doorway on the side would be the only entrance, because making a new doorway was time consuming and unnecessary. Although it was not far from the site of the old kitchen, Ned and Chinoque harnessed two horses to drag the logs to the back of the house. New logs had already been cut, and the young men lifted them onto flat pier stones collected from the banks of the Valley River, raising the entire structure off the ground. In this way, the addition would last longer.

By this time daylight was fading, and hungry people gathered behind the old kitchen. Everyone shared the kettles of soups and stews. The women from Welch's Town were a little dismayed that Betty had no handmade pottery. They, like their mothers and grandmothers, cooked in a variety of clay pots made by women in the community. Although condescendingly referred to by many white people as "dirt pots," Cherokees knew they performed better in many ways than cast-iron or brass containers. For one thing, the thick walls of Cherokee vessels kept food from burning. Also, they were much lighter than cast iron, and not so brittle. They made do with the cast-iron pots Betty provided—heavy, black kettles, Dutch ovens, and skillets. Aqualla had supervised the preparation of a stew made of deer and beans and thickened with crushed chestnuts. Beef stew had simmered all day, near a fire where chicken was fried in a massive skillet. Salkana panfried several large-mouth bass, caught that day with hook and line in the Valley River by John and Betty's youngest son, Lloyd. Cunnooweelih had pounded chestnuts in a heavy wooden mortar and baked the meal, mixed with corn meal and water, into a rich bread. Laid out were pots of beans with thick chunks of pork, milk made from ground hickory nuts mixed with water, roasted peanuts, sunflowers, grapes, mulberries, blueberries, and honey locust. The ears of corn, left roasting unattended, were scorched before Chinoque smelled them burning. Betty called Rebecca's name, and she ran frantically from the house. Betty scolded her sharply, but all Chinoque could think of was his own daughter who would have been Rebecca's age.

Frank and Phillis stopped for a few minutes to eat and talk. Such moments were rare for them during daylight hours. She couldn't believe her oldest son would have been eighteen this year, the same age as Frank. The two boys had been best friends when they were little. She tried for a second to remember what Bill had looked like but quickly asked Frank if he had enough to eat. Even though the new kitchen meant a lot of work for Phillis and Frank, they seized this rare chance to eat as much as they wanted.

If it had been warmer, there might have been a stickball game and dancing. The evening chill was already setting in, though, and people mingled around various fires and in the house. A few dogs wended their way through the groups of people, grabbing bits of food dropped or thrown onto the ground, then scrambling quickly into the darkness to gnaw the remaining bits of meat off a bone. In one group someone pulled out a flask of whiskey. While most Cherokees refused to drink alcohol, a few men gathered to warm themselves with it. Ironically, the green-glass flask was impressed with an image of Andrew Jackson, the architect of the removal. A few of the men left and walked south along the newly built State Road. A few miles from the plantation, despite local outcry, stood a grog shop where Cherokees were served liquor. The Cherokees in Welch's Town had been discussing for a few years the possibility of moving to the Qualla Towns or to Buffalo Town, where there were fewer white people moving in and fewer such problems.

Several men and boys gathered around one of the fires, stoked high with weathered boards from the old roof to provide warmth against the cold. They refused to drink but instead each took out a small, bluish-green stone pipe. Many had carved their own from small cobbles gathered at outcroppings of pipestone along nearby creek banks. Some had purchased theirs from Thomas's store for a quarter. They talked as they smoked, first discussing the progress of the work so far. Lloyd was one of the youngest boys there. Although already eleven, he still stayed close to his father, John, and was usually the first to offer to help him walk to Welch's Town or somewhere else away from the farm, or to get his pipe or some other item he might need. They spoke in Cherokee in the Giduwha dialect, as most of the Cherokees from the Valley River did. Here, John Axe was called "Eteganah" by most people, while miles away in the Qualla Towns, people pronounced it "Etekanah." Cherokee was the first language for all in the group, and it was all the older men spoke. John would normally have been inside already on such a cold night, but he would not miss the chance to visit with so many old friends and hear news and maybe some of the old stories.

Their discussion turned quickly to *anetsâ*, stickball. They discussed the recent stickball game in Qualla, where William Holland Thomas had actually paid the players to play a game for the visitor Lanman. This had not happened before, and the older men were concerned about the game being played for money. Certainly, Cherokees had bet on games, but never had players received pay just so a white visitor could watch a game. The conversation turned to a better game, played a few years ago on Tallulah Creek, not far from Buffalo Town. The western team, players from Buffalo Town and Welch's Town, had played the eastern team, from the Qualla Towns. The game had been so thrilling, and the tales were growing as the stories were retold. The play that was the center of talk had been led by Harry Morris, Gideon and Rebecca's son. He was only a few years younger than Ned, and John thought of how many times the two had played together, at stickball and other games. In the last play, the Qualla players, desperate to stop Harry from scoring, had run two horses across the field. Harry had dived around the first and under the second and scored the final point for the western team. The older men beamed. They had all seen the game, and indeed it had been memorable, even for the older men who had been watching stickball since the days of Dragging Canoe. The Axe, very animated by the discussion, told the small group that he had never witnessed such a game. He noted that Harry was Junaluska's nephew, and that same spirit that had driven Junaluska to charge the Redsticks at the Battle of the Horseshoe had obviously been passed on to Harry. His excitement fell as it occurred to him that he had never had a chance to see his youngest sons play stickball, and he turned his face away from the fire into the darkness.[4]

Like John, Eteganah loved the old stories, and he was a good storyteller. His favorites were the "wonder stories" that told of monsters and spirits. He began to recite the story of Tlanusiyi and the Great Leech. All had heard it before but loved the story when delivered by a good teller. John loved this one especially, because it had all happened so close by. Tlanusiyi, "the Leech place" lay only about ten miles downstream, at the mouth of the Valley River. There, where the river emptied into the Hiwassee, was a deep hole, with a large rock ledge running beside it, across the riverbed. No one walked across that ledge anymore. Too many had been carried off by the Great Leech, red-and-white-striped and as big as a house, diving down into the hole in the rock and sending up such a plume of water that people were knocked into the hole, their mutilated bodies found later along the riverbank. Only a few years ago, two women had, against everyone's pleas, gone out on the ledge to fish. The great plume of water spouted out, and one woman almost lost her baby as the wave swept across the rocks. It was obvious that the leech still lurked, still so dangerous, and few people ventured near the place, although it was a convenient crossing.[5]

By the time Eteganah had finished his story, John noticed the cold seeping through his frail body. Stiffened, he tried to stand, but lost his footing and dropped his pipe. It fell with a sharp clink, as it landed on a large cobble laid against the fire. Lloyd grabbed the pipe for his father and handed it to John as he regained his balance. He looked at it and saw the large chip knocked out of the polished bowl. Muttering quietly, he hesitated and then tossed the pipe into the fire. Lloyd saw the dispirited look on John's face. He would remember these moments and these stories decades later, when serving as Principal Chief of the Eastern Band. As the evening chill deepened, most people said their farewells and walked back to their houses. A few stayed at the farm, sleeping in the house on the floor or in the barn.

Early the next morning a heavy white frost lay on the ground. The women built fires and tended babies shortly after daybreak. The men began the strenuous process of finishing the walls of the kitchen and adding a roof. Betty had hired a local white stone mason to build the chimney base. He had cut limestone from a nearby quarry and carted the large blocks to the site a few days earlier. He worked efficiently with his sons building the solid-stone base and firebox. They constructed several courses of stone, and would raise the stone box about four feet above the ground. The Welches would later finish the chimney with sticks and clay, to a level just above the roof. As the stone mason added levels of cut stone to the firebox, several men nailed wooden planks to the rafters. The kitchen addition was only a single story, and not as tall as the house.

With the roof completed, the Welch household began stocking the new kitchen. Betty had Phillis and Jane haul the table and chairs into the small room. They carried in the dishes and heavy crocks—out the front door of the main house and around to the entrance of the kitchen. All of the sewing materials and other items used by the women in the kitchen were slowly restocked. The brass candle stand that had sat on the table in the old kitchen for so long had been damaged in the move. Betty told Jane to carry it over to the big, open holes of the old cellar pits and throw it in. Phillis watched as Betty gave Jane orders. All the children of Betty, Nelly, and Phillis had grown up together, and yet their lives were so different. Phillis felt her rising anger. Her only friend, Nelly, had died shortly after childbirth, being forced to march to those prison camps in Tennessee. The baby perished on that trip too, as had her own son, Bill. Mrs. Welch was pregnant when the soldiers came, but her children suffered no such fate—they let her stay on the farm, and she could see her children every day. At the same time, she loved Betty's children; she had helped raise them. The people in Welch's Town had lost children too, and they were usually nicer to her and her children than were the white people living along the Valley River. She shook herself out of those thoughts and got back to work—the Welches might stop work at sundown, but she couldn't.

Again the wide variety of foods was available for all. There was no set mealtime—people stopped working when they got hungry and ate as much as they needed, going back to work soon after. The labor continued for the rest of the day, and the kitchen structure was completed by nightfall. The men took breaks and ate and mingled in different groups. Slowly then, families began gathering up their belongings and heading back to their small farms. There was more work to do to get the kitchen ready, but these things the Welches could do on their own.

The last thing to do was fill in the three open cellars that had been beneath the old kitchen, now a hazard. The clutter of the last three days—ashes and food remains, broken pottery and glass, bent nails—was dumped in, load by load. People shoveled the waste into large handmade baskets, made by the women of Welch's Town and traded to the Welches. In some baskets thick beds of ashes still smoldered. Lloyd laughed as Rebecca dumped out the charred remains of several ears of corn. At the same time, children swept the entire yard. The ground around the pits, which had been beneath the old structure for thirty years, was thick with debris. Lost pins and buttons, broken pieces of pottery and utensils, and discarded pieces of tin were swept in as well. Later the holes were capped with fresh dirt. The area of the old kitchen was transformed into part of the swept yard of the main house, the fill and trash in the old cellars eventually becoming hard-packed and invisible, forgotten.

John sat again near the front door of the house, the morning sun warming him. He smoked the new pipe Ned had carved. The small, bluish-green pipe fit easily in his hand, and it worked well enough, but he was surprised at how much he missed the small task of carving it himself. His fingers could no longer do such intricate work, neither could his eyes focus well enough. John looked across the open yard. The old kitchen had blocked his view of the steep, wooded crest line of the Snowbird Mountains. Now he could see, if somewhat blurrily, the small clearings where The Axe and others had built their cabins. It didn't seem to him that it had been over a decade since the soldiers had camped within view of his farm. His frail body reminded him every day of what he and others had endured. John Powell, although no longer in the army, kept up with news of current military campaigns. He had talked a lot about the fighting in Mexico. Supposedly General Scott was a hero. John thought of those four months in Scott's guardhouse and gripped the stone pipe harder. The worst days were over, though. It had been a few years since the government had sent their agents to convince them to move west. The state had even made Junaluska a citizen and granted him land in Buffalo Town. Now other Cherokees were buying land. In spite of all that had happened, John thought, they had succeeded, their survival a triumph.

1

CHEROKEES DURING THE EARLY REPUBLIC

Our company took the liberty of entering all the houses we came to, and as that of Eonah-con-a-heite, or the Long Bear, was the best specimen, allow me to . . . give some notion of his cabin. A small, uncomfortably close room answered for the bed-chamber, dining room, pantry, boudoir, and all, save for kitchen and meat house. The cups, saucers, plates, knives, forks and other things, were of a peculiar whiteness, and were all carefully placed away in the rough cupboard, which the Long Bear had fastened to the wall. Then there were his rifle brightly polished and deposited over the door; his blow-gun, a hollowed cane from one to one inch and a half in diameter, with well thistled arrows, occupying a place on the joists above, and his bow and arrows, whose twang and unerring aim had brought many a squirrel, bird and rabbit to grace his table.

—ALEXIS, "A Visit to the Cartoogechaye Indians," *North Carolina University Magazine*, no. 1 (1851): 116–18

A student from the University of North Carolina with the pen name Alexis and his party made the somewhat arduous journey from Chapel Hill into the mountains of Cherokee County in the southwestern corner of the state in the summer of 1851. There they spent a day intruding into the houses of Sand Town, a Cherokee community on Cartoogechaye Creek, just outside of Franklin, North Carolina. Alexis's observations of Long Bear's cabin, while dripping with a patronizing tone, probably provide a relatively accurate description. Alexis did not see (or at least did not document) handmade Cherokee ceramics, but he highlighted the combination of handmade items and mass-produced, purchased goods. Perhaps Alexis misunderstood the "peculiar whiteness" of the dining wares because he expected everything to be rough and handmade. His preconceived notions regarding Native American culture are clear.

By 1830 the Cherokees had been dealing with Europeans for over a century, exposed to their customs, beliefs, and material culture. In particular, the

early through mid-nineteenth century was a period of transition for many Indian groups regarding perceptions of race and gender. These changes must be
understood within the broader context of American westward expansion and
the growth of capitalism and slavery. Recently, several historians have begun
to investigate these linked issues and how they varied, from the eighteenth
century to the present.[1] These authors have illustrated, through exhaustive research and numerous case studies, the dramatic social changes thrust upon,
and undertaken by, American Indians during this period. These changes occurred on a face-to-face level, and people made personal and economic choices
within this narrower scope. In southwestern North Carolina at the threshold
of removal, Cherokees often resisted a strict racial hierarchy. They supported
a community ethos, clan law, and the right of the individual to reject group
decisions. All of these principles were altered or rejected by the laws of the new
Cherokee Nation, affecting most Cherokees' understanding of society, economy, race, and gender.[2]

Fay Yarbrough reveals that, while race laws hardened in Cherokee society during this period, they retained some fluidity. She found that identity
"remained a complex blend of lineage and legal and social interpretation" and
that issues such as "self-identification, physical appearance, community perception, and behavior" guided racial identification.[3] This transitional period
was marked by different rates of change, making it a nonlinear set of events.[4]
More-acculturated Cherokees accepted race slavery as a part of modern capitalism, a position that also served as a defensive political posture in separating
themselves from an enslaved population. In contrast, most Cherokees continued to reject strict racial separation. To a certain extent, they incorporated
African Americans and members of other tribes into their communities. Their
acceptance was not the same as it had been two generations earlier, when individuals from outside the tribe might be adopted or marry into the tribe and
receive full citizenship. As westernization became more predominant, strict
clan interpretations weakened, but a solidified racial hierarchy was not yet established.[5] While small numbers of free African Americans continued to live in
the southern Appalachians in the 1830s, they could not marry into white society. However, within the Cherokee Nation, free African Americans continued
to marry Cherokees. The Cherokee Nation in the western territory outlawed
this practice in 1839.[6]

Investigating the Cherokee enslavers during the mid-nineteenth century
helps to illustrate the complexities of race during the era. As with white enslavers, the practice in the Cherokee Nation ranged from owning one or a few

people to owning over a hundred, as with James Vann, who possessed a large plantation in northern Georgia. Regardless of the number of people these individuals held captive, this endeavor conferred on them the status of embracing many of the core ideals of Western society, particularly the amassing of individual wealth. This status did not, however, necessarily include a conversion to Christianity. Many Cherokee enslavers, including James Vann and John Welch, rejected Christianity throughout their lives.

Cherokees, including Cherokee enslavers, interacted with enslaved African Americans in ways that differed from whites, including white enslavers, and the people they enslaved. For example, although James Vann brutalized those he enslaved, as he did other people, he did not see it beneath his station to interact in personal, and, in some cases, intimate, ways with his slaves. Historian Tiya Miles documents the repeated social interactions between Cherokees from the Vann house and from the quarters of the enslaved, in particular dances. The enslaved and Cherokees invited each other to their late-night and all-night dances. Cherokees also invited enslaved African Americans to their stickball games, and it seems that, in some cases, enslaved men participated. Moravian missionaries at the Spring Place Mission, near the Vann house, noted these interactions. The white missionaries disdained such dances of Cherokee and enslaved, as well as the stickball games. All were seen as heathen rituals, practices that set back their efforts to educate and Christianize their Cherokee students. For example, in December 1814, a missionary wrote that "the Negro and Indian dance is still continuing in our neighborhood at night. May God have mercy!"[7] Miles also documents at Diamond Hill the sharing of medicine and medical care between enslaved African Americans and Cherokees, as well as friendships and regular social interactions.[8]

Like the Moravian missionaries, most white people did not overcome their racist views, even when presented with the wealth and surroundings of individuals like Joseph Vann, James's son. By 1827 his plantation boasted a two-story brick mansion and gardens. A white visitor from South Carolina, however, commented on the "gaudily painted" house and on the dark skin of Joseph's wife.[9] In this sense, those Cherokee plantation owners found themselves in a liminal space. They were in a very small minority in the Cherokee Nation, but white society would never accept them, not even white people below their economic status.

Perceptions of gender were also undergoing major changes in the Cherokee Nation. During the eighteenth century, the clan system was the foundation of the matrilocal and matrilineal structures of Cherokee life, providing women

with political and economic power not seen in contemporaneous Western society. Married women owned and controlled the family's house and property.
If a man and woman ended their relationship, the man left the town and the
woman kept all the property and the children.[10] Throughout the first half of the
nineteenth century, the viability of the clan system to guide kinship and corporate responsibilities declined. Cherokee men increasingly saw themselves as
patriarchs, and women lost political power and property rights. At the same
time, numerous laws passed by the Cherokee national government encroached
on the power and structures of the clan system, thereby reducing the rights of
women in Cherokee society.[11] The expansion of the Cherokee national government also had the effect of reducing the power of local towns. The majority
of Cherokees rejected much of this, but in many ways it affected women more
than men.

Race, gender, and class in America defined one's rights and privileges, and
increasingly so starting in the 1830s, an era of expanding capitalism, white
immigration, and slavery. During this period, material culture played an important role in defining and signaling racial, gender, ethnic, and class identities.
This material culture included the modified landscape, architecture, clothing,
dining, and personal goods. Groups across the country—white, Black, Indian,
and others, responded by changing their material surroundings to express their
"American" identity or, in some cases, to reject or subvert that identity. For example, in 1813 a small group of Cherokees embraced the directives of the Shawnee "prophet" Tenskatawa to reject white lifestyles. They burned their "white"
clothing, got rid of their domesticated livestock, freed the people whom they
had enslaved, and migrated to the Great Smoky Mountains, where they would
be saved from a great hailstorm with "hailstones as large as hominy mortars"
that would rid the region of white people and Cherokees who did not follow
the prophet's vision. A Cherokee man, James Wafford, was a boy in 1813, living on Valley River. He observed "troops of pilgrims," Cherokees fleeing the
impending disaster as they left the southern parts of the Cherokee Nation for
the mountains.[12] These revitalization movements often occur when a cultural
group observes severe threats to their lifestyle or well-being.

Material culture is also used on a daily basis to signal different aspects of
identity. Often these actions are subtle and contradictory. Individuals within
groups choose many different kinds and combinations of material representation, from small things like the kinds of jewelry they wear, to larger things, such
as the kind of house or neighborhood they lived in.

Acknowledging and observing these details is important. Our surroundings help define us. What we choose to wear and eat, what kind of house we live in, sends signals to others about our status, beliefs, wealth, and politics. For Alexis, certain items in Long Bear's house made sense—a gun represented for him the expected primitive Indian lifestyle, with men focused on hunting and fishing. The blowgun fit this pattern even more so—not only a symbol of the hunt but one that was distinctly "Indian." What seemed to surprise Alexis the most were the dining wares of a "peculiar whiteness." This statement reveals more about the observer than the observed. In all of his preconceived notions about the mountain Cherokees, none included imported whiteware dishes. The description that Alexis gives us of Long Bear's cabin would probably also apply to most of the cabins of Welch's Town above Valley River in the 1850s, as well as most of the other Cherokees living in North Carolina: small, windowless log cabins with few furnishings. Alexis saw only a series of small cabins lived in by "old-time" Indians. For the inhabitants, their homes suited their needs and lifestyle perfectly. In contrast, the Welches built a much larger and more substantial house to serve as the hub of their plantation. It was forty feet long, one and a half stories high, and featured shuttered windows and heavy plank floors. While not as opulent as the Vann house, it visibly set the Welch family apart from their Cherokee neighbors.

The variations in material culture that began in Cherokee communities in the early eighteenth century expanded dramatically during the last decade of the eighteenth century and first decade of the nineteenth century, coinciding with American "civilization" policies designed to transform Indians into yeoman farmers and to coerce more land cessions. Cherokees struggled against cession treaties almost from their first contact with Europeans. The first cession to the British came in 1721, a transaction in which they lost just over one and a half million acres. A series of land-cession treaties during the 1770s cost them another 30 million acres. The first cession with the US government was in 1785, part of the Treaty of Hopewell, and took 4 million acres. Between 1791 and 1828, the American government took another 15 million acres as part of several treaties signed with the Cherokees. Government officials claimed these treaties were voluntary, but, as with colonial governments, the US had a variety of ways to force Cherokees to sign, misrepresented the terms of treaties, and recruited Cherokee signatories who had no representative power within the tribe.[13]

By the 1820s, a growing number of Cherokees were becoming more westernized, embracing a variety of Western practices and beliefs. The creation of a Cherokee Nation and national government at this time was partly an attempt to stem future cessions, and partly an acculturative response driven by a minority of Cherokees. Two decades before the Trail of Tears, the Cherokee Nation was in open conflict with itself. Most Cherokees accepted the need for modernization, as long as it halted land cessions and any talk of removal. However, land cessions continued while the new Cherokee government began to write laws that rejected Cherokee clan-based law and behavior, in some cases criminalizing age-old practices. While Cherokees struggled against external powers, internally the conflict over the future direction of the tribe deepened. The rapid increase in the speed of council laws and the increasingly intrusive nature of them led to an open rebellion against rapid acculturation. Early in 1827 White Path, a respected Cherokee leader, organized a meeting to discuss these issues. Known as the White Path Rebellion, this event proved that most Cherokees resented the intrusion of the national government into their affairs.[14]

This struggle continued into the 1830s, during the passing of Andrew Jackson's Indian Removal Act, the invasion of the Cherokee Nation by the US Army, and the forced march to Indian Territory in the winter of 1838–39. After the removal, the struggle continued, although greatly changed in nature. No longer was it driven by the urgent desire to stop land cessions and removal. For those Cherokees who stayed in western North Carolina, the fight shifted toward saving old towns and communities, those they had fought and died for during the Trail of Tears.

For Cherokees before and after removal, the internal debate entailed defining what it meant to be Cherokee, culturally and socially. Many of the pressures to acculturate to Western practices created binary oppositions, with little middle ground: speaking Cherokee or English, practicing Cherokee religious belief or Christianity, personal wealth acquisition or communal sharing, town or national governance, patrilineal or matrilineal descent, Cherokee or European gender roles. The divisions affected all aspects of life.

Responses by Cherokees throughout this period varied dramatically and depended on their geographic location within the Cherokee Nation, sex, age, family background, and many other factors. In teasing out these varied strands, the interesting challenge becomes not only defining the range of cultural variations but how these changes varied geographically and temporally. Many of the families living in the mountains of western North Carolina prior to removal adhered most strongly to eighteenth-century Cherokee culture, while Cherokee planters such as James Vann, Major Ridge, and John Ross and their families in northern Georgia represented the most acculturated. While the members of Welch's Town honored the deep roots of Cherokee ways, the Welch family would fall somewhere closer to those Cherokee plantation owners of northern Georgia. While their farm was no Diamond Hill, they were owners of a relatively large-scale plantation, especially for the Upper South.

DIVERSE CHEROKEE LANDSCAPES

By the 1810s Cherokees understood too well the growing pressure to cede land to the United States. Embracing the United States' "civilization policy" seemed the answer for some, who remembered the depredations of the eighteenth-century wars and felt that the adoption of Western forms of religion, government, and agriculture might defend them from any future hostilities. However, neighbors exerted an equally strong pressure to continue eighteenth-century practices. These opposing pressures continued to force choices in Cherokee communities throughout the mid-nineteenth century. Some discarded certain aspects of Cherokee culture, while others vehemently held onto Cherokee practices. Most found some compromise. However, there seemed to be no specific pattern in what archaeologist Brett Riggs identified as a syncretic cultural response.[15] Some Cherokees embraced Christianity, while others began pursuing individual financial wealth. Some married non-Cherokees, while others acquired a Western education. The material culture reflected this mixed bag.

When the federal government started the forced emigration in June 1838, many Cherokees still practiced a tribal-held, communal land-tenure system. If land owned by the tribe was not in use, any tribal member could occupy, improve, and "own" it. This system had functioned for centuries. Prior to the nineteenth century, Cherokees had practiced subsistence farming, often with a combination of large communal agriculture plots and smaller, family-owned gardens. By the end of the eighteenth century, the large communal field system had collapsed, as large villages scattered into single-family farms, in response to repeated attacks by the British and later Americans. By 1800 many communities consisted of linear arrangements of houses and farms, lining the banks of rivers and creeks. These communities remained kin-based, however, and families lived a quarter or half a mile away in either direction. In this system a family would improve a farm that encompassed between two and ten acres. At the time of removal, the average Cherokee farm size in western North Carolina was 6.5 acres.[16] Most of this acreage was used for agriculture, predominantly corn. Nearby was a small garden plot for vegetables and an orchard with peach and apple trees. A small log cabin served as residence for the family. Given the population of the Cherokee Nation and the land base they held, even in 1838 this style of subsistence allowed all tribal members enough room to farm.

As this subsistence pattern gave way to westernized forms of surplus production, the uses of Cherokee land changed dramatically. Led largely by second- and third-generation descendants of British traders who married Cherokee women, these families expanded production of livestock and crops, sometimes with the labor of enslaved African Americans. These new types of farms, scattered throughout the Cherokee Nation, caused consternation among the majority of the population. Generating a large surplus of crops or livestock required a much larger amount of acreage. During the early nineteenth century, some farms exploded in size from five or six to hundreds of acres. Claiming and improving fifty or two hundred acres of tribal land caused numerous problems. First, there was some competition for usable land. In the mountainous section of the Cherokee Nation in particular, much of the land was too steep to be used for agriculture, and arable land near waterways was limited. Second, surplus production increased the wealth of the family, sometimes dramatically. Embracing market capitalism flew in the face of many of the communal work and social ethics of Cherokee life. Acquiring money or other resources and not sharing them with the community severely violated normal tribal practice.[17] In the Valley Towns, the Welches may have faced resentment from their neighbors as their farm grew into a plantation during the 1820s, encompassing more land and other resources.

Architecture, in this case the residence and other buildings associated with a family farm, serves symbolic as well as functional roles. The main residence in particular is a symbolic element. It is a representation of a family's place in the world. The location, footage, acreage, and architectural style all reflect a variety of factors that are subsumed under "identity." For Cherokees in the mid-nineteenth century, the range of residential architecture is well documented, archaeologically and in the historical record.

Most Cherokees lived in single-room log cabins, roughly ten to fourteen feet on a side. Alexis's description of Long Bear's cabin—"a small, uncomfortably close room answered for the bed-chamber, dining room, pantry, boudoir, and *all*, save for kitchen and meat house"—illustrates how these small, single-room cabins served multiple functions for the entire family. Alexis's observations suggest Long Bear's family had a kitchen and smokehouse separate from the residential structure, although many Cherokee families did not.[18] Cherokees constructed buildings with cribbed logs. Relatively quick to build, they required few tools and almost no hardware, such as nails. The floor was either packed clay or wooden puncheons (logs split in half, with the flat surfaces aligned side-by-side). A single door granted entry, and there were no windows. A stick-and-clay chimney provided heat and a space for cooking, and wooden shingles were used for roofing. In the spoliation claims recorded by Welch and Jarrett in 1837, the value of these structures ranged from $4.00 to $340, with an average of $24.[19] This style of housing was used by Cherokees throughout the nineteenth century. A photograph of the Cherokee known as Swimmer, taken by anthropologist James Mooney in 1888, shows this style of architecture (Figure 1.1).[20] Although this style of house might seem small and uncomfortable, during the era it was an excellent form for Cherokees who practiced small-scale subsistence farming. Easy and cheap to build, with a lifespan of five to ten years, the house would suffice about the same time a field could be farmed until it had to be left fallow, at which time the family could move to a new field and build a new cabin. During the mid-nineteenth century, most Cherokees did not spend much time inside the house, instead spending more time outside, performing activities in natural light.[21]

Cherokees usually chose a site next to a waterway, near a river, creek, or springhead. This furnished water for use in the house as well as for nearby fields.

FIGURE 1.1. Swimmer cabin. (National Anthropological
Archives, Smithsonian Institution [negative GN1000A])

The house and yard (which was used for work) comprised a very small area, usually less than an acre. This style of architecture would have been used by the members of Welch's Town during the 1840s and early 1850s. Single-room log cabins continued to be the norm during the mid-nineteenth century. However, a small number of Cherokees also adopted other styles of housing, building larger residences, and using different building materials and methods. These structures, built by Cherokee political leaders such as John Ross, James Vann, and Major Ridge, represented those few Cherokees who had gone beyond merely accepting participation in the market economy (as had most Cherokees, if only to gain access to utilitarian items such as metal tools) to competing with the white planter class of the American South. Although the Welch plantation did not match those of Cherokee plantation owners in northern Georgia, it was conspicuously more substantial than most Cherokee farmsteads along Valley River.

The foods that people eat and the ways they prepare and consume those foods often reflect long-held cultural practices. During much of the nineteenth century, Cherokee and white farmers shared many elements of their domestic economies and material cultures.[22] In the antebellum Upper South, most farmers practiced a diverse economy by cultivating multiple grains and vegetables as well as by livestock production. Most raised these foods for home consumption and for sale. In addition, most farmers supplemented their diet with hunting, gathering, and fishing. Cherokee subsistence differed in certain ways, however. Cherokee families usually worked smaller agricultural plots and depended more on wild foods. Occasionally they consumed different animals and used alternate methods of capture and preparation. For example, Cherokees fired blowguns to kill songbirds and other small species, while other people in the region generally hunted larger birds and small game using shotguns and rifles. Cherokees fractured the long bones of wild mammals to extract the marrow. This practice lasted into the mid-nineteenth century and was applied to livestock as well. In contrast, other groups in the region usually sawed or chopped long bones only for dismemberment of the carcass. These different practices leave distinctive marks on faunal remains.[23] While historic documents show that the Welches ran a plantation focused on crop and livestock production, the faunal collection from the site reveals that they still practiced some distinctively Cherokee methods of food consumption.

By the 1830s pork was by far the most commonly consumed meat in the region, for all racial and economic groups. This had not been the case a few decades earlier for Cherokees. Although pigs were brought into the Cherokee country as early as the 1730s, they were not consumed in any great number by Cherokees until the late eighteenth or early nineteenth century. As wild game dwindled, pork was adopted by most Cherokee families. By the time of the removal, families regularly butchered pigs for home consumption, due largely to their ability to preserve the meat by smoking or salting.[24] Alternatively, Cherokees mostly raised cattle for sale to drovers, who moved herds to the lowcountry South for consumption on plantations.

Those without adequate access to domestic livestock for a regular source of meat often turned to hunting and fishing. Fish were a significant natural resource throughout the eighteenth and nineteenth centuries for Cherokees, well documented in the historical record and on archaeological sites.[25] Common methods of collection included stone weirs, gigs, nets, poisoning, and hook and line, used to catch a wide variety of fish, including bass, trout, redhorse, perch, drum, and catfish. Locally, fishhooks were available at outlets such as Hunter's store in Murphy. Small game also represented an important source of meat for most Cherokees. The significance of deer in the Cherokee diet at midcentury is unclear. Although a staple during the eighteenth century, venison had largely been replaced by pork by the early nineteenth century. However, deer and other wild game supplemented meat from livestock for many families.[26]

Cherokees had harvested a variety of nuts for centuries, bringing a large proportion of calories and fat to a diet that was often otherwise very lean. Before a blight destroyed the chestnut forests of the eastern United States in the 1930s, the American chestnut was a common forest species. The thick mast in chestnut forests often obscured the ground.[27] Cherokees also collected hickory nuts in great quantities, and both contributed fat and protein to the diets of people and animals. Cherokees boiled nutmeat for the oil. They dried chestnuts, crushed them into flour, and made bread. They also boiled hickory nuts and mixed the juice with water to make a milklike drink.[28] Cherokees gathered numerous kinds of wild greens that grew in the forest and along open, disturbed areas, such as on field edges.[29] Preparation involved boiling, draining, and frying in fat.[30]

Cherokees also grew an indigenous species of tobacco, *Nicotiana rustica*. For American Indians in the southeastern United States, including Cherokees, *N. rustica* served numerous roles in magic, ritual, and medicine.[31] During the nineteenth century, tobacco (both *N. rustica* and *N. tobacum*, the latter imported from the West Indies) continued to serve these functions but also became used in a social or recreational role.

Archaeological and historical research has repeatedly demonstrated that dining practices signal a range of social behaviors, status, and ideologies of the family.[32] Cherokees had a broad universe of material culture used for preparing and serving food. They crafted many items themselves, as their ancestors had done for centuries, but more and more they also purchased or traded for mass-produced goods imported from Europe and the United States. While these food-preparation and serving wares might seem ordinary and of little note, together they tell a lot about the people who used them every day. For example, most Cherokee families did not all sit down to eat at a given time; rather, each person ate whenever they got hungry. Planned mealtimes for the entire family was a Western practice. Individualized settings and dining were also unknown to Cherokees. Women prepared communal pots of food, and people dipped a spoon into a pot to eat. The associated material assemblages representing these two cultural practices obviously varied greatly. This broad diversity in material culture and behavior can be traced back to the eighteenth century, when sustained contact with the British and French created new challenges and choices, and Cherokees in different regions responded in different

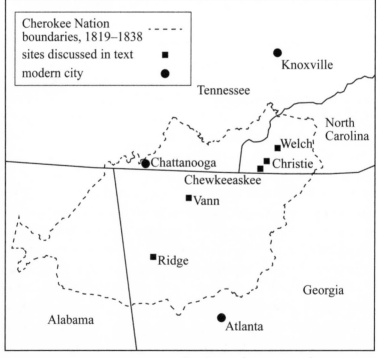

FIGURE 1.2. Locations of study sites. (Lance Greene)

ways. On Valley River the ceramics and other dining artifacts archaeologists recovered from the Welch site show an adherence to Western styles of dining. Hundreds of colorful sherds were from ceramics mass-produced in England, for daily use by the family and to host people from outside the plantation. An absence of handmade Cherokee ceramic sherds shows that Betty did not embrace communal dining practices common in most Cherokee households.

Four different Cherokee families illustrate the diversity of cultural adaptations by Cherokees during this era (Figure 1.2). They pursued contrasting economic and social strategies and chose very different combinations of religious, cultural, and social expression. Historic documents identify the husband as the head of each household. By this time almost all Cherokee families had mostly accepted this shift in the family structure. The matrilineal structure of Cherokee families had largely disappeared by the turn of the century, although Cherokee women managed to maintain some aspects of their power within the family.

Chewkeeaskee

Prior to the removal, Chewkeeaskee and his family lived along the Nottely River, a tributary of the Hiwassee River in southwestern North Carolina. The "fullblood" household included Chewkeeaskee, an adult woman, a boy, and three girls. None were literate in English, but Chewkeeaskee could write Sequoyan syllabary. The family was part of Nottely Town, sometimes called Lawlo's Town, a small Cherokee enclave led by the headman Lawlo, who lived across the river. Like most in Nottely Town, they farmed ten acres along the Nottely River and dwelt in a log cabin, around thirteen feet by thirteen feet, situated on the edge of their cornfields, at the base of a steep ridge that borders the river at this point. Although it lacked windows to let in sunlight, they spent few of their waking hours indoors and rose and slept by the sun. They added a chimney on one end of the cabin, contrived of small logs and plastered with clay. The women cooked in the fireplace, which also provided heat during the freezing winters in the mountains. The only other building on their farm was a corncrib, made of small logs, keeping their corn dry and safe from pests and predators. Next to their cornfield they planted an apple orchard.[33]

The main food source was corn. Chewkeeaskee raised pigs and chickens but spent a lot of time hunting wild game and collecting plants in nearby forests. Small game, such as squirrels and birds, could be killed with a blowgun. He and his family caught fish, turtles, and frogs. Chewkeeaskee did not raise any surpluses to sell for profit; he and his family made just enough to feed themselves. However, their diet was adequate and diverse, fluctuating with the seasons. Excavations at the site by archaeologist Brett Riggs recovered remains of wild game, including fox squirrel, red-bellied woodpecker, box turtle, bullfrog, toad, and fish.[34]

As Cherokees had done for centuries, the women of Chewkeeaskee's family fashioned their own ceramics: globular jars for cooking and storage made from local clay and marked with the distinctive Qualla check pattern, and the everyday bowls for their meals (Figure 1.3).[35] Each evening they filled these bowls with soups and stews of pork and wild game, of wild nuts and greens, enjoying a mix of whatever the season offered. Firing the earthenware took a delicate touch, for it was done near the open flame in the fireplace. Such skills, handed down for generations, were still maintained decades after cheap whitewares became available at nearby stores. Women in many Cherokee households continued to make these ceramics by hand at midcentury, and used them for traditional forms of food preparation, serving, and etiquette. Fragments of this style of pottery were found at the site. The exterior surfaces of the sherds, stamped during production with carved wooden paddles, exhibit patterns including checks and other rectilinear designs and curvilinear designs. At the site handmade Qualla ceramic sherds most strongly represent the kitchen and dining artifacts recovered. During excavations Riggs found more than four hundred ceramic sherds of this kind of pottery, attesting to the everyday use of

FIGURE 1.3. Nineteenth-century Qualla ceramic vessel.
(Courtesy of R. P. Stephen Davis, Research Laboratories
of Archaeology, University of North Carolina)

these pots by the family. In contrast, only twenty-one sherds of mass-produced ceramics were found at the site, including stoneware, whiteware, and pearlware fragments. While the stoneware was used for storage, the other two forms, which represented mostly plates, cups, and saucers, were probably used very little and may have been used only for display. Perhaps the family purchased or traded for these items to serve as decorative pieces or knickknacks. This may also have been the case in Long Bear's cabin and his shelf of dishes of a "peculiar whiteness."[36]

Much of their food was stored underground to protect it from freezing temperatures. Riggs identified and excavated three storage-pit features associated with the Chewkeeaskee cabin. Two rectangular pits lay beneath the cabin and were accessed through a trap door. A third circular pit was just outside, probably protected with a wooden cover. These kinds of cellar pits for storing root crops and other foods were common in the nineteenth century in the region. Historic documents and archaeology both reflect the prevalence of cellar pits. Riggs points out that these cellars were never listed on the Welch and Jarrett valuations or any other listings created during the removal. This was partly due to most Cherokees not allowing these evaluators into their houses but also because cellars were such common architectural features that they did not bother to mention them. The three cellar pits at the site represent the entirety of the archaeological footprint and show the ephemeral nature of these houses. In addition, there is a complete absence of architectural hardware. Nonperishable artifacts such as cut nails and window glass fragments commonly occur on mid-nineteenth century sites in the region, including on some Cherokee house sites. The absence of these artifacts at the Chewkeeaskee site illustrates the traditional nature of the architecture there.[37]

Although Nottely Town was a small kin-based community of houses lining the banks of the Nottely River, they were not far removed from capitalist ventures that had been part of the Cherokee Nation for years. The Unicoi Turnpike crossed the Hiwassee River just a couple miles north of the town. This was a major thoroughfare for the movement of livestock from the Upper South to lowcountry plantations. One of their neighbors, John Christie, operated a ferry at the crossing, and made a comfortable living.

Christie

John Christie and his family thrived in the mountains of North Carolina up to the time of removal. John's father was a white trader in the Cherokee Nation during the late eighteenth century, and John was identified by the US Army as a "mixed blood" Cherokee. His wife was also listed as "mixed blood" and their children "1/4 blood" Cherokee. Prior to removal John Christie and his family lived along the Hiwassee River, about three miles upstream from Chewkee-askee. Their farm sat just below the confluence of the Hiwassee and Valley Rivers. There they built a two-story log house with heavy, hewn logs about sixteen feet on a side. They shaped a fireplace on a solid stone base but finished the chimney with stick-and-clay construction. Archaeologically, architectural remains suggest a structure that had several traits lacking on most Cherokee cabins. Several fragments of flat glass probably represent windowpanes. A large number of machine-cut nails, including nail types for flooring, paneling, and roofing, shows that the Christie house had plank floors, interior battens, and a nailed roof. The family also constructed another cabin nearby that served as the kitchen.[38]

The family was unusually wealthy for Cherokees in the mountains. Their most lucrative business was the operation of an inn or stock stand. Their farm bordered the Unicoi Turnpike, and they made a substantial profit by selling shelter and provisions to drovers moving livestock from eastern Tennessee into Georgia and South Carolina.[39]

They farmed double the amount of land as Chewkeeaskee, growing crops on twenty-one acres. These crops provided for home use and a surplus for feeding droves of cattle and other livestock. With the money gained from the stock stand, the Christies probably purchased more corn from other Chero-kees, most likely members of John Christie's extended family. He had siblings, nephews, and a son living nearby.[40]

Because the Christie family ran a business, they probably spent much less time hunting and fishing than Chewkeeaskee. Their wealth allowed them to buy plenty of livestock and other foods. Although the Christies may have eaten wild foods that they purchased from or traded with neighbors, their diet resembled that of white people in the region. It also reflected class dif-ferences; they would have gotten most of their meat from their domestic animals. Unfortunately, very little bone was found during the excavations at the Christie cabin site. However, the artifacts associated with dining show a very different pattern from the Chewkeeaskee family's. Several hundred sherds of mass-produced ceramics make up the bulk of the artifacts. Most of these are pieces of whiteware and pearlware dishes, such as plates, cups, and saucers. Decorative patterns such as blue shell-edge, blue transfer print-ing, and hand-painted polychrome designs are common. The large number of mass-produced ceramic sherds shows that the Christie family had embraced

Western ideals of dining. During excavations Riggs also found almost 150 handmade Qualla sherds.

In contrast to the very low number of imported ceramics at the Chewkee-askee site, in the Christie house these were the main items used every day for dining. If this is the case, what were the Qualla ceramics at the Christie house used for? Riggs surmises that the combination of imported and Cherokee-made materials in the Christie household "may reflect a form of cultural blending that resulted in an expanded repertoire, a new type of material identity."[41] If this is the case, perhaps openly embracing either dining style actually served the Christie family's best interest. The use of imported ceramics in the house, particularly of teawares that suggested "refinement," showed local white people, including passing drovers, that the Christies were "civilized." The continued use of Qualla ceramics, in contrast, indicated to nearby traditional Cherokees, like Chewkeeaskee, that they still practiced Cherokee forms of production and methods of consumption. The combination also shows that, at least in this household, one could actively promote both systems simultaneously.[42]

Ridge

The Ridge was born in the early 1770s to a Cherokee father and a mother who was the daughter of a Scots trader and Cherokee mother. When he was a child, the family moved to a secluded area in eastern Tennessee to avoid the repeated attacks on Cherokee towns by American forces, particularly those led by John Sevier. In 1788, at the age of seventeen, The Ridge joined in the attacks on frontier settlers and became renowned for his part in the attack of militia troops south of Knoxville, Tennessee. As a young man, he was named Kah-nung-da-tla-geh, "the man who walks on the mountaintop," supposedly reflecting his penchant for traveling on foot along ridge crests as well as his ability, metaphorically, to see far. To English speakers he became known as The Ridge. He continued to fight on the frontier until 1794, when the Cherokee Nation and the United States established a permanent peace. After the fighting had ceased, he returned to his home in the town of Pine Log in northern Georgia, where he had originally settled with his family to avoid the fighting. During the mid-1790s, he married Sehoya, whose Anglicized name was Susanna Wickett.[43]

By the end of the eighteenth century, The Ridge began to make a name for himself in Cherokee politics. He was an early supporter of Cherokee national laws that challenged many clan-based practices. The Ridge adopted other Western practices. He and Susanna accepted the "civilization policy" of the United States, switching to larger-scale agriculture and cloth and livestock production.

Part of this policy included dismantling towns, and having Cherokee families improve larger farms, farther away from other families. One consequence of this was the loss of the corporate nature of traditional Cherokee society and government. By the early nineteenth century, the Ridges had fully embraced the market economy. They both enjoyed this new standard of living and viewed acculturation as the best way to maintain a tribal land base in the east.[44]

In 1811 The Ridge rejected the movements to return to more traditional ways, such as the message being spread to many tribal groups by the Shawnee leader Tecumseh and others. In 1812 he joined Andrew Jackson's force, along with numerous other Cherokees, to fight the "Redstick" Creeks in Alabama. The Redstick movement, named for the red clubs carried by its fighters, gained widespread support among the Creek Indians and reflected the rejection of the pace of cultural change driven by Creek leaders, much as most Cherokees were rejecting rapid change in their society. The movement expanded into internecine warfare in 1813. After an attack on Fort Mims by Redstick fighters, the United States entered the war. Andrew Jackson led a military force, including Cherokee men, to attack the Redstick force. At the Battle of Horseshoe Bend on March 27, Jackson's forces defeated the Redsticks. The Ridge, who fought at the battle, became well known for his charge across the Tallapoosa River to attack the Redsticks. During this time, he became known as Major Ridge.[45]

In the first decade of the nineteenth century, the Ridges had lived in Pine Log, but by 1820 they had settled on a plantation along the Oostanaula River, a Cherokee settlement in northwest Georgia. Their home on the Oostanaula from about 1819 to 1837 was called Chieftains. The house at Chieftains was originally a "two-story hewn log dogtrot house" measuring fifty-four feet by twenty-nine feet. Dogtrot is a style that refers to a central hallway that runs perpendicular to the long axis of the house, creating a covered breezeway between rooms. This substantial hewed-log house had glass-paned windows. After a short time, the log house was framed with sawn lumber, and the breezeway was covered. By the mid-1830s, the house was painted white and had four brick fireplaces, eight rooms, and thirty glass-paned, shuttered windows.[46] At Chieftains, Ridge operated a large-scale plantation complex, including the main house, two kitchens, a smokehouse, corncribs, stables, and cabins for the people they held in slavery. Soon after settling on his new farm, he entered into a partnership with a white man, George Lavender, and they operated a store near Ridge's house and a ferry.

The scale of Ridge's holdings was rarely matched in the Cherokee Nation. By the mid-1830s, more than two dozen enslaved African Americans farmed his 280 acres, grew corn, cotton, tobacco, and other crops, and maintained his large herds of cattle, swine, and sheep. They resided in cabins built behind Ridge's house. Numerous Cherokee and white visitors frequented Chieftains and the Lavender store, to talk with Ridge and to buy and trade at the store.

Although Ridge spoke little English, he provided his two oldest children with a Western education. His oldest son, John, attended a Moravian mission in northern Georgia and later attended other mission schools in Tennessee and Connecticut.[47] On his return John settled within a few miles of Chieftains. John was a founder of the *Cherokee Phoenix*, a newspaper that began publication in 1828 and was printed in English and Cherokee syllabary.

The kitchen wares recovered from the Chieftains site clearly depict a family who had embraced Western ideals associated with dining. The vast bulk of ceramics (almost 15,000 sherds), for example, are imported wares: pearlwares and whitewares with a wide variety of decorative designs, Chinese porcelains, and alkaline-glazed stonewares.[48] In contrast, fewer than four hundred sherds of handmade Cherokee ceramics were found, and many of these might have predated the Ridge occupation of the site. Archaeologist Patrick Garrow interpreted this small number of Cherokee potsherds as evidence that Cherokees were trading or selling handmade vessels at Lavender's store but that no one in the Ridge household actually used them.[49]

Major Ridge and Susanna were two of the earliest Cherokee converts to Christianity, although Ridge's conversion took years of persuasion by Moravian, Baptist, Presbyterian, and Congregationalist missionaries. Susanna announced her conversion and was baptized in 1819. Even though they had sent their children, Nancy and John, to missionary schools, Major Ridge resisted conversion for much of his life. His reason for sending his children to mission schools was more for the education they would receive, in particular for John, whom Major Ridge knew had the potential to become an influential leader.[50]

In 1835 Ridge signed the Treaty of New Echota, an act not sanctioned by the Cherokee Nation, and seen as treasonous by the majority of Cherokees. Ridge and his family emigrated west in 1838, and he and his son, John, were assassinated in June 1839 because of their involvement in the treaty.

Vann

James Vann was the son of a Scottish trader and Cherokee mother. Born in the late 1760s, he spent his early years amid the almost constant warfare between Cherokees and the United States. His parents moved the family into northern Georgia in an attempt to avoid this conflict, but troops led by John

Sevier burned these towns in 1782. During the 1790s James Vann embraced the market economy and began establishing his own businesses. By 1800 he had established residence along the Conasauga River in northern Georgia and, over the next nine years, built it into the largest Cherokee-owned plantation in the nation, called Diamond Hill.[51]

Vann had been key in convincing the Cherokee Nation to allow the construction of a Federal Road through tribal land. The United States rewarded him by having the turnpike routed directly past Diamond Hill. He also received a contract to operate a ferry. Vann's holdings included large-scale agricultural and livestock production, ferries, stores, taverns, and over one hundred enslaved African Americans. As historian Tiya Miles points out, Vann had joined the planter elite microculture. During the same period, Vann also purchased land near his plantation for the construction of the Moravian mission called Spring Place. Although Vann welcomed missionaries into the Cherokee Nation and sent his children to be educated in missionary schools, he never converted to Christianity. The Diamond Hill plantation complex and surrounding area included cultivated fields, rows of cabins for the enslaved, animal lots, orchards, and the Spring Place mission.[52]

Little is known about the original house Vann built in his early years at Diamond Hill, although by the time of his death in 1809, the plantation complex included two houses, cabins for the enslaved, a workshop, a corncrib, a blacksmith shop, and a stable. While Vann was an adept businessman, he was not interested in creating the perception of an elite southern planter, as was his son after James's death. However, he did adopt some of the attitudes and behaviors of what Miles describes as "white southern masculinity," including gambling, drinking, and abuse of his wife and the people he enslaved.[53] Moravian missionaries at Spring Place documented over a period of several years the physical, emotional, and mental domination and abuse of the people Vann enslaved and of Vann's female family members. Vann had embraced the sense of power, pride, and self-worth that grew from the total authority of a plantation master. A strong sense of personal honor, fueled by alcohol, caused frequent and intensive physical abuses against Vann's mother, sisters, and wives, as well as many of the enslaved on the plantation. Although rape and sexual assault of the enslaved by white plantation owners is well documented,[54] relatively little is known about these abuses regarding Cherokee masters. James Vann was known to have physically abused many of those he enslaved. We can only imagine the level of sexual abuse by Vann.[55] He had long been known as a violent man, especially when drinking. Abusive to strangers and family members alike, in more than one instance, he murdered an enslaved person for insubordination. In February 1809 an unidentified group of men assassinated Vann.[56]

Joseph inherited the entire plantation in 1809. Ambitious like his father, Joseph had learned more about white society, having been sent to private schools in Georgia and South Carolina. He immediately began expanding farm operations. To accomplish his goals, he tightened controls over the enslaved he had inherited, creating an environment in some ways more repressive than his father's.[57] His main achievement was the construction of a two-story brick house (Figure 1.4). In 1819 he engaged an architect to design a grand plantation house. He then hired a white brick mason and other white skilled laborers to build a grand estate home. Some of the enslaved helped in the construction, and Cherokee wood carvers produced many of the ornate decorative pieces. By 1821 it was "a handsome Federal and Georgian style home embellished with glass windows, venetian blinds, ionic columns, square pediments, sunken paneled walls, medallion cornices, carved Cherokee roses, scalloped bead board, newel posts, a garret with wainscoting, outdoor porticos, a mantel festooned with wood-carved snakes and lizards, and the pièce de résistance: a mystically suspended stairway that would become an architectural marvel generations later."[58]

FIGURE 1.4. Vann House, Chatsworth, Georgia, 2017. (Thomson, Creative Commons)

This was something not seen before: a Cherokee family living the life of the southern enslaver elite, with a plantation estate to rival most white plantation owners. Many visitors to the estate marveled at the new house and commented favorably. Others were not so impressed, such as a white plantation mistress, who commented on factors such as the "gaudily painted" colors of the house and the dark skin of Joseph's wife.[59] These kinds of comments help clarify the overarching racial politics of the day. For many, ostentatious wealth could not overcome the "darkness" of the Vann family. Their respectability would not save them.

Although much has been written about the Vanns, relatively little is known about the everyday details of their lives. The diet of the Vanns at Diamond Hill is poorly documented but was probably luxurious in quality and quantity. When Joseph inherited the plantation, it comprised 1,000 head of cattle, 250 horses, 150 pigs. Given the quantity of agricultural and livestock pursuits, the bulk of the Vann diet was probably domesticated foods. However, there were traditional Cherokee communities nearby, and it is possible, as at the Welch plantation, that the Vanns had access to wild foods.[60]

A clear sign that southern white people placed race before class occurred in 1830. In that year a Georgia law went into effect that extinguished Cherokee law and government within the boundaries of the state. Two years later the state established a land lottery in which white men purchased chances to win Cherokee land. In December 1832, Col. William Bishop, a leader of the Georgia Guard, claimed he was the rightful owner of the Spring Place mission, and he also claimed Vann's brick house. Although Joseph struggled to build a legal case to remain in Georgia, he and his family were forced to flee the plantation and settled in Tennessee.[61] The Vanns were then forced to emigrate west with the vast majority of Cherokees. However, given their wealth, their travel to Indian Territory was not as horrific as for the majority of Cherokees. Joseph traveled west before the mandatory removal date and established a new farm before most Cherokees arrived in early 1839. He died in October 1844, when the boilers of his steamboat *Lucy Walker* exploded, killing dozens of others on board as well.[62]

POLITICS

Thus, we see that Cherokee lifestyles ranged enormously in the early nineteenth century. How did this impact the political atmosphere among the tribal members? At the turn of the nineteenth century, the Cherokees in the southeastern United States were still recovering from the warfare and disease of the second half of the eighteenth century. The new government of the United States had supported a program of "civilization" but had done little to carry it out. In 1803 Thomas Jefferson formally initiated Indian removal policies. Although Jefferson originally considered trying to convert Indians into yeoman farmers, he concluded that such a scheme would take too long, and the possibility of westward emigration became more feasible with the Louisiana Purchase in 1803. Although Jefferson's removal plans were never realized, his idea was embraced by every successive president.[63] Partly in response to these pressures, a council meeting of the entire Cherokee Nation was held in 1809. At that meeting, a national committee was formed in an effort to stop land cessions to the United States. While the committee began the first national attempt to end land cessions, it also began modifying internal affairs, including many practices based in clan- and town-level governance. These two actions by the newly formed national government foretold changes to come. The first aimed at an external group: ending white annexing of tribal land, which most Cherokees supported. The second was internal. Laws against long-held practices, many of which stripped both clans and towns of their authority, alienated most Cherokees. These problems intensified during the first four decades of the nineteenth century, as the struggle to maintain sovereignty grew progressively more difficult.[64]

The belief of those Cherokees who established a national government (and the belief of many white people as well) was that acculturation would be the most successful strategy for maintaining their lands, which was the key to survival. This minority group of Cherokees wanted to secure their homeland for themselves and for other Cherokees, at least during this early period of government formation. Ending land cessions and forced-removal efforts had long been one goal for Cherokees who embraced Western practices.

A struggle had begun in earnest within the Cherokee Nation during the first decade of the nineteenth century, as the Cherokee national government became formalized and a series of laws began to dismantle older Cherokee structures of governance. In 1808 the government organized the Cherokee Light Horse, an internal police force, to monitor horse theft and other crimes. In 1810 a much more controversial law was passed: the responsibility of clan, or blood, revenge was negated. Clan revenge, considered a moral obligation by most Cherokees, became a capital crime. Limiting clan revenge was a rejection of the code that placed social controls at the clan level.[65] Other laws of the nation in direct opposition to clan and town laws followed quickly.

Cherokee national laws replaced clan-based practices with a patriarchal system of ownership, kinship, and power. Increasing centralization of the government culminated in a set of articles established in 1817, including the creation of a thirteen-member executive committee. This committee was given decision-making power in many internal and most external issues. This move by the standing Cherokee government and without the approval of most of the nation shocked many Cherokees. This was especially because it came at the same time as the 1817 treaty, which surrendered 650,000 acres to the United States.[66]

Between 1808 and 1827, the National Council passed numerous laws addressing such internal affairs as matrilineal inheritance, polygamy, conjuring, gambling, ball plays, dances, and Christian faith for holding office.[67] Another major change came in 1825, when the Cherokee Council passed a law that endowed the children of a Cherokee man and a white woman with full citizenship. Another attack on clan structure as well as eighteenth-century gender roles, this law stripped Cherokee women of the sole power to bestow Cherokee citizenship.[68] As the reforms began to turn inward and affect Cherokee culture, most Cherokees resisted. They agreed that acculturation, for the sake of holding together the tribe and the tribal land base, was happening too fast. The nation was becoming a place that Cherokees did not recognize. Many of the legal strictures passed between 1810 and 1830 were based on European laws and founded in patriarchal and patrilineal societies. As such, they were unfamiliar to most Cherokees. Cherokees who rejected the rapid shift to national governance responded with rage, with resistance, and, as a common Cherokee practice, by sometimes separating themselves geographically from the nation. By 1817 several groups, totaling roughly three thousand Cherokees, had already left the nation and moved to the Arkansas Territory. Another seventy-five Cherokee families took individual reservations under the acts of the 1817 and 1819 treaties, including the Welch family.[69] Most left because they rejected the effects of Cherokee nationalism.[70] The flight of whole communities from the Cherokee Nation, starting more than thirty years before the removal and coincident with the creation of national laws, illustrates the internal discord created by these changes.

This was all part of the larger rift that was quickly expanding within Cherokee society. By the first decade of the nineteenth century, the heated debate involved many interwoven facets: a national government versus town government, Western agriculture and personal wealth acquisition versus small-scale subsistence farming, Christianity versus Cherokee religious belief, and the redefinition of gender roles, property rights, and many other issues that affected every aspect of Cherokee life.

The fault lines of such debates did not perfectly mirror white delineations of race, but it appeared to white observers that they did. Calcifying Western perceptions of race in America during the early to mid-nineteenth century are well documented. Understanding perceptions of race within Indian groups is more difficult.[71] The racial terminology for Cherokees employed by the US army in the 1830s, based on "blood quantum," included terms such as "full blood" and "mixed blood." This was not the view of race held by most Cherokees. The military used blood quantum as both physical trait and behavioral determinant. "Full blood" was used either for a person whose lineage was perceived as entirely Cherokee or for a person who embraced what was considered "traditional" Cherokee practices. In contrast, "mixed blood" meant someone whose lineage included a white person, as well as someone who accepted at least some Western ideologies or practices. Later in the century, as government rolls continued to link "blood" to identity, Cherokees gradually accepted this viewpoint.

Maintaining the Old Towns

Although white Americans regarded Cherokees as the "civilized" tribe, "beneath the upper socioeconomic level was a surprisingly durable stratum of traditionalism, especially in North Carolina."[72] Cherokee clan and town structures in the mountainous region continued to organize daily life and formed the basis for behavior within and between communities. Rejection of large-scale government had been a core trait of Cherokee society since the first sustained and documented contact with Europeans. In Fred Gearing's study of eighteenth-century Cherokee social and political structures, he noted: "Early in the 18th century there was no formal political system beyond the villages. Then, the Cherokee tribe was an aggregate of politically independent villages; there were no structures to facilitate decisions by the tribe at large, or to permit the systematic coordination of tribal actions. After the creation of a tribal state at mid-century, the villages remained political entities within the larger, sovereign state."[73]

In eighteenth-century Cherokee society, a carefully designed set of intertwined political, kinship, and social structures helped maintain a balance within and between towns, as well as with relations with non-Cherokees. These were based on both the clan system and the town. A town did not signify a precise geographic location but a group of people whose primary identity was membership in that town. Geographic location might change as a result of war or depletion of natural resources, but the town would continue to exist as a group of people. Some towns contained several hundred people, although most were one hundred to two hundred. Political control was lodged at the town level; each functioned as a discrete governing body. Local government was organized with formal offices, led by the chief, or headman. However, governing bodies had no power of coercion, only persuasion. The entire community, male and female, had a voice in discussing issues relating to the town. Geographically, a town usually looked like a cluster of houses surrounding a community town-house, accommodating community-wide discussions and debates. Discussion could last for days, and the headman was charged with facilitating a consensus view. Preserving harmony and balance was central to proper behavior, and if someone held an opinion that differed from the majority view, they eventually withdrew from the proceedings.[74]

The offices and laws of the town worked in close conjunction with clan laws. The clan system was the basis for much of Cherokee behavior. First and foremost, the system of the seven clans in Cherokee life controlled marriage and kinship. Clan identity was inherited from one's mother. If she was non-Cherokee, her children often lost much of the support of Cherokee society. Marriage to someone of the same clan was strictly forbidden. Most towns had members representing all clans. If someone visited another town, it was the duty of a clan member to take care of that person.

By the early nineteenth century, Cherokee towns were much smaller than their eighteenth-century counterparts. Spatially more linear, they consisted of a series of log cabins stretching along the banks of a creek or river. In many of these towns, the local headman served a leadership role, and the bulk of town membership included his adult children and their families. The town often took the headman's name, such as Lawlo's Town, of which Chewkeeaskee was a member.[75] The town offices and organizations also evolved, in large part because there were not sufficient numbers to uphold the old ones. This is also one of the main reasons the clan system began to lose significance. However, town-level governance remained a foundational belief, and Cherokees shunned any attempt to enforce laws from a higher level, Cherokee or white. This belief was sternly guarded and would drive many Cherokees outside the Cherokee Nation.

One of the town organizations perpetuated in modified form through the nineteenth century was the gadugi—the communal work party. The ga-dugi had close associations with the eighteenth-century (and earlier) Cher-okee towns. Certain forms of the word meant "town" or "settlement."[76] This linguistic overlap suggests that one of the basic meanings or tenets of the town originally was a place of communal activity. Well into the nineteenth century, the modified forms of towns and the gadugi fulfilled many of the original goals of their predecessors, including the redistribution of wealth and the support of communal labor.[77]

The Treaties of 1817 and 1819

A series of land cessions between 1805 and 1807 had led to Cherokee assassinations and a national law making land cession a capital offense. In 1817 and 1819, crises occurred within the Cherokee Nation, again involving land cessions and federal pressure to migrate to territories west of the Mississippi River. Nancy Ward, who had lived through the turbulent years of the American Revolution, signed a petition with eight other Cherokee women who demanded no more land be ceded: "We do not wish to go to an unknown country which we have understood some of our children wish to go over the Mississippi but this act of our children would be like destroying your mother. . . . Your mothers your sisters ask and beg of you not to part with any more of our lands we say ours you are our descendants & take pity on our request, but keep it for our growing children for it was the good will of our creator to place us here and you know our father the great president will not allow his white children to take our country away."[78]

Ward was a highly influential person in Cherokee politics for decades. She was a Beloved Woman, a title which earned her a variety of privileges and power. In council meetings Ward was a vocal opponent of the Treaty of Hopewell in 1785, because it included land cessions to the US. This was the last Cherokee council meeting in which women formally participated, although women continued for decades to make their voices heard. In 1817 and again in 1819, Ward and other Cherokee women protested proposed land cessions. Although the cessions were accepted by the male-controlled Cherokee national government, it is likely that the vocal statements by Cherokee women against them were why the proposed removal treaty in 1835 was rejected by all the national and district leaders and could be achieved by the US government only by coercing a small group of wealthy Cherokee men who were not government officials. Even as Cherokee society shifted toward a patriarchal structure, women continued to exert political and economic power well into the nineteenth century, and later.[79]

Despite Ward's faith in President Monroe expressed in the petition, both

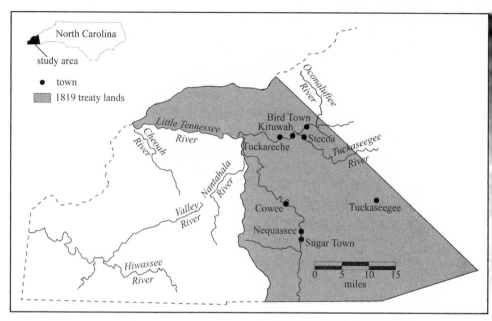

FIGURE 1.5. Reservee towns within the 1819 treaty lands. (Lance Greene)

poor settlers and wealthy speculators (such as Andrew Jackson) applied pressure to seize Cherokee lands, which led to a land exchange in 1817 and another in 1819. In total, these two treaties relinquished four and a half million acres of Cherokee land in the east.[80] As allowed by article 8 of the 1817 treaty and articles 2 and 3 of the 1819 treaty, many Cherokees, including the Welches, left the Cherokee Nation. These citizen reservees accepted 640-acre parcels of land from the United States outside the Cherokee Nation, in exchange for becoming United States citizens and renouncing Cherokee citizenship.[81] Their reservation parcels on the ceded lands were along the northern boundary of the Cherokee Nation in southwestern North Carolina. Several reasons counted toward their choice. First, the old towns were seated on rich agricultural soils. Second, often communities had occupied those lands for some time, and taking a reservation on a certain tract allowed one to stay in one's home. These towns were located along key trails in the mountains and were considered the hub of social and political interactions. They were also often important sites of religious, historical, and mythical significance (Figure 1.5).[82]

Historian William McLoughlin claimed that, during the 1819 treaty land cessions, many of the political leaders of the new Cherokee Nation, including Chief John Ross, did not want people to take reservations or to see the reservees succeed—a failure of Cherokees trying to form their own communities outside the boundaries of tribal lands would support the cause of Cherokee nationalism.[83] As would occur twenty years later during the removal crisis, there was open debate about the town versus the nation, and during both events Cherokee national leaders, as well as white politicians, would try to undermine those attempting to leave the nation and maintain their local towns.

John Welch, Catahee, Junaluska, The Axe, and Gideon Morris were all reservees. They resettled many of the old towns in the area, such as Kituwah, Cowee, Nequassee, Sugar Town, Tuckareche, Bird Town, Stecoa, and Tuckaseegee.[84] Town leaders and others worked together to decide where and how to claim reservations. Gideon Morris met with the community to discuss where he should make his claim. Betty Welch attended that meeting, and she, along with other witnesses, claimed that all decided he should make his claim on the land that had been held by a Cherokee leader called Long Blanket or The Clubb.[85] Morris's 640-acre claim ran along the Little Tennessee River and encompassed the old town of Nequassee, which included a large earthen mound. The community selected the site for Morris because "he could talk the white people's language[;] by fixing him on that place he could do their business."[86]

Not only did they make communal decisions regarding where to make claims, they also claimed adjacent tracts to maintain both old town lands and to keep communities intact. Yonaguska, a well-known headman in the region, accepted a tract on the Tuckaseegee River that encompassed the old mother town of Kituwah. Within Yonaguska's reservation was a large earthen mound, at the time roughly fifteen feet high and eighty feet on a side, and the center of the ancient site of Kituwah. Nearby was the reservation of Yonah Equa, or Big Bear, at the old town of Tuckareche, or Bear's Town. Like most of the reservees, Yonaguska and Yonah Equa had selected tracts that encompassed these old villages.[87] Welch, Catahee, Euchella, and others settled on or near Cowee, a town that had been prominent in the eighteenth and early nineteenth centuries. The mound at Cowee was reserved by Euchella. Adjoining Euchella's tract around Cowee were the reserves of The Old Mouse (Euchella's father) and Catahee (Junaluska's father and Gideon Morris's father-in-law). To the south was the Welch tract: 640 acres on Iotla Creek.[88]

By 1821 the reservees found themselves under siege. Euchella filed a lawsuit against a white man, Joseph Welch (no relation to John Welch), who had purchased a portion of the reserve in a state land sale. The case, *Euchella vs. Welch*, reached the North Carolina Supreme Court, which found in favor of Euchella. Euchella soon discovered, however, that legal right did not guarantee possession. White men flocking into the vacated lands coerced many reservees. Because of this pressure and the resulting confusion over multiple claims to the same tracts, the state offered to purchase back the reservations they had just granted. Euchella and many other reservees accepted the offer. Euchella moved to the Nantahala River, which was still part of the Cherokee Nation.[89]

Like many other reservees, John Welch was forced from his land after only a couple of years. In 1822 he sold his tract to a white man, Benjamin Brittain, for a fraction of what it was worth. Welch's mother-in-law, Ann Blythe, claimed that he was threatened that he would be arrested for his alleged participation in a revenge killing of the Cherokee man Ah Leache, should he refuse to sell.[90] Welch and his family then moved back into the northern edge of the Cherokee Nation, along Valley River.

The flight from the reserves in the early 1820s saw many of the reservees resettle back in the Cherokee Nation. The Welch, Morris, Euchella, Catahee, and other families settled along the northern boundary of the nation, mostly along the Valley River. The area was one of the most isolated parts of the Cherokee Nation, thus allowing them to remain at a distance from the central Cherokee government. A ring of steep-sided mountains—the Snowbird Mountains

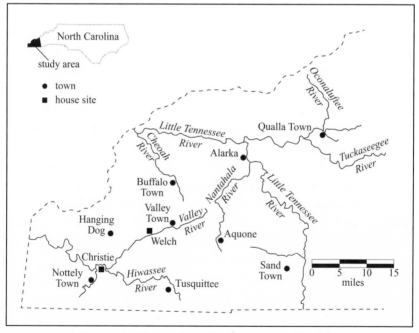

FIGURE 1.6. Removal era Cherokee towns and key sites
in southwestern North Carolina. (Lance Greene)

to the north and west, the Valley River Mountains to the south, and the Nantahala Mountains to the east—kept the region relatively isolated. Here, the Valley Towns were settled in close proximity around the head of the Valley River.

To the northwest of the Valley River settlements sat three major towns in the Cheoah Valley: Cheoah, Buffalo Town, and Connichiloe, or Tallulah. Cherokees also lived along Hanging Dog Creek, west of the Valley River, along Tusquittee Creek, farther east, and in other, smaller towns (Figure 1.6).[91]

The Welch family moved to Valley River in 1822, choosing prime agricultural fields just south of the core of the Valley Towns. Along with the Welches, several other Cherokee and intermarried white individuals had moved into the area in the early 1820s. Constituting a small portion of the Cherokee population in southwestern North Carolina, these individuals nonetheless had significant social and economic power. John and Betty Welch were among the wealthiest of these families in North Carolina, as were their neighbors and associates Gideon and Rebecca Morris, who lived just upriver.

The Welches built their farmhouse on an elevated knoll overlooking the river, surrounded by more than 150 acres of rich agricultural land. Based on archaeological evidence and later descriptions of the farm, their first home was relatively modest compared to their plantation fifteen years later. They initially constructed a log house, about fourteen feet on a side. It had a puncheon floor and a stick-and-clay chimney with a stone foundation and firebox. At some point in the late 1820s or early 1830s, with a growing family and increasing wealth, the Welches decided they needed a larger house. This new log structure, twenty feet by sixteen feet, was one and a half stories high, with a plank floor, glass windows with wooden shutters, a split shingle roof, and a stick-and-clay chimney with a stone foundation. Sawed planks for flooring and window glass were expensive architectural items at the time. The plantation expanded from 1822 through the 1830s. By 1832 the Welches had constructed a private road, downriver, to join the Unicoi Turnpike built in 1816.[92] A map drawn by a cartographer from Tennessee, Matthew Rhea, shows a road leading from the Welch farm, south to the mouth of Valley River.[93] Although their initial farm was relatively modest, in twenty years they developed a plantation rivaling any in the region. At the time of removal, the family held captive nine African Americans, grew 1,200 bushels of corn annually, and owned 316 head of livestock.[94]

The failure of the reservees to hold their land grants, and their return to the Cherokee Nation, pleased many white people and some Cherokees. As Robert K. Thomas, a Cherokee anthropologist who studied nineteenth-century

Cherokee history and culture, observed, "The drive toward centralization was expressly a move to curb individual town autonomy and thereby control the erratic, to Cherokee eyes, behavior of individual town chiefs."[95] The reservees, in accepting the terms of the 1817 and 1819 treaties, severed ties with the Cherokee Nation in exchange for keeping their old towns and their communities. However, the desire for land by incoming white families proved to be too much for these scattered Cherokee communities, even though they held legal title to the land. In some ways the outcome of the 1817 and 1819 treaties was repeated twenty years later by the Treaty of New Echota; the state and federal governments trampled the legal rights of the reservees, allowing the illegal usurpation of land held by Cherokees and their abuse by local white people, the army, and the state.

2

"Leave Home and Take to the Mountains"

Resisting Removal, 1836–38

I collected yesterday about 80 Indians. They had all received orders
from Welsh of Valley River to leave home & take to the mountains.

—John Gray Bynum, "Letter to General Winfield Scott," June 13,
1838. John Gray Bynum Papers, Southern Historical Collection,
University of North Carolina, Chapel Hill, 1838

As the internal cultural struggles continued, pressure from outside the
Cherokee Nation for tribal emigration westward rose dramatically. In
1830 Congress passed President Andrew Jackson's Indian Removal Act. Prior
to 1836, however, most in the Cherokee Nation did not seriously consider the
possibility of forced emigration. At least a portion of the Cherokees had exhib-
ited a willingness and ability to conform to Western views of "civilization." In
addition, Cherokees employed numerous legal representatives in Washington,
DC, where they found many sympathetic to their cause. However, these ac-
complishments ultimately meant little in the face of a southern-planter president acting in a climate openly hostile to nonwhite people and noncitizens.
Jackson moved swiftly to enforce the emigration that would ultimately occur
after he left office.

By the spring of 1838, federal troops and state militia loomed at several
forts in southwestern North Carolina as well as in other parts of the nation
(Figure 2.1).[1] Their mission was to remove all Cherokees (excepting roughly
seven hundred Cherokees in the Qualla Towns, who, with the support of William Holland Thomas, claimed exemption from removal) from the region.[2]
However, almost one-third of the Cherokees in North Carolina avoided removal, either through tentative federal exemptions or through active resistance in the form of fleeing into the mountains for several months, until the

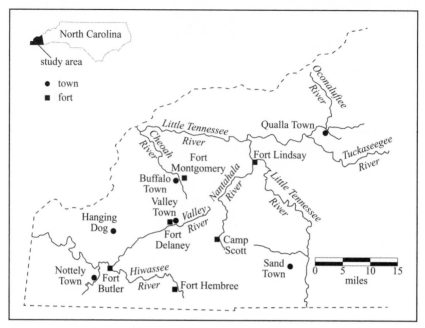

FIGURE 2.1. Military forts and Cherokee towns in southwestern
North Carolina, 1836–38. (Lance Greene)

occupying armies withdrew. Their decision to remain, even in the face of tre-
mendous loss, was sustained through not only a desire to stay in the land of
their birth but also their allegiance to eighteenth-century political and kinship
structures. The Welches shared these beliefs and worked to keep local Cherokee communities intact.

In contrast, the US government instituted a plan for the modernization
of a land and its people.[3] Modernization of the lands previously within the
boundaries of the Cherokee Nation was achieved through a series of steps that
legitimized, in the eyes of the state, the takeover, sale, and settlement of these
lands. The military performed the initial steps, followed by state governments
and civil servants. The undertaking assigned to the US Army was substantial.
The military occupation of a sovereign nation and forced emigration of its people constituted only part of the job. The army was also charged to prepare the
land for settlement by white people, and this entailed improving infrastructure
and mapping and recording valuable natural resources, such as timber, iron,
minerals, metals, water, and fertile soil.

By the beginning of 1835, the Cherokee Nation stood as one of the last
large tribal groups remaining in the Southeast.[4] The US Army, dealing in Florida

with increasing Seminole resistance to removal, eyed warily the Cherokee resistance and discussed the possibility of armed Cherokee uprisings, particularly in the mountainous portion of the nation.[5] To impose control over sixteen thousand people required a detailed census. Prior censuses of Cherokees had generally counted only adult men, or "warriors," to estimate fighting strength. The systematic removal of the entire tribe demanded a more detailed list of all individuals.

The census, often referred to as the Henderson roll, after David Henderson, the enumerating agent for Tennessee, began in June 1835.[6] A census taker was assigned for each state containing part of the Cherokee Nation. In North Carolina, Nathaniel Smith, an army officer, recorded the census, assisted by two men living in the Cherokee Nation: John Timson, a Cherokee, and Preston Starrett, a white man married to a Cherokee woman.[7] The 1835 Henderson roll lists 3,436 individuals living in the portion of the Cherokee Nation within the boundaries of North Carolina.

The census takers sent by the War Department into the Cherokee Nation in 1835 used six racial groups in which to place the people they were to record—fullblood, half blood, quadroon, African Cherokees, intermarried whites, and Black slaves—often based on judgments of physical appearance and sometimes on judgments of behavior by the census taker. The multitude of categories for the offspring of Indians and Europeans, versus the single category "African Cherokee," reveals the basis for racial classification. By the mid-1830s the federal government had accepted the theory of hypodescent, expressed as the one-drop rule, for African Americans. The dramatic expansion of cash crops in the South led to increased value for enslaved labor, followed by a hardening of the classifications needed to separate the enslaved population from everyone else. Although people of European descent generally saw American Indians as inferior to themselves, the classification of their "blood" was by degree, and therefore a "fullblood" was expected to be less able or willing to accept "civilization" than an Indian of "mixed blood." These Western racial categories were understood as indicators of innate social and behavioral traits. This was a shift from the Enlightenment thinking of a generation earlier, when the federal government attempted to institute civilization policies in order to "improve" Indian populations.[8]

These categories, beyond reducing identification to "blood," poorly suited the racial and ethnic diversity that existed in the Cherokee population, which included, minimally, Cherokee, Natchez, Creek, Catawba, African American, and white individuals. "Fullblood" Cherokees constituted almost 90 percent of the North Carolina population. In many areas, such as in the communities in the Cheoah River Valley, 100 percent of the population was identified as "full-blood" Cherokees. Nearly 10 percent were labeled as various forms of "métis" Cherokee, children of a Cherokee and a white parent. Cherokees married to people of African descent were categorized as African Cherokees, regardless of perceived blood quantum. In addition to 3,354 Cherokees, Smith recorded twenty-two intermarried white people, twenty-three people of African Cherokee descent, and thirty-seven enslaved African Americans.[9]

Congressional approval, required for removal of the Cherokees, came in the form of the infamous Treaty of New Echota, signed in December 1835 by removal agents and a tiny minority group of Cherokee leaders.[10] Chief Ross and most in the nation condemned the Cherokee signers, later known as the Treaty Party, as traitors. By signing away tribal land, they broke one of the original laws of the Cherokee Nation. The first decades of the nineteenth century had witnessed the murders of several Cherokees for the sale of land, and many in the Treaty Party would pay the same price for their actions.

President Jackson had decided to remove all Cherokee presence from the Southeast and did whatever he deemed necessary to achieve this end, including striking articles from the signed treaty before sending it to Congress. The original version of the Treaty of New Echota, signed by the members of the Treaty Party, included article 12, which gave Cherokees, with some limitations, the option to remain in the Southeast, receive 160 acres from the federal government, and become US citizens. Article 13 enabled Cherokees who lost land under the 1817 and 1819 treaties to claim the same amount of land. The option to claim land had been provided to the Cherokees in treaties in 1817 and 1819 (although in these earlier treaties they were given 640 acres; see chapter 1). President Jackson, afraid that a large number of Cherokees would accept the offer as they had twenty years earlier, unilaterally struck articles 12 and 13 from the treaty before sending it to Congress for ratification. Few people are familiar with Jackson's striking of articles 12 and 13 of the 1835 treaty, although it had major repercussions at the time. This unconstitutional act created chaos on the ground; for much of the two-and-a-half-year military occupation of the Cherokee Nation (1836–38), officers assumed every Cherokee would be removed, while many Cherokees thought they had the choice to avoid removal by claiming land and US citizenship under article 12. Jackson's act also exacerbated the confusion regarding Cherokees' claims to American citizenship, a significant issue that could have derailed much of the removal process (e.g., see discussion of Wachacha, this chapter).[11]

Congress ratified the treaty on May 23, 1836. With document in hand, Jackson quickly launched the removal. Article 16 of the treaty stipulated that removal must occur within two years of ratification (May 23, 1838). Military occupation of the nation began immediately. Jackson heard the rumors of impending Cherokee violence in the mountains. Needing little prodding for military intervention, he dispatched Gen. John Wool to the mountains of North Carolina in June 1836. Wool arrived in the Cherokee Valley Towns in July with roughly two thousand men.[12] Once on the ground, he took the rumors of an impending Cherokee uprising at face value and instituted harsh measures to prevent it. He confiscated the firearms of Cherokees in the region.[13] Most Cherokees acquiesced. They hoped that Chief Ross, who continued his efforts in Washington, DC, might slow or halt removal. Ross advised them to refuse to acknowledge the treaty. By the end of the summer, Wool realized his heavy-handed tactics were unwarranted. The Cherokees refused to remove, but their resistance took the form of noncompliance.

The timing of the treaty ratification in May 1836 and Wool's subsequent military actions had serious repercussions in southwestern North Carolina. Despite Ross's continued attempts to stop the removal, some Cherokees in the mountains assumed ratification meant they would be forcefully removed immediately. Many families did not plant crops, for fear they would be out west by the time they were ready for harvest. While Wool confiscated firearms to prevent uprisings, in reality it hindered the ability of Cherokees to hunt for wild game. These combined actions made the threat of starvation very real for many Cherokee families by the summer of 1836. Wool realized the danger. He offered the Cherokees provisions, which they refused: "Those in the mountains of North Carolina during the summer past, preferred living upon the roots and sap of trees rather than receive provisions from the United States. . . . Many have said they will die before they will leave the country."[14]

This prophetic statement was one of Wool's last in the mountains. At his own request, he was reassigned in May 1837, and Col. William Lindsay took command of operations.[15]

While Lindsay took control of federal troops, troops from the Tennessee militia patrolled southwestern North Carolina, considered a potential hotbed of violent resistance. The two-year deadline for removal had not yet arrived, and the soldiers were supposed to convince the Cherokees to move peacefully, while maintaining order between the Cherokees and the increasing number of white settlers. These settlers had reacted to the ratification of the treaty quickly, and by the summer of 1837, numerous white families squatted on Valley River, although it remained Cherokee land.

The Welch plantation lay nine miles upstream from Fort Butler, the headquarters for removal in North Carolina. Their prominent farmhouse served as a meeting place and was a hub of activity for the military. Betty, having lived most of her life with a Cherokee man within Cherokee communities, spoke both English and Cherokee fluently. Federal and militia officers kept a regular presence at the Welch house, using it as a place to deal with issues between local Cherokees and recently settled white people. Betty Welch served as an interpreter for Joseph Powell, a lieutenant colonel in the Tennessee militia. Joseph Powell, his brother, Capt. John Powell, and his troops mustered into service in July 1836, were among the first troops to occupy the Cherokee Nation.[16]

Despite the views of many of the soldiers, officers Joseph and John Powell enjoyed the company of the Cherokees. In their dealings at the Welch farm, they became acquainted with the family. Some of these relationships grew intimate. The Welches' oldest daughter, Mary, charmed John Powell, and the two married in 1837. This put the Powell brothers in a difficult position, situated between the local Cherokee communities and the soldiers posted at Fort Butler. Mary (Welch) Powell claimed a separate residence from her parents in 1837, and John Powell probably lived there even while stationed at nearby Fort Delaney.[17]

Within a few months of their arrival, military correspondence reveals that some of the officers stationed at these posts questioned the Powells' loyalty to the mission of the removal. In mid-November 1837, Joseph Powell defended himself in a court-martial convened at Fort Butler in response to two charges: that he was "trespassing on the citizens of the state" and "giving opinions calculated to incite opposition to the treaty." The first charge stemmed from a petition prepared by white civilians and officers of the North Carolina militia. It stated that Powell, in dealing with conflicts between white and Cherokee individuals, had consistently found in favor of Cherokees. It also claimed that Powell had openly told Cherokees that they could ignore the current treaty and avoid removal. During the proceedings, Powell conducted his own cross examining of the witnesses against him. He also called character witnesses in his defense. The testimony shows that many of the complaints against Powell focused on interpersonal conflict between local Cherokee and white people; white complainants saw him as a traitor to his race when he acknowledged Cherokee property rights.[18]

The more severe charge from a military standpoint was that Powell allegedly told Cherokees they could ignore the treaty and remain in their homes. Several of his character witnesses disputed the charge. Preston Starrett, a white man married to a Cherokee woman who served as an interpreter for the army, testified, "Your ability was good, your influence among the Indians great, and on frequent occasions you used it to aid in the execution of the treaty, from the confidence you possessed of the Indians, you were able to do as much as any other military officer in the country." Another of Powell's character witnesses was "Mrs Betsey Welsh." This rare opportunity to hear her own words confirms that she acted as an interpreter for Powell and that many of the cases he adjudicated were carried out at the Welch plantation. She concurred with Powell that he urged Cherokees, including her husband, to participate in the dispersal of claims and to follow the terms of the treaty. The military tribunal found Powell innocent of all charges. However, complaints against Powell, focusing on his leniency toward the Cherokees, continued throughout the removal. In March 1838 Cherokee claims commissioners John Kennedy, Thomas Wilson, and James Liddell wrote to Col. William Lindsay, commanding officer of the federal troops participating in the removal, and demanded Powell be arrested for endangering the removal proceedings. Lindsay refused to arrest a fellow officer without evidence of wrongdoing.[19]

In addition to military occupation, the removal efforts included other activities. Article 9 of the New Echota treaty stipulated that Cherokees would be reimbursed for lost property and improvements. Another purpose was to identify resources for future use. Benjamin Currey, superintendent of Indian removal, appointed two local white men, William Welch (no relation to the Welches) and Nimrod Jarrett, to record valuations of the Cherokees residing in North Carolina. Welch and Jarrett began evaluating Cherokee wealth in November 1836, four months after the military occupation began. They worked through February 1837, recording valuations for more than seven hundred Cherokee properties. These valuations describe architecture and agricultural improvements and assign line-item monetary values for each farm. Although a few officials sincerely attempted to compensate Cherokees for their losses, the government never intended to reimburse the Cherokees for many kinds of resources. For example, article 9 made no provisions for payment for the presence of or potential for timber, water, gold, marble, and iron, although they were often measured in the censuses, surveys, and valuations.[20]

Welch and Jarrett spent a considerable amount of time along the Valley River. The detailed information they collected for the Welches shows an expansive plantation, especially in comparison to other nearby farmsteads. The Welch farm had been occupied for fourteen or fifteen years, with a collection of structures of different ages and construction techniques. While the main house was valued at $191, the team estimated many of the other structures such as the external kitchen and several other smaller cabins to be worth $20–30. The Welches raised large numbers of cattle and hogs for years prior to the removal. In 1838 the Welches claimed "one Hundred & fifty head of cattle twenty-six head of Sheep one hundred and twenty five head of Hogs fifteen head of Horses."[21]

A lingering fear in Washington, DC, of a Cherokee uprising led to the authorization for the creation of a detailed map of likely the most dangerous part of the Cherokee Nation: the mountains of southwestern North Carolina. Members of the Topographical Engineers, under the command of Maj. William G. Williams, went to the region in November 1837.[22] Williams understood that one of the main goals was to map the mountainous terrain for troop movements and for locations of Cherokees, considered possible enemies of the state: "The surveys which are now in operation will present a mass of valuable information in relation to the topography of the country, and enable such dispositions to be made in reference to troops and munitions of war as will in case of emergency, we hope, contribute greatly to the prompt suppression of the evil."[23]

Five field-survey crews were sent to cover the area. Most survey crews, operating a chain and compass system, consisted of five or six men. The mapping in southwestern North Carolina was performed with state-of-the-art methods and equipment. These crews worked until January 1838, recording in three months the main river and creek drainages in the entire portion of the Cherokee Nation within the boundaries of North Carolina. A composite map generated from the survey data shows important landmarks, including the Welch plantation, listed as "Welsh (half breed)" (Figure 2.2).[24]

The state intended to auction the land vacated by the Cherokees. However, this could not be accomplished until a cadastral survey was performed. Modern cadasters are maps that show discrete property boundaries (plats or plans). Cadasters also provide information on land ownership, dimensions, and value. Prior to the removal, land within the Cherokee Nation was not allotted through deeds or discrete property boundaries as throughout most of the United States. Instead, a tribal rule of right of occupation guided land use. If a particular plot of land was not in use by another Cherokee family, its occupation or cultivation was deemed acceptable.[25]

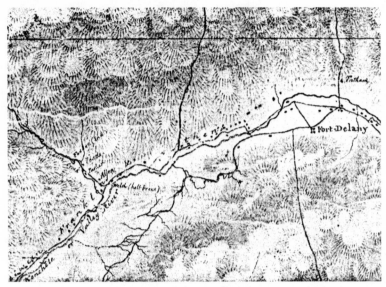

FIGURE 2.2. Section of 1838 composite map, showing Welch farm. (National Archives, identifier 78116890)

Surveyor Reuben Deaver led the survey and creation of these property boundaries for the anticipated sale of the vacated lands. Surveyors invented these boundaries in 1837, establishing 1,400 individual tracts ranging from fifty to four hundred acres. The Welch farm was designated Tract 71, including four hundred acres, in District 6 (Figure 2.3).[26] The Deaver maps showed newly created property boundaries and ranked each property in terms of quality of land, including arable soils, water, and timber. The combination of the Williams army map and the Deaver property map created the necessary geospatial grid for immediate settlement by white farmers and businessmen. Many current property boundaries were initially delineated during the surveys in 1837.

In January 1838 the US government launched preparations for forced emigration, stipulated in the treaty to begin on May 23, 1838. Commissioners John Kennedy and Thomas Wilson arrived at the Cherokee agency in eastern Tennessee to adjudicate Cherokee claims for loss of property and improvements. The commissioners expected to hear claims until the deadline of May 23, at which time the hearings would close. In early 1838, however, Cherokees resolved to support Chief Ross's attempts to alter the terms of the treaty and therefore ignored the commission.[27]

Gen. Winfield Scott, the newly appointed commander of the oddly named Army of the Cherokee Nation, arrived at Fort Cass in eastern Tennessee in

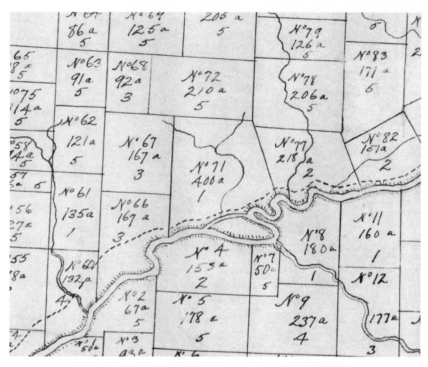

FIGURE 2.3. Section of Deaver survey map showing Welch
farm (Tract 71). (Cherokee County Register of Deeds)

early May 1838, less than two weeks before the commencement date. There
he commanded a multitude of institutions, including a massive, sprawling
concentration camp and a military jail and court.[28] Scott had at his disposal
approximately seven thousand men: federal troops, militia, and volunteers,
representing numerous infantry, artillery, and cavalry companies, stationed at
posts in Tennessee, Georgia, and North Carolina.[29] He had almost one soldier
for every two Cherokees. Scott personally declared the removal a war and effected the migration of as many Cherokees as possible by, among other things,
holding prisoners for extended periods without charge and declaring, with no
legal authority, that Cherokees were aliens.[30]

The US Army moved the Cherokees out of their homes in North Carolina
at gunpoint between late May and late July. The Chewkeeaskee family and many
others of Nottely Town were marched to Fort Butler a few miles to the northeast. From there the soldiers took them to Fort Cass in eastern Tennessee. By
mid-June the bulk of the mission was complete. The mass of North Carolina
Cherokees found themselves imprisoned in Fort Cass. In the third week in June,

the state disbanded their militias, and many federal troops moved out of the nation.[31] A small force of federal soldiers guarded the prisoners at Fort Cass.

The first several detachments under armed guard, totaling roughly six thousand Cherokees, left in June. These detachments traveled mostly along water routes, and General Scott's plan was for the entire Cherokee Nation to soon follow along these routes. However, disease was widespread in the heat of the summer, and the mortality rate in most of the detachments was outrageously high. Drought conditions also made some of the rivers unnavigable. Chief Ross and other Cherokees proposed that the removal of those held in east Tennessee be postponed until the end of the summer. Ross also proposed that the Cherokees be allowed to conduct their own travel. Scott agreed and set a new start date of September 1 for the remainder of the detachments. The Cherokee delegation, led by Chief Ross, was given oversight of the removal proceedings. Ross's brother was awarded the contract for providing food and other resources along the routes for the thousands of forced migrants who would depart in September and October.[32]

By late summer Fort Cass was a sprawling prisoner of war camp.[33] The scene there in the late summer was horrific. Most Cherokees camped without adequate food, water, shelter, clothing, or medicine. Several people died every day, mostly infants, small children, and the elderly. Diseases such as cholera, smallpox, dysentery, and whooping cough spread rapidly. Daniel Butrick, a Baptist minister who spent much time in the camps, wrote in his journal of tending the sick, presiding over numerous burials, witnessing white men being allowed into the camps to sell whiskey, and hearing accounts of beatings, rape, and murder by the soldiers.[34] The bulk of the North Carolina Cherokees then marched west in detachments of roughly a thousand people each in late August and September 1838.[35] Chewkeeaskee, his wife, and their children marched with one of these large detachments to Indian Territory.

RESISTING REMOVAL

Scott commanded a force of federal troops and state militia ordered to keep watch over fifteen thousand Cherokees and oversee the dispersal of funds to Cherokees by the federal board of commissioners. But something else was happening along the Valley and Cheoah Rivers that the military was slow to perceive. While Scott originally hoped to leave Fort Cass with all his troops by the end of September, the resistance to deportation by Cherokees in the mountains held him and his troops in the region until December.

A small contingent of "fugitives" gradually came to the attention of Scott. Developments along the Valley River between July 1 and December 1 illustrate the determination of the holdouts to preserve their communities intact in the mountains. The events and actions surrounding this small group of resisters posed serious problems for Scott and, at one point, almost derailed the removal for thousands of Cherokees. The Welch family was in the middle of the entire affair, and they would emerge from the events a different family. Also involved were many of the same people who had been reservees twenty years earlier. As they had then, they chose to protect their local communities and avoid control by the state. People from the preremoval communities along the Cheoah, Nantahala, and Valley Rivers and along Hanging Dog Creek fled into the mountains and hid from the troops.

Until mid-summer of 1838, the Welches felt relatively safe from removal. John Welch, as a reservee of the 1819 treaty, was a US citizen and, as such, legally entitled to compensation for property and improvements lost through that treaty. However, Scott discovered that the Welches and others supported other Cherokees avoiding removal. On June 13, 1838, John Gray Bynum, commander of the North Carolina militia at Fort Montgomery (now Robbinsville) reported, "I collected yesterday about 80 Indians. They had all received orders from Welsh of Valley River to leave home & take to the mountains."[36]

Another officer, Capt. George Porter, reported: "I have, with my company, taken post here convenient to two points (one of which is Welch's, the other Colvard's) where the Indians are fed and harboured and where the trails from the mountains, on both sides of the river, concentrate. . . . Welch's family and Nancy Colvard . . . should be apprehended and sent in. . . . Welch's people I understand have liberty from Genl. Eustis. These two families are doing a great deal of mischief."[37]

On June 20, 1838, just as the army began seizing Cherokee families, John Welch transferred power of attorney and the ownership of all chattel property, including those he held enslaved, livestock, and farm equipment, to Jonathan Blythe and Jonathan Parker.[38] Jonathan Blythe was Betty's father, and Parker a close neighbor. They designed this legal action to protect the Welch holdings on Valley River by placing as much legal power and property in the name of white men.

In late July, John rode with his oldest son, Ned, John Powell, Gideon Morris, and Morris's brothers-in-law Junaluska and Wachacha, to Fort Cass, where they planned to settle their claims with the board of commissioners. All the Cherokees in the group claimed US citizenship as reservees or children of reservees and considered themselves protected from forced emigration. The next morning, as they approached the fort, soldiers arrested all the Cherokee men in the group, John, Ned, Junaluska, and Wachacha, without charge and locked them in the fort guardhouse, described later by John Powell as a "loathsome dungeon."[39] Gideon Morris immediately rode fifteen hours back to Valley River, to inform the people there of the arrests and warn of possible further actions by the military. Scott's knowledge that the four Cherokee men had no intention of moving west spurred his arrest order. At the time, however, his main focus was still on the thousands of prisoners of war at Fort Cass.[40]

While federal troops monitored the movements of the Welch family, Wachacha, an "active, powerful, full-blooded Cherokee" held in prison at Fort Cass with John Welch and the others, attempted another strategy aimed at remaining in North Carolina. He filed a writ of habeas corpus with Charles Keith, a Tennessee circuit court judge serving in Athens, a small town near the fort. Wachacha claimed American citizenship because his father, Katatahee (or Catahee), had been a reservee in 1819. Judge Keith immediately ordered General Scott to appear in his court in Athens to defend Wachacha's imprisonment and to bring Wachacha. Although seen by Scott as an ignorant "fullblood" Indian, Wachacha was in fact a Cherokee headman who had long understood Western law pertaining to individual rights. Wachacha's claim of citizenship, if supported by Judge Keith, would make the forced emigration of hundreds of Cherokees (those with connections to the reservees, and perhaps others as well) held in the camps illegal. Upon realizing this, Scott took the case much more seriously. It could potentially undermine the entire removal process, just as the first Cherokee-led detachments were leaving for the west.[41]

General Scott's correspondence with H. R. Poinsett, the secretary of war, not only reveals the seriousness of the case but lays out the arguments he presented to Judge Keith. Scott began by arguing that the Cherokees, by refusing to emigrate as stipulated by the Treaty of New Echota, initiated a state of war between the Cherokee Nation and the United States. If true, then a civilian court would hold no sway in the actions undertaken by the army. Scott makes very clear that he considered the removal an act of war: "some confusion of ideas had evidently arisen on the subject from the fact that no battle or skirmish had preceded the captures in question; that under instructions and the obligations of war as well as of humanity, the troops had in their operations, and over all in their power to avoid bloodshed; that their bloodless success, gained by discretion, entreaty and kindness, did not change the character of our operations which were those of war in all its array, and it was finally submitted whether a prisoner so made and detained could be legally remanded and discharged by a state judge on any judicial authority whatever, unless, indeed, it should appear, on evidence, that he were a citizen of the U. States and therefore not liable to be held as a prisoner of war."[42]

In describing those "bloodless" and supposedly kind actions, Scott overlooked the numerous acts of theft, assault, and rape documented at Fort Cass by his soldiers against the Cherokees. Scott also argued strongly against the citizenship of reservees and their families. He stated that the articles of the 1817 and 1819 treaties did not automatically provide citizenship but allowed Cherokee reservees to apply for it. Scott then argued that Wachacha, whom Scott deemed "confessedly a Cherokee and alien by birth," if indeed a citizen, needed to provide the original certificate, under seal, from the clerk of the court who provided it.[43]

Judge Keith found in favor of Scott's argument, declaring that Wachacha was not a US citizen and thus bound by the removal treaty to emigrate. In mid-September, Scott returned Wachacha to the Fort Cass guardhouse. There he remained until placed into one of the emigration detachments leaving Fort Cass. But Wachacha was determined to remain in North Carolina. Before the detachment had left Tennessee, he and his brother, Junaluska, gathered a group of roughly twenty-five Cherokees and guided their escape back into the mountains of North Carolina. Wachacha successfully escaped with the other Cherokees, but Junaluska was caught and traveled with the detachment to Indian Territory. Upon his return to North Carolina, Wachacha joined a group of "fugitive" Cherokees led by a headman called Euchella. Junaluska soon returned from Indian Territory and remained in North Carolina.[44]

Scott stayed busy organizing the departure of the majority of Cherokees from Cass and then mustering out the state militias and most of the regular soldiers. However, he saw collecting those Cherokees who evaded capture as his last duty of the removal, and he began with the Welches. On August 22 Lt. H. L. Scott of the Fourth Infantry reported: "I found that the families of Welsh, of Morris, and of Wat-chut-cher [Wachacha] had fled at daylight yesterday morning. The two former families have gone to South Carolina and the latter to Lufty [Qualla Towns] in Haywood County N.C. This flight I understand was caused by information communicated by Morris who I understand immediately after the arrest of Welsh left Calhoun [Tennessee] at 12 o'clock on one day and reached this place by 3 o'clock the next morning."[45]

Most of the Cherokees still in the area had fled to the Qualla Towns or to South Carolina or hid in the mountains. Lieutenant Scott made camp around the Welch house in an effort to trap the Welch children and other "fugitive"

Cherokees. Betty was pregnant at the time. Her children were not faring well. While her oldest son suffered in prison with her husband, her other nine children, five of whom were under ten years old, were in hiding with the Morris family in South Carolina. She remained at the farm with the eight people they held enslaved, one of whom, Nelly, was also pregnant. Betty could only watch as the soldiers camped around her house and pilfered the farm. Scott sent his next order, to seize the enslaved from the Welch plantation. John Powell later described the event: "Affiant states that he told the gard that took the negroes away that if they moved the woman . . . that it would kill her & they replied that they could not help it that it was Genl Scott's orders to bring [Elizabeth] Welch & children if they could get a hold of them & if they could not, to bring all his Welches negroes at all hazards. I then told the gard that the negro woman Nelly had only a few days since had a child & that it would not in my opinion do to move her as she had been out of her bead [bed] [not] more than an hour at a time since she had been confined to her bead as affiant had been told by the family."[46]

The oldest African American on the plantation was Isaac, "about 40." He was probably married to Nelly, four years younger than he. Nelly had a daughter named Jane and a newborn babe in the summer of 1838. Phillis, twenty-six years old, had three children, Bill, Claire, and Henderson. There was also a boy, six years old, named Frank.[47]

The soldiers marched all nine of the enslaved African Americans eighty miles from Valley River, across the Long Ridge, to Fort Cass. As Captain Powell had warned the officers in charge, Nelly delivered her baby ten days before the march, and was unfit to travel. Nelly, her newborn, and one of the boys died at the agency in Athens.[48] Powell also observed that a lack of medical care caused the deaths of these three people: "Affiant [Powell] was at the agency at the time. One negroe boy died & [affiant] believes that if the boy had been attended to he could have [been] saved, the negroe woman [Nelly] died before affiant went to the agency[.] some short time before the boy died the woman died as affiant was told & affiant believes that the treatment the woman received that was got by affiant & brought home was the cause of her losing a child in a very short time after getting her [the baby?] home."[49]

Imprisoned at Fort Cass, John Welch was regularly questioned by General Scott and others in his office, where he was very poorly treated. Several witnesses hinted at torture of Welch and the other prisoners.[50] An "oppressive insolent" lieutenant abused him while in the guardhouse.[51] Both John and Ned Welch became gravely ill while imprisoned. Ned, considered near death, was finally released in early September, although John continued to be confined.[52]

Although the attempts at including the Welches in one of the removal detachments failed, the imprisonment of John, Ned, Junaluska, and Wachacha left Betty and several other women as temporary heads of household, forced to spend more than three months attempting to stop soldiers and squatting white civilians from looting their farms. With most of the family imprisoned or in flight, agents auctioned off much of the Welch property, including cattle, hogs, corn, wheat, oats, potatoes, and other crops.[53] Their house was broken into and, among other things, $225 in gold and silver coins was stolen from a trunk.[54] Whatever was not auctioned by the government was also stolen. John Welch later claimed "that as a consequence of his arrest and long confinement not only entirely lost his health but that nearly the whole of his large crop of corn wheat rye oats potatoes cattle & hogs were lost and destroyed there being no person left at his home able to take care of his property, himself and oldest [son] & negroes confined in a loathsome dungeon while [illegible] Florada soldiers with a horde of other equally worthless white men were rioting in and plundering him of his property."[55]

"Florada soldiers" refers to federal troops who had recently fought in the Second Seminole War. These soldiers scoured the mountains in search of runaway Cherokees. To the best of their knowledge, there were not more than a few dozen, a hundred at most.

The state auction of the vacated lands began during General Scott's search for the runaways. The Welches decided to repurchase their own land at the state auction in Franklin, through their son-in-law, Capt. John Powell. On November 2, 1838, Powell bought back the Welch farm.[56] By this time a trusted member of the family, he carried with him to Franklin $1,000 of Welch money in gold and silver for the down payment required by the state. Powell purchased 1,274 acres, including roughly 150 acres of arable agricultural land along Valley River, as well as the houses of John and Betty Welch, Ned and Emily Welch, and Mary and John Powell. These tracts also included hundreds of acres of wooded uplands. The Welches planned to use these upland, wooded tracts for the settlement of Cherokee refugees (Figure 2.4).[57]

John Welch was released from the Fort Cass guardhouse in early November. Upon his return to Valley River, it was obvious his physical health had been destroyed. Nearly blind, he could barely walk. Powell testified, "Many times affiant has seen said John Welch when he could hardly find his road in a fair sunshiny day."[58] Preston Starrett described Welch after his release as "unable since to do anything of consequence still drag[g]ing out a lingering miserable existance [sic] without hope of recovery to human appearances."[59]

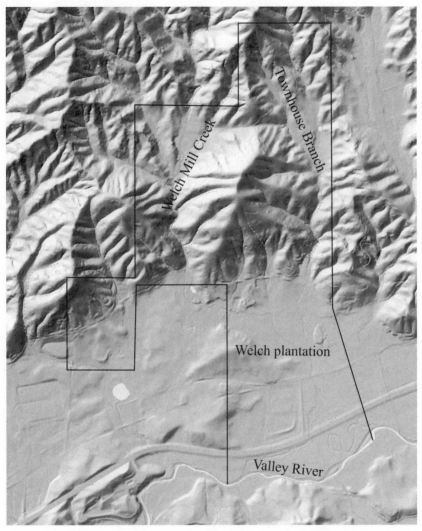

FIGURE 2.4. Welch 1838 property boundaries on digital elevation
model, showing uplands. (US Geological Survey, Lance Greene)

Despite his very ill health, John continued to act pragmatically to fore-
stall any other removal efforts by the government. On December 24, 1838, he
signed power of attorney to Betty, and she became responsible for claims and
suits filed for the benefit of the family as well as sole owner of the Welch chattel
property.[60] This legal document gave Betty significant powers in dealing with
claims against the government for loss of land and property. The document
also made Betty a wealthy woman.

The military occupation in the mountains continued after the main Chero-kee detachments had started westward. Federal troops combed the steep ridges and valleys, searching for the Cherokees in hiding. The occupation might have continued for several months if not for the incident involving Tsali. He was an older Cherokee man who had lived with his wife, Nancy, and their children along the Nantahala River. They, like many other Cherokees in the region, fled into the mountains to escape the army dragnet. In late October, Tsali, Nancy, and their three grown children and their families were captured by Lt. Andrew Jackson Smith and three enlisted men of the US Army Dragoons, accompanied by William Holland Thomas. Thomas had agreed to help locate some of the Cherokees in hiding. He was concerned that they would jeopardize the tentative authorization by the army for the Qualla Town Cherokees to remain in the mountains.

Thomas left the small detachment as it began marching the prisoners. On the march to Fort Cass in eastern Tennessee, the soldiers were physically abusive to members of the group. The form of abuse and who first responded is unclear, but Tsali, one of his sons, Nantahala Jake or Lowen, or his son-in-law Big George, killed a soldier by hitting him in the forehead with an axe. A second soldier was quickly killed and a third wounded. Lieutenant Smith fled on horseback. The army, unable to locate Tsali and his extended family, coerced Euchella and other members of his group, who had also been in hiding in the mountains, to capture him. Members of Euchella's group then executed Nantahala Jake, Big George, and Lowen on November 23, 1838, and Tsali himself two days later. Wachacha, who had only two months earlier been held in the Fort Cass guardhouse, had forced General Scott to justify the imprisonment and removal of the Cherokees, and had escaped from a detachment with two dozen other Cherokees and returned to the mountains, aided Euchella in Tsali's capture and execution. Because of their involvement in the "Tsali affair," the members of Euchella's group were given permission by the army to join the Qualla Town Cherokees and remain in North Carolina.[61]

Tsali's capture and execution held paramount importance for all Chero-kees still in the east, because it signaled the end of military occupation of their communities. General Scott was ready for the costly, unpopular occupation to come to an end. Likewise, the officers and soldiers in the field were hoping to avoid winter in the Southern Appalachians; living in tents and scouring the countryside on horseback or on foot amounted to extreme physical hardship. Scott used the execution of Tsali to send a message that the few Cherokees thwarting capture had been brought to justice, and therefore the massive, forced removal of the Cherokees had been a military success.[62]

By early December, word had spread to those Cherokees holed up in the various mountain ridges and valleys of the deaths of Tsali and his sons and of the deal effected by General Scott and William Holland Thomas. The Cherokees remaining in North Carolina drew a collective breath. The agonizing period of military occupation had ended. Immediately after the troops had been dispatched, most of the Cherokees who had hidden in the Snowbird Mountains retreated to the Cheoah Valley or the Valley Towns. Some returned to their homes on Hanging Dog Creek, roughly seven miles southwest of the Welch farm.[63]

Those individuals who chose to seek safety from military detention in the Smokies paid a huge price. The homes they had fled five months before had been looted, and in some cases burned, and crops, livestock, and household goods stolen. What had been thriving communities were barren of activity. In 1840 William Holland Thomas recorded a census of Cherokees, by community, in North Carolina. He also recorded information on where every family had lived in 1835 (at the time of the Henderson roll), and how many had died "during emigration." In 1835, some 202 individuals lived in Buffalo Town. Of that number, 78 died during the removal, a loss of almost 40 percent of the population. For the families living on Valley River, the number lost was about 13 percent. Out of the two communities, a total of nearly 100 people had died during the removal. In Buffalo Town, 32 of the 51 families grieved at least one family member and others lost to emigration. Several families lost three or four members. Death hit mostly the young and the elderly. Starvation, hypothermia, and disease killed people at a tragic rate.[64]

Those families, although exhausted and suffering anguished grief, began immediately to rebuild their communities. Most of these Cherokees quickly found patrons who provided land and other forms of support. Many moved to the nearby Qualla Towns, where William Holland Thomas, a white businessman who had worked with the Cherokees for decades, provided aid. Roughly a hundred moved onto land provided by the Welch family, creating a community that would thrive for fifteen years.

In February 1839 the six enslaved African Americans taken from the Welches who survived the march to Fort Cass were returned to the farm. Nelly, her newborn infant, and one of the young boys had been buried in unmarked graves at Fort Cass. Isaac, probably the father of Nelly's baby; Phillis, probably the mother of the boy who had died; and four children were returned. Having endured the forced march along eighty miles of rough trail, imprisonment, and the return trip, they were again held in bondage on the

Welch plantation. A year after removal, the Welches held two more people in bondage.[65]

Within a year of the army's departure, people in these communities had reconstructed core governmental structures and reestablished dance grounds and townhouses. They had survived military occupation, but the next decade would bring challenges they could not have predicted. As during the removal, they would struggle to adapt to these changes while maintaining their identity as Cherokees.

The events of the removal illustrate the racial hierarchy firmly entrenched in nineteenth-century America. The American state performed a massive military occupation but was only partially successful in removing the Cherokee presence from the Southern Appalachians. Hundreds were allowed to remain, and hundreds more sought refuge in the mountains until the troops dispersed. Cherokees found ways to resist, through hiding, legal loopholes, changing ownership of land and property, or marriage to a white person. Even though they would stay in North Carolina, the bitterness of the occupation and the devastating losses of family members, land, and property would not be forgotten.

Those four hundred Cherokees who had fled an advancing army in the summer of 1838 fled into the unknown. They were unsure of the outcome, unsure of their connection to the tribe, to the US, and to their land. But they were defiant in their belief in their community. They suffered immeasurable loss. But they thwarted the power of the US government and an occupying army and won their right to stay and to keep their communities intact. A quarter of those who had evaded the army, those who built Welch's Town, relied on community cohesion and cooperation, as they had two decades earlier when they left the Cherokee Nation, in 1819. Their identity, based in community autonomy, was guided by age-old Cherokee beliefs in localism. Their ability to remain was dependent on support from people outside the community. They relied on people who controlled wealth and land, two things that they could not acquire.

Those people living in the Valley Towns and Cheoah Towns in 1839 stand out as important figures in American history. The Welches, Axes, Owls, Morrises, Wachacha, and many others actively resisted and outlasted the military might of the US. Their persistence derived from their unified community response to forced emigration. Community members understood how to sidestep military occupation, although at a severe cost. While their story wrecks the national narrative of Manifest Destiny, it fulfills another—those who risk their lives for independence.

3

"A Settlement of Indians on Valley River"

A New Community on the Welch Farm

The Cherokees are "forming Settlements, building town houses, and Show every disposition to keep up their former manners and customs of councils, dances, ballplays, and other practices, which is disgusting to civilized Society and calculated to corrupt our youth, and produce distress and confusion among all good thinking people."

—Andrew Barnard, "Letter to Governor Edward Dudley," April 6, 1840, Governors papers, State Archives of North Carolina, Raleigh, 1840

By January 1839 all members of the Welch family had finally returned to their farm along the Valley River. John, around forty-eight years old, was prematurely aged, blinded, and permanently disabled by his treatment at the hands of the army. Betty, now thirty-eight, was pregnant. She gave birth to a daughter, Stacey, later that year. Stacey was Betty's tenth and last child and the one she had carried throughout the removal the previous fall. All of their children, infant, young, and adult, were close by. Their oldest son, Ned, and his wife, Emily, farmed just downstream. Ned and Emily had married around the time of removal and moved to the property since then. Their first child, Laura, was born in 1840. South of the Welches and east of Ned and Emily was the farm of the Welches' daughter Mary and her husband, Capt. John Powell. The rest of the children still lived with Betty and John. In 1839 Mary was eighteen, and the next-oldest child, James, was thirteen. Betty and John had eight children at home with them, ranging in age from one to thirteen years (Figure 3.1).[1]

In the third week of November 1839, John Powell transferred the deeds of the seven tracts of land purchased at state auction, 1,274 acres in total, to Betty (see Figure 2.4).[2] The original purchase of the land in November 1838 by Powell (while John was still imprisoned at Fort Cass) was a conscious choice by the family to choose the person least likely to be questioned or harassed by land agents or other white people who had interest in purchasing the land themselves. In addition to being the only white male in the household, John Powell served as a militia officer. The Welches would have, ideally, purchased the land themselves or performed the transfer immediately. Postponing the transaction for a year suggests they feared the social climate. The threat of removal persisted, and displeasure at the continued Cherokee presence prevailed among the growing local white population.

The transfer of land to Betty Welch in November 1839 signified a critical step in an evolving legal and cultural battle between business and political elites and the Cherokees on Valley River. The transfer established Betty as the sole owner of the Welch farm: she legally held all real estate and chattel

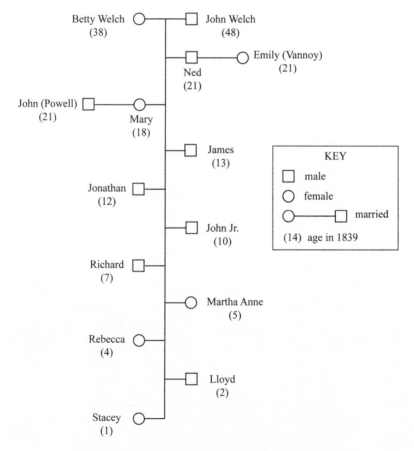

FIGURE 3.1. Welch family tree, 1839. (Lance Greene)

property, including buildings (several houses, a blacksmith shop, a grist mill, barns, stables, corncribs), goods, livestock, and eight enslaved African Americans. She also retained power of attorney for John and was therefore entitled to all funds owed him by the federal government through the Board of Cherokee Commissioners that convened several times in Murphy. Beginning in 1839 and increasingly throughout the 1840s and 1850s, Betty served as the public figure associated with the Welch plantation, expanding her role as the farm manager and as the spokesperson for the Cherokees who had settled there.

Attitudes toward Betty varied dramatically among the different groups she dealt with on a regular basis. The Cherokees of Welch's Town likely saw her as a strong benefactress who had repeatedly shown her support for them. Her role as matron after removal and after John had returned in ill health was an easy transition for them for several reasons. First, they barely subsisted through the winter of 1838–39 and reached out for help to any who offered it. They had known Betty and her family for years and trusted her. Cherokee society enjoyed a long history of women participating in town politics, owning property, and being economically independent. In the Powell court-martial in 1837, Powell reveals that Cherokee women continued to hold property separately from their husbands when he asked a witness, "Among the Indians do not husband and wife hold their property separately and each trade for themselves?" Therefore, Betty's control of the farm fit certain aspects of long-held Cherokee culture.[3]

In contrast, white men who dealt with Betty—military officers, Indian Office agents, businessmen—often expressed contempt for her. For decades, white men had bemoaned what James Adair, an eighteenth-century trader, and others called the "petticoat government" of the Cherokees and the power women exercised in Cherokee society.[4] Numerous acerbic comments directed at Betty, observing her "shrewdness" and "demonic" behavior, are founded partly in this view. The removal had transformed John Welch into a person with few or no rights, including ownership of land. Betty gained those privileges. This surprising shift in household power galled men like Indian agent Thomas Hindman and local businessman J. W. King, whom Betty would deal with in the 1840s. The head of the household was a married woman. She acted like a man, daring to deal with white men as equals. Her wealth elevated her power.[5]

Betty's control of the property is also coincident with the era of the cult of domesticity. This ideology stressed the role of women as nurturers who belonged in a domestic setting, away from the arena of business and politics.

Betty may have been one of the few married women in the patriarchal American South at the time who not only owned and controlled property but interacted on an equal footing with government officials and business elites. Betty's ability to advance beyond many of the legal and social constrictions of the society at large was due in part to her willingness to ignore them. Primarily, she had ignored the social strictures on a white woman marrying a nonwhite man, seen as a member of an inferior race. Ironically, it was this marriage that allowed her to become wealthy and powerful. Her husband's nonwhite, noncitizen status hindered his ability to own land or property, or to enter into certain kinds of legal contracts, such as serving as power of attorney. If married to a white man, Betty would have forfeited these rights. Betty Welch represents an unusual case of the failure of the cult of domesticity. The negation of feme covert for two decades prior to the Civil War is one of the most radical parts of this story and was made feasible only by Betty's marriage to a nonwhite man, which was in itself another negation of a supposedly inviolable social contract. John Welch's imprisonment and blindness forced Betty to take on the role of head of household, usually reserved for men. She was not the only one. Nancy Hawkins, a single Cherokee mother, owned and operated a farm and controlled extensive wealth. The ability of such women to reject Western gender roles was based both in the contrasting view of women's roles in Cherokee society and in the marginalized status in which they found themselves.[6]

Betty's actions should not be mistaken as modern liberalism, as revealed by her continued enslavement of African Americans. The Welches practiced enslavement prior to the removal. They were fully aware that slaveholding provided security in addition to wealth after the removal. Betty, as a woman married to a nonwhite man, was in a precarious position. Her wealth and her status as an enslaver diminished those threats. Referring to the limitations on white, married women during the nineteenth century, Stephanie Jones-Rogers writes "for them, slavery was their freedom . . . slave ownership allowed southern women to mitigate some of the harshest elements of the common law regime." She describes how "women's economic investments in slavery, especially when they used legal loopholes to circumvent legal constraints, allowed them to interact with the state and their communities differently."[7]

In the antebellum South, plantation mistresses were seen as the arbiters of civilized life and domesticity. They stood apart both from the master, who was supposed to carry out the daily management of the enslaved, and from the enslaved themselves, whom white people regarded as dirty and ignorant.[8] White enslavers taught their children from a very young age how to manage their captive laborers. In the antebellum South, it was common practice for men to inherit land and women to inherit enslaved people. These women understood the economic power and freedom represented by slaveholding, and many attempted, often successfully, to hold onto it after marriage. Plantation mistresses were often involved in daily interactions with the enslaved. In contrast to widespread perceptions, many practiced harsh forms of punishment, including beating and whipping, either through an overseer or by their own hands.[9]

Betty's extensive local political power derived in large part by her control of the plantation and the enslaved labor of people held there. It is unclear what training, if any, Betty received early in life. We do not know if she grew up in the Cherokee Nation or if her parents were enslavers. While the Welches embraced plantation life and the enslavement of African Americans, did they incorporate the image of white female domesticity? How did Betty see herself in the role of plantation mistress?

During military occupation the Welch plantation had been ransacked, and livestock and crops stolen. Luckily, however, the buildings suffered very little damage. The central feature of the farm was the main house, carefully situated on a prominent knoll overlooking the Valley River (Figure 3.2). The location

FIGURE 3.2. Location of Welch farm, facing south
toward the Valley River. (Lance Greene)

provided a panoramic view. This large, level area was high enough to avoid flooding and provided easy access to surrounding crops and pasture. It over-looked the Western Turnpike, not more than a hundred feet from the front door. People traveling on the turnpike viewed an impressive structure for the period. The orientation of the house served two purposes. First, it faced the Western Turnpike. Second, it faced southward, in order to receive as much sunlight as possible during the winter months. This "southern exposure" was a common practice in the region in the nineteenth century.[10]

The Welches built their first house, a one-room log structure, on the prop-erty in 1822 or 1823, after losing their reservation near Cowee. Although roughly the same size as most Cherokee houses, it stood out because of the family's im-provements. They added a stone base to the chimney, to support the upper stick-and-clay chimney, and added puncheon floors. Army surveyors noted these two architectural elements. Glass-paned windows, evinced by the recovery of several thin, flat pieces of glass, provided sunlight and heat in the winter and ventilation in the summer. Other architectural elements, such as large machine-cut nails and daub (clay packed around the chimney), attest to the construction methods of the house. This served as their home for several years.

At some point, as the family grew, they needed more space. They built a much more substantial house about fifty feet from the old one. This new home was a one-and-a-half-story log structure, forty feet long and sixteen feet wide. In contrast, most Cherokees and many white people lived in single-room log cabins that were twelve or fourteen feet on a side. The Welches cut timber from their land and hewed massive logs. The house had a stone fire-box, but most of the chimney was stick-and-clay. Instead of rough puncheons, they laid plank floors. They constructed the house in stages, and one side had a wooden-shingle roof, while the other had boards nailed on. As with their earlier house, the Welches added windows with glass panes. Heavy wooden shutters hung with hand-wrought iron hinges.[11] With this new house occupied by a growing family, the old one became the kitchen, a common practice for the period. Cooking in a separate structure reduced the likelihood of fire in the main house. This was particularly important with structures that contained fire hazards such as wooden, clay-covered (stick-and-clay) chimneys. This practice also kept the main house cooler in the summer and provided more space by relocating the tools and labor of food preparation. Both the main house and the kitchen had large, below-ground cellar pits dug near the chimney to store crops during the cold months, another common practice in the region.

The three archaeological features excavated at the site were originally used by the Welches as cellar pits beneath their first house on Valley River, which they later turned into a kitchen. The three pits were dug in the same alignment; they were all open at the same time or constructed in succession. Their alignment also reflects the alignment of the structure that stood over it.

Several lines of evidence reveal that the artifacts and other remains found in the cellar pits occurred over a brief period. There are several ceramic sherds and fragments of bottle glass that fit back together, including ceramic sherds found in different pits. The faunal assemblage also supports this. The pits contained approximately 1,100 bones, but only five show any sign of chewing: two were gnawed by dogs, two by rodents, and one had unidentified gnaw marks. This suggests that the bones were deposited in the pits and covered quickly. In addition, almost 40 percent of the faunal assemblage could be identified to the level of species, showing that many of the bones were deposited in a complete or nearly complete state.

The soils in each pit included three or four discrete zones, identified by differences in soil color and texture, and by the presence or absence of charcoal. Each zone also contained distinctive collections of artifacts and food remains, representing the preparation of different kinds of food. For example, all of the remains of cottontail rabbit, fifty-three fragments in all, are from the upper two zones of a single pit. All of the bones from turkey are from another pit. The faunal remains from the third feature are almost entirely cow and pig, plus several unidentified, broken long bones, suggesting both cow and pig were processed by crushing the long bones.

In addition, archaeological remains show that the old kitchen was dismantled, not burned or left to rot in place. There were few architectural artifacts in the pits. Several cut nails were found, but these were all bent or broken. Fragments of burned or sun-hardened clay, representing the pieces of chinking between logs, fell off while the structure was taken apart. If it had been burned, there would have been large pieces of burned wood, as well as unbent nails. If left to rot in place, thin zones of rain-washed soils would have been deposited in the pits, as well as more architectural debris (Figure 3.3, Figure 3.4).[12]

The kitchen was largely the domain of Betty, Phillis, and the younger women and girls. Here they prepared a wide variety of foods grown and harvested on the plantation. They also used the space for other activities, including cloth and clothing production. The plantation was also home to numerous other structures, mostly situated behind the main house. These included two small cabins, a smokehouse, a lumber house, a blacksmith shop, a stable, and a corncrib.[13] It had taken them fifteen years to build such a complex.

FIGURE 3.3. Exposed surfaces of three cellar pits. (Lance Greene)

FIGURE 3.4. Cellar pit Feature 1 during excavation,
showing profile wall. (Lance Greene)

The two small cabins on the Welch farm were probably occupied by the enslaved. They were both single-room log cabins, twelve feet on a side, with puncheon floors and stick-and-clay chimneys. Nearest the main house was the smokehouse. This structure was also a small log house and had a board roof. Pork could be preserved through smoking or salting, common meat-curing methods in the region. Although called a smokehouse in the evaluation, it is also possible that the Welches salted pork there. Whichever process was used, the small structures used to "cure" and store pork were called smokehouses.[14] Farmers liked the smokehouse to be near the main home, often within the house or yard lot. This provided quick access to meat and minimized danger of meat being stolen or damaged. Welch and Jarrett valued the structure at $18, roughly two-thirds the value of the kitchen. Most of the other buildings were of single-pen, log construction and valued at $15 each by the army.

Beyond the core of the farm complex were several other areas of activity. Shortly after moving to Valley River, the Welches built a water-powered grist mill on Welch Mill Creek, where it flows from the uplands into the valley floor. By the time of removal, the mill was already falling down. The construction of a grist mill in 1837 by Gideon Morris suggests that the two families, and perhaps the wider community, shared many such facilities. The agricultural fields maintained by the Welches, amounting to roughly 150 acres, were situated to the north, east, and south of the farm complex. These fields were used to grow corn, wheat, rye, and oats.[15] To the southwest of the main house, they gathered water at a springhead. A spring house was constructed over the springhead, and a small log cabin nearby was occupied by enslaved people or tenant workers.

Mary and John Powell lived in a small log house five hundred feet south of the main house, on the other side of the turnpike. Their farm overlooked the largest of the Welch agricultural fields. They also had a second, smaller log cabin on their property, which was sometimes occupied by Phillis, who worked in the house and farmed the large field nearby. Mary's grandmother also lived in the house and was cared for by Mary and Phillis.[16]

Ned and Emily Welch also lived close by his parents. Although theirs was a smaller farm than John and Betty's, it contained several buildings. Their main property had two single-room log cabins and a loom house. They also owned another property with two more log cabins.[17] Perhaps they rented these out to white tenants, as their parents had done before the removal. Or as plantation tasks changed seasonally, the living arrangements of the enslaved might have changed. This is suggested by the presence of the loom house. Enslaved women or girls might have slept there if they were weaving cloth or clothing.

The six enslaved people who survived the ordeal at Fort Cass were marched back to the Welch plantation in early 1839. Within a year the Welches held two more people captive. Isaac and Phillis were the only adults. Jane and Claire were two of six children; the names of the other four went unrecorded, as did their ages. Prior to Nelly's death at the hands of the army, Isaac and Nelly were a couple and had at least two children together. Nelly's newborn baby had died on the march to Fort Cass, but her daughter, Jane, survived, as did Phillis's daughter, Claire. Phillis, about twenty-five years old, had three children, but there was no other adult male in the enslaved community who could have been the father. Perhaps the Welches purchased Phillis with her three children, or the father may have died or was sold prior to the removal. He may have lived on a neighboring plantation. It is also possible that John Welch or his son Ned fathered Phillis's children. Ned was about the same age as Phillis and did not marry until 1837, probably after Phillis's children had been born. The men in the Welch household might have identified with "white southern masculinity" and seen rape as a right of their plantation authority.[18]

Phillis, Isaac, and the children interacted on a daily basis with the Welches and regularly moved between the three farms that made up the Welch plantation. Each of the farms had spare log cabins for them to sleep in, as they moved from house to house depending on the season and tasks. One of these cabins was just behind the Welch main house. Placement of cabins for the enslaved behind the main house and near activity areas was common, to situate the enslaved close to their work areas, including the kitchen, smokehouse, and stable.[19] These cabins on the Welch plantation were poorly constructed. The Welch and Jarrett appraisal for the two structures was $15 each, three dollars less than the value of the smokehouse. Although the same size, the smokehouse was either of newer construction or more substantial, or it contained better materials or more improvements than the cabins.

While there is no documentation of Betty's treatment of or interactions with the enslaved people on the plantation, we can surmise something about life there. Thousands of plantations across North Carolina held fewer than twenty enslaved laborers. In most cases enslaved people worked relatively closely with their captors. Enslaved women performed a multitude of tasks both indoors and outdoors. Historians Margaret Smith and Emily Wilson documented enslaved women in North Carolina "cooking, cleaning, washing, spinning or weaving, sewing, preserving foods; outside, tending animals and gardens and performing other domestic tasks; and, at harvest time, working in the field."[20] In contrast to their view of white women as pure and domestic, white society viewed enslaved women as dirty and uncivilized. Ironically, then, enslaved women, especially those working in a plantation house, were declared impediments to civilization and female domesticity, while their labor actually created and maintained the image of a successful plantation. They refused to go happily along on the "civilization" program while also being treated as lesser. This ongoing struggle infused the daily environment of slavery. Enslaved people subverted the language of the civilizing mission by rebelling against it. Enslaved women fought to challenge what historian Thavolia Glymph called the "ideology of white female supremacy" in a variety of ways. The violent responses of a master or mistress also gave the lie to the facade of southern civility.[21]

Most of the enslaved on the Welch plantation were children. Of the six with known ages, only Isaac and Phillis were over twenty years old. Although the ages of the African American children on the plantation are unknown, it is likely that they had Welch children of similar age to play with. Even in the low-country antebellum plantations, Black and white children commonly played together until around eight years old, at which time they would be separated and begin to learn their roles within plantation society. Tiya Miles has documented at Diamond Hill in northern Georgia that well into adulthood Cherokees and enslaved African Americans continued to interact socially.[22] Did this apply to the Welch plantation? The rigid social hierarchy based on race of the lowcountry South was less severe in the Upper South. The vast wealth to be made on cash crops such as cotton was not possible in the mountainous terrain and climate. Although their views on slavery are unknown, the people of Welch's Town probably had not completely accepted the Western ideology of race, including Black inferiority. It is possible they rejected the idea of enslavement, which they viewed as a central part of the capitalist ethic as practiced in the South.

How aware were John and Betty of the difference in the survival rates of the members of their family compared with the people they enslaved or with the families from Welch's Town? John and Ned had been imprisoned and abused. However, all of the Welch family members survived the removal. In contrast, 30 percent of the African Americans on the farm in 1838 died. This percentage was much closer to that of some of the Welch's Town families. Did this shared trauma connect the enslaved and members of Welch's Town after removal? How much time did the enslaved people living on the Welch farm spend in Welch's Town, roughly a mile away, hidden in the steep Snowbird Mountains? In other parts of the Cherokee Nation prior to removal, Cherokees and enslaved African Americans had attended each other's dances and

shared medicines and medical care, and similar events may have occurred between the enslaved community and the people of Welch's Town.[23]

POSTREMOVAL TOWNS

Of the roughly 3,600 Cherokees living in North Carolina in early 1838, only
1,100 remained a year later.[24] These Cherokees found themselves going home
to a world greatly altered, an environment with a palpable sense of the unknown. Those who had eluded capture in the mountains assumed they were
fugitives in the eyes of the United States. Citizens of neither the Cherokee Nation nor the United States, their stolen lands had been divided into tracts and
sold at auction while they were hiding. Although still in the Cherokee homeland, they seemed to be a people without a home. Out of this surreal environment, they began to assess their situation and make pragmatic choices about
their own survival. This was a monumental task, for they faced racism from
local white people and from state and federal institutions. The purpose of the
removal had been to rid the region of any Cherokee presence, and many local
white individuals seethed that any Cherokees continued to live in the area. At
both the state and federal levels of government, racism was expressed through
a reluctance to grant or even discuss any kind of citizenship or other rights.
This marginalization left the Cherokees in North Carolina in a legal limbo for
years after removal.

A primary impact of removal for those who remained was the loss of any
land on which to live or work.[25] To overcome these immediate problems, the
Cherokees found sympathetic patrons willing to help them. With their help
Cherokees established three major town clusters, as well as smaller settlements. The largest group of settlements was known as the Qualla Towns, led
by William Holland Thomas, a white man who had grown up near the Cherokee towns along the Tuckaseegee River. Thomas had helped negotiate a tentative removal exemption for the roughly seven hundred Cherokees living in the
Qualla Towns in 1838. After the removal Thomas continued to purchase land
for the Qualla Town residents to live on (Figure 3.5).[26]

A few miles south of Franklin, North Carolina, the Cherokee community
of Sand Town occupied the lands along Cartoogechaye Creek and Muskrat
Branch. This town was much smaller than the combined towns of the Qualla
settlements. The headman of Sand Town was Chutasottee, or Woodpecker.
William Siler, a local white entrepreneur, had provided land on which the
Cherokees could resettle. At first, Siler maintained ownership of the land,

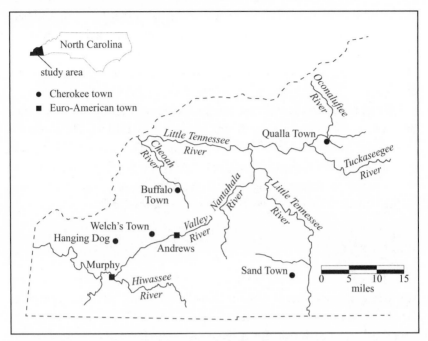

FIGURE 3.5. Postremoval Cherokee towns in
southwestern North Carolina. (Lance Greene)

but the complete economic relationship is unclear. The Cherokees may have
worked for Siler, or he may have allowed them to continue their preremoval
lifestyle unhampered. The Siler family had been among the first white settlers
in the area and involved in taking some Cherokee lands in 1819. In spite of
this, there seem to have been some close associations between the family and
at least some of the Cherokees in Sand Town, for now Cherokees lived safely
on Siler's property.[27]

Another group of Cherokees returned to their homes along the rivers and
creeks of the Cheoah River drainage. Cherokees lived in three major towns
in the Cheoah Valley in 1835—Cheoah itself along the Cheoah River near
present-day Robbinsville, Buffalo Town along the Cheoah River near the
mouths of East and West Buffalo Creeks, and Connichiloe or Tallulah along
much of Tallulah Creek.[28] Although many of the Cherokees of Cheoah and
Tallulah were removed west, most members of Buffalo Town remained in the
mountains. Labeled "incorragible savages" by Col. John Gray Bynum, the officer in charge of removal in the Cheoah Valley, the people of Buffalo Town
refused to cooperate with any removal efforts.[29] Many people from Buffalo

Town and smaller numbers from the other Cheoah Valley towns moved back
to this area because of its isolation and community ties, led by Lawlo and
Dickageeska, the headmen.[30] These groups stayed relatively safe from white
incursions, for the Cheoah Valley was and is one of the most isolated areas in
the region.

Other Cherokees found their way back to smaller preremoval communities. Several families returned to their homes on Hanging Dog Creek, roughly
seven miles southwest of the Welch farm. Hanging Dog Creek had long been
settled by Cherokees. Families such as the Axes and the Owls, who had lived
there in 1835, initially reclaimed their farms. A few families returned to Alarka
on the Nantahala River, and Peachtree Creek, east of Murphy.[31]

WELCH'S TOWN

Over the course of 1839, a group of Cherokees settled on the lands of the
Welch family. The Welch property included more than 1,200 acres, composed
mostly of steep, mountainous land in the Snowbird Mountains. While the
larger settlement of Buffalo Town could sustain itself, Cherokees from smaller
towns found that their preremoval communities had been so thinned by emigration and death that they would be too sparsely populated to cope. They also
feared reprisals by local white people and further removal attempts by federal
agents. So many of these individuals quickly gathered on the Welch land and
established a town with people from other small, preremoval communities.[32]
Thomas Hindman, a temporary federal agent sent to the area in 1841 to effect a
second removal, noted, "Mrs. Welch . . . has purchased some twelve or thirteen
hundred acres of land from the state of North Carolina at something near the
sum of $8000, one eighth of which is only paid for, the largest portion of the
Indians are settled upon this land."[33]

The newly formed community of Welch's Town situated itself on two par-
allel, narrow creek valleys in these mountainous tracts. One was Welch Mill
Creek (see Figure 2.4) The creek, originating near the central ridge spine of the
Snowbird Mountains, flows year round and is fed along its course by several
springheads. The level, arable land along this creek encompasses roughly sixty
acres. At a slightly higher elevation, just above this flat land and ringed by it, are
numerous small benches and knolls forming ideal cabin sites. Another creek to
the east was, and is, called Townhouse Branch. This larger branch and the fertile
land around it, also owned by the Welches, lay roughly half a mile east of Welch
Mill Creek. A trail that led through a small gap in the ridgeline connected the

two creek valleys. Townhouse Branch produces more water than Welch Mill Creek, and its level ground encompasses around fifty-five acres.

Most of the families of Welch's Town made their home along these two creeks. They built small, single-room log cabins with chimneys built from cribbed logs packed with clay. Most had hard-packed dirt floors, although a few had rough puncheon floors. These cabins lined both sides of the two creeks, taking advantage of low natural rises where the steeper slopes break along the edges of the creek valleys. The seclusion offered by the uplands proved a crucial factor for the Cherokees on Valley River and in surrounding communities. Few white people ever ventured into these steep, narrow coves, due to the difficulty of traversing on foot or horseback. The density of the chestnut/oak forests kept visibility to a minimum, particularly in the warmer months when leaf cover could greatly obscure line of sight. During the years following removal, this seclusion was very desirable. The memory of occupation hung heavily, and the threat of a second removal was very real.

Welch's Town grew throughout the year as Cherokees from scattered settlements heard about the safe community. Although left in relative peace, the Cherokees in these areas knew that the state of North Carolina provided them no legal rights of citizenship or land tenure. They were now largely out of hiding. However, they had returned to their farms too late to gather any crops the army had not pilfered, and they therefore found themselves still fending off hunger. Those who had returned to the Cheoah, Valley, and Hiwassee river valleys turned for help to sympathetic neighbors. Several local white families later filed claims with the federal government for compensation for feeding Cherokee families for up to a year after the removal.[34] Although the Welches filed no such claims, they engaged in similar practices, providing food, clothing, and shelter. This year-long subsistence by white and Cherokee families on Valley River staved off desperation for those who had evaded the army.

By 1840 the members of Welch's Town (and other communities) were rebuilding townhouses, ball fields, and dance grounds. The members of Welch's Town and those of other small Cherokee communities had risked everything to stay in North Carolina so that they could maintain their community, beliefs, and local government. The daily actions and interactions that stemmed from these social structures required physical structures and spaces. They also reestablished formal town-level social structures to deal with community affairs. Community members were elected to formal positions in charge of local council and work-party institutions. These community-support organizations evolved from eighteenth-century (and much earlier) organizations.[35]

In the years following removal, Welch's Town was largely synonymous with what many people referred to as the "Valley River Cherokees," although a few other scattered households, such as Nancy Hawkins and Greybeard across the Valley River on Vengeance Creek, did not live on Welch land. William Holland Thomas recorded town rolls on a regular basis, partly in his role as a claims agent. He maintained power of attorney for many of these towns throughout the 1840s and 1850s. His records, along with censuses taken by the government, reveal the changes in town membership throughout the period.[36] In March 1839 Thomas listed seventeen families as "Valley River Cherokees." A year later he clarified the phrase and recorded twenty-seven families, totaling eighty-five people, "living at John Welches," showing the town continued to grow through 1839 (Table 3.1).[37] In August 1843 John Owl and Wa haw neet were selected as representatives "by the Cherokees living on Valley River commonally called the Welch Indians" in appointing power of attorney for the group.[38]

Thirty families dwelt in Welch's Town in 1840. The creation of a new community from several small preremoval communities was driven by realities of the postremoval environment. Too many members of the smaller towns were dead or had been pushed west. However, all the members knew each other, and many were closely related. More importantly, they dedicated themselves to the goal of sustaining a small community. Eleven of the Welch's Town families in 1840 originated in Hanging Dog Creek. Many of these families had known the Welches for decades. The Axe had taken a reservation near the Welch reservation in 1819. John Owl and others on Hanging Dog had tended cattle for the Welches before the removal. Ten of the Welch's Town families had lived on Valley River, in the Valley Towns. Five families came from the Wacheesee community on Beaverdam Creek, fourteen miles away. Prior to removal, the patriarch Wacheesee led the community, composed largely of his descendants. The army marched Wacheesee and his extended family to Fort Cass in the summer of 1838. Wacheesee died there, but his family escaped and walked back to the Beaverdam Creek area, where they were assisted by a white family for a year. The members of Welch's Town in 1840 from Beaverdam, or Wacheesee Town, included Wacheesee's widow, the families of his sons, Sam Wacheesee and Chinoque Wacheesee, Toononailuh, and Caluska, also called Locust. Two families came from Fighting Town, Georgia, and one from Duck Town, Georgia. One family had lived in Tusquitta Town, east of Welch's Town. The connection of these last families to the Welches is unknown, but they probably had long-term family ties. Members of Betty's family made their homes in Tusquitta Town

before removal. One family from the old Hanging Dog community, led by
Alkinnih, a widow, settled in Buffalo Town. Several families who had lived on
Valley River also moved to Buffalo Town, illustrating the intermarriage and

TABLE. 3.1. Heads of Households, Welch's Town, 1840

Name	# in family	Residence in 1835
Tecanequeloskih or Gray Beard	5	Valley River
Tiyestah	2	Hanging Dog
Jackson	2	Valley River
Tenutlahee	2	Valley River
John Towih	1	Hanging Dog
Old Axe	8	Hanging Dog
Etekanuh	4	Hanging Dog
Chunowhinkuh or Chinoque	3	Hanging Dog
Dickageeska or Oogatulla	3	Hanging Dog
Wahya netuh or Young Wolf	4	Hanging Dog
Cossehe la	2	Hanging Dog
Walla	4	Beaverdam
Sam Wah chee suh	6	Beaverdam
Kalouskuh or Locust	3	Beaverdam
George an orphan	1	Valley River
Chicke eh	3	Valley River
Johnson Connel	2	Valley River
Arsena	3	Hanging Dog
Annohee	2	Tusquitta
Culleskella	3	Duck Town, Georgia
Chinoquih (Wahcheesuh)	3	Beaverdam
Tu non na luh	2	Beaverdam
Little George	2	Fighting Town, Georgia
Chuno whin ka	10	Hanging Dog
Chu la lo ga	2	Fighting Town, Georgia
Tlunoskeeska	1	Valley River
Little Dickageeska	2	Hanging Dog
	85	

Source: William Holland Thomas, "Census of the North Carolina Cherokees, 1840," William
Holland Thomas papers, David M. Rubenstein Rare Book and Manuscript Library, Duke
University, Durham, North Carolina.

other close connections between these two communities divided by the steep Snowbird Mountain range.[39]

The geographic locations of Welch's Town and the Welch plantation accurately represented their separate social and political economies. The Welch plantation was prominently situated on an elevated knoll overlooking a broad, fertile floodplain and the Western Turnpike. The town stayed invisible in the steep, wooded Snowbird Mountains. Only one mile apart, the leaders and inhabitants of these two communities chose contrasting adaptations to a postremoval environment. While the members of Welch's Town resided in the more-isolated, mountainous parts of the area, the Welch family began expanding their plantation holdings in an effort to expand their strong political and economic position. Even in the Upper South, plantation owners enjoyed an elite status. However, for the Welches, this status was greatly affected by race. Although they possessed wealth and holdings beyond the reach of most, they had learned firsthand in 1819 and again in 1838 that class did not outrank race in the antebellum South.

December 1839 marked one year since the last of the soldiers had marched out of western North Carolina. The Cherokees now in the Valley, Hiwassee, and Cheoah river valleys had spent the year recovering from the loss of family members to death and removal, finding sustenance, and attempting to understand their status within the newly acquired lands of the United States. Forced removal remained a possibility, and reactions to a continued Cherokee presence by local white people varied. As local outcries were made against these "uncivilized" people, the concept of "otherness" became increasingly codified by the United States government. The growing power of state control during the late federal and antebellum era defined, legally and socially, what it was to be an American. This was particularly true in the South, where these divisions were increasingly based on race. Whiteness entitled one to both citizenship and property ownership.[40]

The community mixed old and new Cherokee practices. The households were established (or at least recorded by Thomas) as headed by men. However, a townhouse and dance grounds with deep history in Cherokee society revealed a continuation of town-level governance. This may reflect the continuation of political power for women in the community. The older women in particular—Liddy Owl and Aqualla Axe—probably wielded significant influence, even though William Holland Thomas regularly recorded John Axe and John Owl as the "headmen" of Welch's Town.

Very few transactions with members of Welch's Town appear in the Thomas and Hunter ledgers throughout the 1840s. Women in the town likely contin-ued to make pottery and baskets, and men resumed carving wood and stone tools. Items that required purchase were limited to iron tools and to cloth and sewing items like pins and thimbles. Even though Cherokee society had been shifting to a more patriarchal society in the early nineteenth century, women would not relinquish all of their economic and political power.

The members of Welch's Town refused to embrace an American identity. They had witnessed the birth of the Cherokee Nation and the attempts of its leaders to westernize, and realized that, given their "otherness," in both physi-cal and cultural difference, they would not be welcomed, because white people saw them as outsiders. In any case, that was not their goal. These Cherokees had, for decades, inhabited geographic and cultural borderlands, where they could guard their communities and local governance. They had rejected the Cherokee Nation in 1819, long before their flight from the US Army in 1838. They had lived near one another on the 1819 reservations, guided by the Cher-okee form of localism that seated real political power in the town. The peo-ple who created and built Welch's Town in 1839 and lived there throughout the 1840s were dedicated to the idea of not only staying in the mountains but maintaining their communities. Even though the Welches embraced wealth accumulation, they too rejected large-scale government in favor of community or town control. They were all connected by family ties and by the need to rees-tablish town life. Although they remained in North Carolina and reestablished their towns, life would continue to be a challenge throughout the decades fol-lowing removal.

4

"COUNCILS, DANCES, BALLPLAYS"

New and Old Ways on Valley River

This settlement are principally full blood Cherokees and completely subservient
to the will of Mrs. Welch, a white woman (wife of John Welch, Cherokee) and
she under the control and influence of Mr. Thomas. Mrs. Welch has considerable
shrewdness—and understands how to manage ignorant Indians to suit her
purpose ... they labor for her, almost constantly and answer every purpose of
slaves—she spares no pains to keep up their prejudices against the West and tells
them they can always have the privilege of using her land and residing upon it.

—THOMAS HINDMAN, "Letter to Thomas Hartley Crawford, Commissioner
of Indian Affairs, December 20, 1841." Letters received by the Office of
Indian Affairs, 1824–1881, M-234, roll 86, pages 582–84, 1841

In 1841 Thomas Hindman, a temporary federal agent to the Cherokees in
North Carolina, sent a letter to Commissioner of Indian Affairs Thomas
Hartley Crawford about Betty Welch. His views on Betty and Welch's Town
are reflected in his language: her "shrewdness" contrasts with their "ignorant"
state. Part of his dislike of Betty was her association with William Holland
Thomas, whom Hindman distrusted.[1] Hindman convinced Commissioner
Crawford to strip Thomas of his job as disbursing agent and award the position
to Hindman. In this role he attempted to convince the remaining Cherokees
in North Carolina to participate in a "voluntary removal." He was one of the
first to question the motives of the patrons such as Thomas and the Welches.
Were these individuals exploiting the Cherokees' tenuous situation to acquire
a cheap, almost slavelike labor pool? Or were they acting in an altruistic man-
ner for groups of refugee Cherokees for whom they had sympathy?[2]

Thomas has been accused of extorting cheap labor from Cherokees in
the Qualla Towns, while others have seen him in a more altruistic light, as

the "white chief of the Cherokees."[3] Thomas's motives may have been quite different from the Welches'. Thomas strove to win a high profile for himself and the Cherokees of the Qualla Towns roughly forty-five miles northeast of Welch's Town. He spent years in Washington, DC, and Raleigh, North Carolina, as agent, lawyer, and state senator, and was a booster for turnpike and railroad construction in the area.[4] The Welches, in contrast, attempted to keep a low profile. They acquired wealth and served as spokespeople for the Welch's Town Cherokees. However, they helped the Cherokees establish a traditional community removed from the view of local white people, and they themselves never invited publicity. Except for their trips to the nearby town of Murphy to address the boards of Cherokee commissioners, they rarely left their plantation. Interactions with military officers, government agents, and businessmen all took place at their house.

By 1840 the Welch plantation incorporated a large and diverse workforce. The Welches sustained many relationships with the various groups of workers on their land, including enslaver-enslaved with eight or nine African Americans, patron-client with roughly eighty-five Cherokees in the steep uplands north of the plantation, and landlord-tenant with one or more white families. Did the Welch family risk their lives during removal to help Cherokees in hiding solely because of their prior connections, or did the Welches see this group as a source of labor? What was the economic relationship between the Welches and people of Welch's Town?[5] Did the Welch family expect remuneration for their assistance during removal and for land to inhabit for the following fifteen years?

This chapter attempts to address two of the main research questions: What was the relationship between the Welch family and the members of Welch's Town, and did it include exchange of goods or services? What was life like for the enslaved people, mostly women and children, held captive by the Welches, and how was it different for them compared to those held by white enslavers on Upper South plantations? To answer these questions requires looking at all three communities—the Welch family, the enslaved community, and Welch's Town—and the interactions between them.

THE WELCH FAMILY

The plantation complex included the households of John and Betty Welch, Ned and Emily Welch, and Mary and John Powell. The location and organization of the farm was designed to be conspicuous on the landscape and to

enable surplus production of livestock and crops for profit. Despite the afteref-
fects of the removal, by the spring of 1839, the Welches had resumed most of
their regular farm activities. With a workforce of eight enslaved African Americans and several adult members of the family, they maintained agricultural
fields of roughly 150 acres. In the 1837 valuation, the family cultivated 164.5
acres. In the 1850 federal census, they cultivated 160 acres. Their production
varied little before and after the removal. In 1850 the combined agricultural
production for the Welch plantation was 1,500 bushels of corn, 215 bushels of
rye oats, and 200 pounds of potatoes.[6]

In addition to providing needed resources and income, reinstituting farm
activities brought a sense of stability and normalcy to their lives. Operating
an upland plantation required a high level of organization. By April 1839 the
Welches began the yearly cycle of producing numerous kinds of crops, with a
focus on corn. In 1839 they grew roughly a thousand bushels of corn. They also
harvested smaller amounts of rye and potatoes.[7] The family sold most of their
surplus grain locally. They found a ready market in the numerous innkeepers
along the Unicoi Turnpike, who sold grain to drovers moving livestock to the
lowcountry South. The Unicoi Turnpike, extending from eastern Tennessee
to northern Georgia, passed through Cherokee County and connected the
Tennessee Valley and the southern tip of the Appalachians to the Lowcountry South. During the early and mid-nineteenth century, thousands of drovers traveled the turnpike, transporting cattle, sheep, hogs, turkeys, and other
livestock and game to the lowcountry for consumption on cotton plantations.[8]
The economy of Cherokee County, as in other nearby counties, depended on
this business. Stock stands, or inns, sprang up every eight to ten miles along
the route, the distance a drover could move a large herd in a day. Local farmers
sold surplus grain to these innkeepers, who in turn sold it to the drovers. More
importantly, drovers regularly purchased livestock from local farmers, who
otherwise would have had difficulty in converting them into cash.

Plowing the fields in preparation for planting started in April. The fields
were plowed once or twice, followed by harrowing to break up dirt clods and
smooth the rows left by plowing. A single-horse shallow-draft plow had been in
use by white farmers for some time and had been slowly introduced to Cherokees through the late eighteenth and early nineteenth centuries.[9] Men, women,
and children planted in early May, after the last frost had occurred. Once the
seed was planted, little was done until the corn sprouted.

In the spring of 1839, the Welches were also tending livestock. The Welches
raised cattle and swine throughout the 1840s and 1850s. The family regularly

drove hogs to Murphy, where they were sold and driven along the Unicoi Turnpike. Gradually the Welches rebuilt their stock, and by 1850 they had regained roughly the same numbers as before removal. Through the spring and summer, most of the cattle had to be grazed on grasslands along the river valley, requiring labor from people on the Welch farm. Almost all people on the plantation, young and old, male and female, over the age of eight or ten, contributed to the care of the livestock. A lot, delineated by a wooden split-rail fence, confined part of the livestock and was listed for the Welch farm in 1837.[10]

Livestock—cattle, swine, horses, sheep—represented substantial profit for the Welches. Cattle and swine were used for home consumption but could also be driven downstream to Murphy and the Unicoi Turnpike to fetch a good price. Prior to the development of railroads, there was no efficient or cheap method of shipping grain out of the region, so livestock represented for many the best way to increase their wealth. The members of Welch's Town expanded that wealth, by providing labor to care for and feed the animals. By feeding the hundreds of head of Welch livestock on rich mast in the wooded uplands, they also saved the Welches substantial amounts of grain.[11] This may also have been a task that members of the enslaved community shared, perhaps drawing these two communities closer together. Archaeology shows that the family owned a wide variety of other animals, including chickens, turkeys, and domesticated European hares.

In early summer much of the labor became focused on tending crops, particularly corn. The main task was regular hoeing to kill weeds that would choke out the grain. Weeding was done by hand with large-bladed iron hoes. As with tending livestock, almost all those living on the plantation would have been involved in these tasks. In a letter to John Taylor, dated July 23, 1855, John C. Welch Jr. apologized for not writing sooner, describing "having so much corn to hoe" as the reason.[12] Corn production using these methods usually yielded between eight and twenty-five bushels of corn per acre.[13]

Harvesting became the central task for most of the laborers on the farm in the late summer and early fall. In 1850 the Welches harvested 1,500 bushels of "Indian corn."[14] In 1841 William Holland Thomas paid $0.50 per bushel for it.[15] Although the price was volatile throughout the 1840s, corn continued to provide a substantial portion of the income for many Cherokee and white farmers in the area.[16] The rectangular corncrib near their house was recorded during the removal-era property valuations as "7–20 [feet] Round logs board R.[oof]."[17] The structure was the same size and value of the small log cabins nearby and could have stored roughly a thousand bushels.

The Welches produced large amounts of grains throughout the 1840s. In 1850, in addition to 1,500 bushels of corn, they raised 215 bushels of rye oats (as well as two hundred pounds of potatoes).[18] The processing and consumption of corn is well documented at the Welch site. Numerous carbonized maize cupules, kernels, and cobs reflect its importance in the family diet. A much smaller number of carbonized wheat and rye grains show up.[19] The 1850 agricultural census records that the family harvested 90 bushels of rye.

The presence of wheat grains in the assemblage is interesting, because the Welches did not claim wheat production in 1850.[20] They may have rotated different grains from year to year. Grains of oats and rice appear in the archaeological assemblage in small numbers. Rice cannot be grown in the mountains; Betty purchased it from Thomas's store, which supplied rice and other foods shipped from the Lowcountry South.[21] Oats can be grown in the region, although there is no documentation that the Welches raised it. Oats were often used as fodder for animals, and therefore the presence of the grain in small amounts in the house area may reflect its use elsewhere on the farm.[22]

The diversity of foods raised on the farm was astounding. The food remains from the Welch site reveal this complexity as well as the contextual nature of foodways. The assemblage is unique, with evidence for the consumption of beef, pork, chicken, corn, oats, and wheat, but also a wide variety of wild plants and game. This assemblage derived from the Welch family's wealth and their association with Welch's Town, by which their already rich diet was heavily supplemented. The Welches ate better than anyone else in the region. They grazed cattle on rich pastures. In the fall months, people from Welch's Town drove the cattle and hogs into the mountains to graze on thick beds of acorns and other nuts. While most farmers ate a diet heavy in pork, the Welches also ate a lot of beef. In butchering the cattle, the family kept alive one of the older Cherokee practices. They cracked the dense long bones into pieces with hammers or axes. This provided access to rich marrow, a practice used by Cherokees for centuries.[23]

As with foods, the materials used to prepare and serve food in the Welch house were abundant and varied. Ceramics give clues to the functional and cultural aspects of food preparation and dining.[24] The collection of dining-related artifacts from the Welch site help reveal how the Welches situated themselves within the different communities along the Valley River. Betty's cupboards hosted an astonishing array of imported dishes she bought at Thomas's store. In contrast to the few dishes in most Cherokee households, she had dozens of plates, cups, and saucers, and could set a table for large numbers of guests. Half the dishes were plates, many decorated with a blue shell-edge pattern, a common style at the time, or with printed patterns of romantic English landscapes (Figure 4.1, Figure 4.2). Bowls of various sizes, adorned with sponge-printed patterns, held side dishes. Betty served coffee in delicate hand-painted cups and saucers from a large tin coffee pot. While dining with the Welches, visitors saw several ceramic patterns and styles, in blue, brown, red, purple, green, yellow, black, and tan. Betty purchased dishes from Thomas piecemeal, and did not worry about matching any of the styles or colors.[25]

The Welches had regular visitors, including many white people, who dined at their house. They embraced Western styles of dining but rejected some of

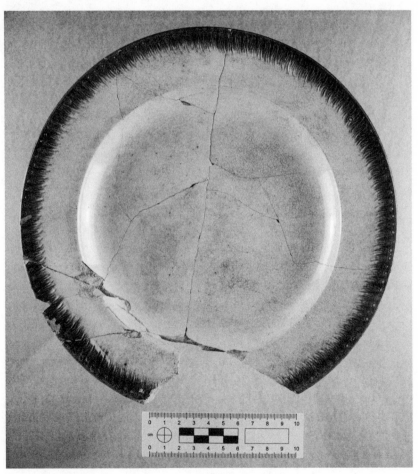

FIGURE 4.1. Reconstructed blue shell-edged whiteware
plate from Welch site. (Lance Greene)

FIGURE 4.2. Decorated ceramic sherds from Welch site. (Lance Greene)

the fancier, more formal dining wares. The vast majority of ceramics for both families were inexpensive. William Holland Thomas, a successful lawyer and businessman, crafted a different image. Matched sets of dishes, large platters, and pressed glassware decorated his table.[26]

Betty also purchased large stoneware crocks. She stored them in the kitchen, and in the fall the family stored food in them for use throughout the winter.[27] But she chose not to use one form of pottery available to her: hand-made Cherokee pots. She could have ordered these vessels from Thomas's store or from women in Welch's Town, and at less cost than the imported wares she used every day. By not using them, Betty rejected some aspects of eighteenth-century Cherokee culture, particularly in food production. Perhaps she was never comfortable with Cherokee eating habits, or she might have felt a need to downplay any association with Cherokee culture. Betty was fully aware of the visual impact of their plantation on the landscape, and, particularly after removal, the display of Cherokee foodways and associated handmade vessels may have been too conspicuous. Perhaps the role of plantation owner and enslaver that the Welches maintained limited their ability to publicly express their connection to Cherokee practice. Their plantation house served, during and after the removal, as a meeting place for white military officers, government officials, and businessmen. The Welch family established a set of cultural patterns that reflected the acceptance of both Cherokee and Western practices. This composite of behaviors and material culture enabled them to retain connections in both worlds.[28]

In contrast to a large collection of mass-produced ceramics, some artifacts were handmade and reflect eighteenth-century Cherokee practices. Many Cherokee men continued to carve their own stone pipes from chlorite-schist (pipestone) pebbles readily available in local streambeds. These pipes were elbow shaped, with a small bowl and a short, stub stem (Figure 4.3). After carving, a hollowed section of cane or sourwood was inserted into the short stem for smoking. One hand-carved chlorite-schist pipe, fragments of two others, and fragments of a molded clay pipe were found in the Welch artifact assemblage. Although molded clay pipes were inexpensive, the manufacture of a stone pipe by one's own hand still harbored significance in a historical connection to a

FIGURE 4.3. Top and side views of chlorite-schist
pipe from Welch site. (Lance Greene)

Cherokee past and to the formalized activity of tobacco smoking. The selection of proper raw materials, the carving of a specific size and form, and the continued use of the pipe, all related to the personal and social significance of this activity. For John Welch and his adult sons, smoking a carved-stone pipe served as an intimate statement for those within the household and for the Cherokees of Welch's Town.[29] After Betty served his dinner on a "Western" plate, John smoked his pipe—the hybrid material culture of a cross-cultural marriage.

THE ENSLAVED COMMUNITY

As opposed to lowcountry South plantations in which hundreds of enslaved workers harvested cotton, the enslaved population on an upland plantation usually numbered fewer than twenty. In the mountains, the climate and terrain did not allow for large-scale cash-crop production. Therefore, enslavers exploited captive labor in many other activities, such as blacksmithing, grist and saw milling, carpentry, ironworking, tanning, and gold mining.[30] This was true for the Welch plantation, in which Isaac, Phillis (and Nelly prior to the removal), and the enslaved children were involved in a multitude of tasks, from cooking and cleaning and childcare to planting and harvesting, tending livestock, producing cloth and clothing, clearing fields and digging ditches, and panning and mining gold. The immense variety of tasks performed on mountain plantations is striking and was organized to maximize productivity of the entire labor pool. To a certain extent, farm and household tasks were divided by race, ethnicity, gender, experience and training, and age.[31]

Both agriculture and livestock were central for the Welch family in terms of subsistence and income. The mountainous region was tied closely to the lowcountry cotton economy, and the enslaved community on the Welch plantation produced an assortment of commodities for export. On most Southern Appalachian plantations, family members both oversaw and worked with the enslaved people. It was common for the adult sons of a plantation owner to work side by side with captive laborers. It is unlikely that, after the removal, John Welch's health allowed him to participate in any of these demanding activities. However, Ned, James, and John Jr. would have been capable of these tasks. John Jr.'s comment about "having so much corn to hoe" reflects his daily work but ignores the labor performed by enslaved people there.[32] For much of the year, all of the African Americans were involved in agricultural activities. Enslaved men and women worked in the fields for major activities like planting, weeding, and harvesting. Enslaved children as young as five performed tasks, such as pulling weeds, in agricultural fields.[33] The relatively small number of enslaved individuals on the Welch plantation, in addition to most being women or children, meant that all worked doing difficult outdoor tasks.

This proximity in work did not mean the treatment of the enslaved was any less cruel. In contrast to the common perception of the treatment of enslaved in the Southern Appalachian region as being less harsh than in the lowcountry, the captive workers were exposed to the same privations and punishments. These included severe shortages of food, clothing, shelter, and medical supplies, while physical punishments included beating and whipping, and threats of sale into the lowcountry South. Enslaved people in the mountains were more likely to be whipped than their counterparts on larger plantations farther south, and both white and Cherokee enslavers carried out these abuses.[34]

On the Welch plantation, Isaac performed a variety of jobs. The plantation included a blacksmith shop, and Isaac likely worked in the shop year-round making and repairing a variety of tools and hardware from small items like nails and buckets to plow and wagon parts.[35] Regular maintenance on the farm also included repair of outbuildings, fences, and machinery. Isaac spent part of his time working at the grist mill owned by the Welches. The mill, abandoned around the time of removal, stood on Welch Mill Creek at the base of the Snowbird Mountains, serving the needs of the entire community to grind flour and wheat. The mill was replaced by a new one built by the Morris family upstream from the Welch plantation.[36]

On the Valley River, gold mining could be an economically rewarding endeavor. Several Cherokees from Valley River claimed losses during the removal of both gold and gold-mining equipment, including pans and rockers.[37] In 1837 George Featherstonaugh commented on Cherokees panning for gold on Valley River, and a gold survey performed in 1860 shows the segment of Valley River adjoining the Welch farm as a probable area for placer deposits.[38] Although there is no direct documentation for gold mining on the Welch land, it is probable that such work was performed seasonally, most likely by enslaved workers. Gold mining was a regular task assigned to enslaved people in the Southern Appalachians, particularly during "down" times in the agricultural seasons.[39] Gold mining may have been a significant seasonal source of income for the Welches.

Phillis, like Isaac, performed a multitude of jobs. The federal census lists the Welch plantation "value of home manufacture" for 1850 as $170. The bulk of this income came from the production of cloth and clothing, and tasks related to these took up much of Phillis's time. While most plantations and smaller farms supplied some of their own textiles for farm use, larger plantations generated fabrics for the market. The Welch family raised sheep, and Ned and Emily Welch's holdings included a loom house. In 1838 the Welches bred twenty-six sheep and in 1850, thirty-five. In 1850 the Welches produced seventy pounds of wool. The entire plantation, including the farms of the Welch children Ned and Mary, yielded 155 pounds, amounts considerably higher than needed for family use.[40]

Isaac was involved in the shearing of sheep and the skirting of fleeces. Phillis, like the women in the Welch family, spent much of her time processing the raw wool and converting it into cloth and clothing. She first washed the wool, to remove the lanoline and dirt, then carded it to align the fibers. The fibers may then have been dyed, or dyeing may have occurred after the fabric was produced. The women and girls worked long hours in the loom house spinning wool on a spinning wheel and weaving the spun wool. Census records from 1850 show that the Welches did not grow flax, so at least in that year the women were processing wool but not linen. Phillis also tailored fine clothing; the Welches regularly purchased finer cloths such as silk from William Holland Thomas's stores. They then sold the finished garments back to Thomas. Intensive cloth and clothing production is visible in the Welch household through the archaeological record. A large number and variety of clothing-related artifacts in the Welch assemblage include brass pins, bone, brass, pewter, iron, and gilt buttons, brass hooks and loops, and cloth and leather fragments. The Welches used a variety of sizes of brass pins, revealing the diverse kinds of sewing they did, from producing fine silk clothes to manufacturing rough homespun clothes.[41]

The enslaved women also churned butter. In 1850 the Welch plantation produced three hundred pounds of butter. For the three Welch families combined, the amount was seven hundred pounds. These commodities were sold for local use and to shop owners for export. Phillis would have also taken care of the infants and small children on the plantation. Enslaved women were often forced to care for small children as they continued other tasks such as cooking, cleaning, spinning, or sewing.[42]

The enslaved community—men, women, and children—performed many more tasks that went undocumented. For example, enslaved workers in the Southern Appalachians often were involved in the production of commodities as varied as iron, whiskey, brandy, and cigars. Captive workers toiled as carpenters, coopers, and stonemasons. Enslaved men strained in coal mines and in the timbering industry, and they worked in exporting all of those goods along waterways, roads, and canals.[43]

WELCH'S TOWN

Living along Townhouse Branch and Welch Mill Creek, the members of Welch's Town were situated in the uplands and near the crest of the Snowbird Mountains. In contrast to the Welch family's large-scale agriculture, families there grew corn and other vegetables for their own consumption on 3–5 acre family plots.[44] The acreage of tillable land on Welch Mill Creek and Townhouse Branch (approximately 115 acres) provided an adequate space for crops and gardens for the thirty families of Welch's Town who resided there. Most of the level ground along the two creeks was plowed and planted each year in corn. They sowed squash and beans in the cornfields after the corn had sprouted. Bean plants require a frame to climb in order to thrive, and the corn stalks provided this structure. Additionally, beans return nitrogen to the soil. This style of gardening had been practiced by Cherokees for centuries. Cherokees also raised peas, potatoes, cabbage, sunflowers, pumpkins, and watermelons in small garden plots. Orchards provided peaches and apples.[45] The methods and the scale of agriculture practiced by the people of Welch's Town were in sharp contrast to those practiced along the Valley by the Welch family.

These two creek drainages were on the edge of an extensive tract of steep, wooded, and unsettled land to the north—a perfect landscape in which to acquire natural resources. These hardwood forests boasted a broad diversity: red, white, and scarlet oak, shagbark hickory, beech, chestnut, maple, and locust. Beneath this canopy, in an equally diverse understory, dogwoods, eastern redbuds, mountain laurel, and rhododendron thrived. Narrow coves with abundant fresh springs sheltered shrubs, wildflowers, and ferns. Foot trails led from these two creeks in two directions. To the south the trail headed downslope to the Valley River and the Welch plantation. To the north a steep trail wending back and forth brought one to the northeast-southwest-oriented ridge spine of the Snowbird Mountains. At the crest of the mountains, a trail meandered down through the Cheoah Valley to Buffalo Town.

In the 1840s the steep, rugged, densely wooded terrain teemed with wild game: deer, turkey, bear, and rabbit, along with numerous other species. Cherokees fished and hunted birds with blowguns.[46] They also collected plant foods. The fall brought a vast variety of nuts, or mast. Falling chestnuts, hickory nuts, acorns, and hazelnuts created beds so thick that they masked the ground. The

forest and forest edges offered several kinds of wild greens harvested by Cherokees. While the Welches raised surpluses of crops and livestock for the market,
the members of Welch's Town continued to practice subsistence-level agriculture and to hunt, fish, and collect wild game and plant foods. They gave some
of these foods to the Welches.

While the Welch family (and perhaps the enslaved African Americans as
well) may have hunted, the people of Welch's Town spent more time in the
wooded mountains, where wild game abounded. Several bones from at least
two raccoons in the Welch cellar pits probably represent hunting by Cherokees, although perhaps Frank or one of the younger enslaved men trapped
them. Squirrel remains were also found among the faunal remains, probably
brought to the farm by Cherokees from Welch's Town.

Numerous species of wild game, including deer, bear, turkey, rabbit, squirrel,
raccoon, mallard, bobwhite, and turtles complemented the diet of the Welches.
One of the most common sources of meat was white-tailed deer. Remains of
deer found in the cellar pits reveal not only that the family enjoyed venison but
that deer were butchered in November or December.[47] The Welches used deer
bone and antler for tools around the house. Someone carved two antler tines
into handles for kitchen utensils; both were broken in production along the
drilled shaft and discarded.

The only fish species identified on the archaeological site was largemouth
bass, which is unusual. Cherokees historically ate a variety of fish native to the
waters of the Appalachians. The fish remains may represent a single episode
of fishing, probably by hook and line, in which the fishermen or women were
using bait specifically to catch largemouth bass. A brass pin converted into a
fishhook was recovered in a soil zone immediately beneath numerous largemouth bass bones, and may have been dumped into the pit still attached to a
disarticulated fragment (Figure 4.4).

The uplands also served as free range for cattle and hogs, which subsisted
very well on the mast. Cherokees and white people agreed that mast-fed cattle
and pigs tasted much better and richer than those fed on corn.[48] Tasks associated with caretaking livestock also shifted in the early fall. Part of the Welch's
focus on livestock was due to the unusually high labor pool they were connected with: not only enslaved African Americans but this much larger force
of Cherokees. Members of Welch's Town tended the Welch livestock (cattle
and hogs) as well as their own in these mountains.[49] Throughout the fall and
winter, these areas provided the necessary mast, such as chestnuts and hickory nuts, to fatten livestock, particularly hogs, much better than could be done

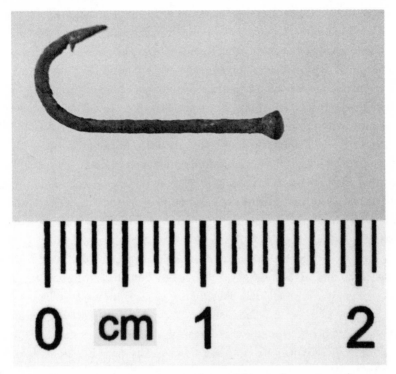

FIGURE 4.4. Brass pin converted into a fishhook. (Lance Greene)

with grain and hay.[50] This made the Welch livestock more valuable and, more importantly, saved them a substantial amount of grain. It is possible that the enslaved people helped with these chores in the fall months. Although not documented, livestock was such a major part of the Welch income that many people would have been involved in caretaking these animals, both on the farm and foraging in the mountains.

In addition to tending livestock in the mountains, the Cherokees of Welch's Town also collected wild plant foods for themselves and for the Welches. The Cherokees of Welch's Town gathered a diverse variety of plant resources, as revealed by the abundance and variety of floral remains from the Welch site. Seeds of wild greens from the Welch site include amaranth, chenopod, poke, smartweed, evening primrose, carpetweed, and purslane. A variety of native fruits were also consumed by the Welches, including grape, blueberry, elderberry, blackberry, mulberry, plum, honey locust, ground cherry, nightshade, and sumac.[51] The members of Welch's Town, who had readier access to these wild species, probably shared these items. Fragments of carbonized chestnuts, hickory nuts, hazelnuts, and beechnuts show the importance of these foods in the Welch diet.

The archaeology shines a light on the social world within which the Welch family chose to exist. The material culture in the Welch household circa 1850 can be classified into two distinct groups: mass-produced goods and handmade goods. These two groups also coincide with gender divisions of the period. The mass-produced goods are mostly dining wares, and the handmade items mostly goods used by men (e.g., smoking pipes, talc pencils used in blacksmithing). With the guidance of the historic documentation, we can argue that Betty, as both the woman of the house and the head of household, was in charge of the kitchen and of entertaining guests, whereas John, unable to serve as head of household after 1838, maintained ties with the Welch's Town Cherokee.

John and Betty lived a complex cultural existence that allowed them to function in both white and Cherokee societies. Betty took control of the plantation after imprisonment destroyed John's health. However, even before that, she had embraced certain Cherokee practices and rejected others. For example, Betty did not opt for household items that could have signaled her desire to achieve an elite planter status. For the Welches, financial success did not mean associating with elites or exhibiting wealth. Instead, it meant achieving a level of financial security. Particularly in periods of marginalization such as the removal era for the Cherokees, life was precarious, and therefore cash was often hoarded.[52]

Betty laid her table with imported ceramics, like the tables at the Ridge and Vann plantations. Archaeology has shown, however, that these other households, even Ridge's, still used handmade Cherokee ceramics in the house, although in much smaller numbers than imported ceramics. Why was Betty so stringent in her rejection of these wares when Cherokee households of every economic level used them? To complicate the matter even further, the food remains from the Welch site show that, even though she rejected Cherokee ceramics, Betty did allow traditional foods to be served, including bear, turtles, and small birds, as well as wild plant foods such as chestnuts, amaranth, and chenopodium. Someone on the plantation fractured the long bones of livestock to access the marrow, another Cherokee practice. The presence of these artifacts and food remains, along with the absence of Qualla pottery, suggests the particulars of Betty's cultural hybridity.

While many of Betty's statements made through material culture were directed at the outside world, John's display his connection to Cherokee beliefs and principles. This was increasingly the case after the removal, when Betty became the primary leader of the farm, and John played a lesser role in external affairs. These associations were also reflected in their differing spheres of exchange. Betty participated more fully in local markets and acquired, through cash purchase, mass-produced goods circulating in the market economy. John, alternatively, participated in a local sphere of exchange marked by intimate personal, family, and clan relationships through which he acquired and disseminated a range of handmade goods and foods.

While the Cherokees of Welch's Town provided labor for the Welches, they did not provide sustained labor for agricultural purposes, such as planting or harvesting. Instead, the Cherokees performed activities in the mountains, around their own community. In the upland setting of Welch's Town, they had access to wild plants and animals, and could tend their gardens and fields without the prying eyes of white people. While their labor provided income for the Welches, it was not a constant or sustained part of the plantation labor. The Welches' motives in helping the Cherokees during and after the removal were guided not by greed or the desire for cheap labor but by the ties that had bound the two groups for at least two decades. Events that would happen throughout the 1840s and 1850s would continue to reveal the support the Welches provided and the close connections they felt to the members of Welch's Town.

5

"Their Determination to Remain"

Evading Agents, Lawyers, and Other Swindlers

On December 14, 1841, Thomas Hindman rode up the Franklin Road to the Welch farm on Valley River. Betty Welch greeted him upon his arrival at the log house on the hill. The Welch house served as a central meeting place, and forty-five Cherokees, roughly a third of Welch's Town, awaited him there. Hindman was there for one purpose: to convince the Cherokees in North Carolina to migrate west.[1] This "voluntary removal" marked the latest in a series of attempts by the federal government to unite all Cherokee people. The government's underlying motive was to simplify the task of settling past treaty obligations by organizing all Cherokees into a single group.[2] This event, only three years after the removal, was the first of many such challenges for the people of Welch's Town throughout the decade. In addition to the constant fear of forced emigration, they faced uncertainty regarding their rights of citizenship and land tenure.

Less than a week after his meeting at the Welch plantation, Hindman reported to Commissioner Crawford and Secretary of War Albert Lea that William Holland Thomas was cheating the North Carolina Cherokees and convinced them that he could arrange a "voluntary" emigration:[3] "This settlement are principally full blood Cherokees and completely subservient to the will of Mrs. Welch, a white woman (wife of John Welch, Cherokee) and she under the control and influence of Mr. Thomas. Mrs. Welch has considerable shrewdness—and understands how to manage ignorant Indians to suit her purpose."[4]

His dislike for Betty Welch was in part because of her association with William Holland Thomas. Hindman worked with Chief Ross, who had an adversarial relationship with Thomas. Ross endeavored to move all Cherokees west as a group, leaving none in the Southeast, and saw Thomas as a major hindrance. In addition, Thomas had accused Ross and Hindman of making fraudulent claims to the government. Hindman then claimed Thomas and others were defrauding Cherokees in North Carolina and convinced Commissioner Crawford in the Indian Office to remove Thomas as a disbursing agent and replace him with Hindman.

Hindman's dislike for Betty Welch also stemmed from his distaste for a woman of such considerable wealth and clout. It is clear from Hindman's letter that Betty stood as the unquestioned leader of the Welch plantation and wielded significant influence over the Cherokees of Welch's Town. Like other white men who tried to conduct business with Welch's Town in later years, Hindman would not have been used to dealing with a woman in such a position, and it rankled him.

In addition to the issue of Betty's power, her marriage to a Cherokee upset social norms. Despite her substantial wealth, she carried the nineteenth-century stigma of racial "mixing." Numerous statements at the time by both locals and visitors reveal the widespread nature of this view. A year before Hindman's appearance on Valley River, Andrew Barnard had stated he would rather see his children "in the grave" than married to an Indian.[5] In 1843 a North Carolina joint committee was formed to discuss the presence of Cherokees in the state. They strongly recommended the Cherokees be removed, because the mixing of white people and Cherokees (including the "refuse" trickling back from the west) would have a "demoralizing" effect on the population.[6] The fear of miscegenation pervaded Cherokee County, given its unusual demographics. In 1850, the first year that the population was enumerated in detail, the county resembled other rural Southern Appalachian counties. The portion of the population designated as white numbered 2,939 and included landless tenants and farm laborers, numerous small-to-middling landowning farmers, a small group of slave-owning farmers, and a small group of professionals, many of whom were enslavers and part-time farmers.[7] The African American population in Cherokee County in 1850 was 446, consisting of 337 enslaved and 109 free Black individuals.[8] What set Cherokee County apart was the Indian population: 553 Cherokees, enumerated in the 1851 Chapman roll, lived in Welch's Town, Buffalo Town, and a few other, smaller enclaves around the county.[9]

Racist views added to the difficulties faced by the Cherokees in North Carolina, who were struggling to solidify their rights regarding citizenship, land tenure, and even residency. Conflicting statements at the state and federal levels, plus a general refusal by anyone in power to make a clear determination on the rights of Cherokees, placed them in an incredibly marginalized position. They remained in this position for at least a decade, during which none of these issues were settled. However, it became increasingly apparent throughout the 1840s that, although the federal and state governments wished to remove the last of the Cherokees, they had little inclination to provide funding for it.

By convincing Crawford and Lea of Thomas's dishonesty, Hindman replaced Thomas as disbursing agent on September 29, 1841.[10] This "second" or "voluntary" removal attempt of the early 1840s was a concerted effort by the federal government and supported by the government of the Cherokee Nation west of the Mississippi River. The "eastern Cherokees" had been a problem for the Indian Office since the removal. They claimed US citizenship but were owed funds as members of the Cherokee Nation. Federal officials in the Office of Indian Affairs and the War Department felt pressure to settle claims as stipulated in the 1835 Treaty of New Echota. Articles 1, 8, and 9 of the treaty set aside large sums to compensate Cherokees for lost property and improvements to their farms, for travel west, and for subsistence in Indian Territory. In lieu of Article 13, they also settled similar claims for lost property and improvements stemming from the 1817 and 1819 treaties.[11]

The funds still owed the Cherokees by the Treaty of New Echota could be settled only when issues such as citizenship could be clarified. It was obvious to government officials this would be easiest if all of the Cherokees were in one place: Indian Territory. Once assembled together, they would all supposedly receive the funds equitably. Cherokee Nation officials, particularly John Ross, supported these efforts; otherwise, his community must await their money. In addition, Ross strongly desired to locate all members of the Cherokee Nation together. Some officials in the federal government carried a paternalistic belief that the North Carolina Cherokees would be better off in Indian Territory. Others wanted the remaining Cherokees far from white society.

The struggle to settle claims against the federal government regarding the loss of real estate, chattel property, and travel monies dragged on for years, and Cherokees became familiar with many unsavory characters who saw the confusion as an opportunity for profit. For the reserves in North Carolina, including John Welch and several people in Welch's Town, the claims also included the loss of land and improvements stemming from the 1817 and 1819 treaties, and considerable sums of money were at stake.

Although Hindman presented his task in the mountains as relatively simple to Commissioner Crawford and Secretary Lea, in reality it was a nearly impossible goal, especially because the frugal Tyler administration refused to finance any such move. Hindman rationalized that it was in the best interest of the Cherokees to emigrate, to separate them from corrupt white individuals.

Once in North Carolina, he considered Thomas and Betty Welch the worst of these. Shortly after his arrival in December 1841, he recognized the enormity of the task he had taken on: Cherokee farms were scattered throughout miles of steep mountains, and most Cherokees still despised the idea of removal, "voluntary" or otherwise.[12]

Regarding his meeting with the Welch's Town Cherokees at the Welch farm, an excerpt from his journal is worth recounting at length:

> Set out this morning (14th) from Murphy for a settlement of Indians on Val-
> ley River fourteen miles distant, to whom I had previously sent a request
> to meet me on the 15th at the house of John Welch, a half breed Chero-
> kee, where I arrived the same evening and saw several Cherokees, to whom I
> made known my business . . . a number had gone to the mountains on a hunt-
> ing expedition before my invitation was received, therefore, out of about
> one hundred and twenty who reside in this neighborhood, only forty five
> attended, but to those, I read, and had interpreted [by John Timpson] first,
> my instructions in relation to the business with Mr. Thomas, second, in rela-
> tion to collecting their claims against the government . . . and while reading
> all those documents they gave good attention and shewed every disposition
> to treat me with respect and kindness. I then endeavored to impress upon
> them the great advantage that would result by adhering to the advice given,
> and also endeavored to shew them their true situation, and what would even-
> tually be their fate provided they neglected this friendly offer and continued
> to live within the states.[13]

Hindman's account reveals several interesting aspects of life at the Welches. As it had been since at least the early 1830s, the Welch house was a hub of polit-ical and social activity for Cherokees and white people. Hindman figured ap-proximately 120 Cherokees lived in the neighborhood, the largest portion of whom resided on the Welch farm. Although Hindman wrote that most of the Cherokees had gone on a "hunting expedition," he also reported that Thomas revealed to the Cherokees that Hindman's purpose was to gather them for re-moval, and many fled into the mountains as they had done only three years be-fore.[14] Indeed, Hindman's visit occurred only two years after federal troops had left the region. Within these communities there was palpable fear of another attempt at forced removal. The ongoing undefined status for the Cherokees kept them in a perpetual state of uncertainty and wariness during the first de-cade after the Trail. Visitors to these communities, especially those working for the federal government, earned no trust, although usually they were met with civility. Cherokees were still mourning the widespread loss of family members. Of the thirty-three families listed as residing in Welch's Town in 1840 (including the Welch families), seven had lost at least one member to starvation or disease during the fall and winter of 1838. The number of Cherokees living in Welch's Town and along Valley River in 1840 was 129. A total of nineteen people, or 13 percent of the original group, had died during the removal.[15] These numbers make the meeting between Hindman and the members of Welch's Town seem surreal. The respect shown Hindman camouflaged the mistrust and loathing held by many toward the government and its agents.

The interaction of Hindman and the forty-five Cherokees present was mediated and translated by John Timson. Hindman urged the Cherokees to consider his proposal:

> As but a small portion of their people were present, I considered it proper they should defer an answer untill all could be together, and consult among themselves. . . . Chinequah [John Owl], the speaker, stated they were then ready to reply, and preferred doing so at that time, and then proceeded to say, those of the Cherokees, who composed that settlement, had separated from their Nation, and was now opposed to removal, neither did they consider their interest as identified with the other settlements, therefore could see no necessity for a counsel or of appointing any one to visit a country with a view to examine it when it was their determination to remain where they were, and that they protested against any one but themselves receiving any funds from the United States which belongs to them, either private claims or per capita . . . I insisted that this answer could only be for those present, as the others had not heard the Talks could not know their purport, and of course he could not answer for them. His reply was that he had been instructed to answer for all, therefore as their determination appeared to be fixed, and that their answer had evidently been prepared in advance, I considered it useless to remain longer with them at this time.[16]

Chinoque, or John Owl, was a community leader and served as representative for the group. His comments are particularly enlightening regarding the motives and attitudes of the Welch's Town Cherokees. At the core of his statement is the idea of community-level identity: the Welch's Town Cherokees not only felt no connection with those Cherokees west of the Mississippi River, they felt no close connection, at least politically, with Cherokees in nearby communities. This community-level identity, driven by long-term settlement in a specific landscape and strengthened through long-standing kinship ties and recent trauma, bound the Cherokees of the Valley and Cheoah river valleys only to each other.

Hindman would also claim that the Cherokees in "Cheohee" were "completely subservient" to Betty Welch.[17] Although they were unlikely subservient, the statement does show that Betty and the Cherokees of Cheoah (Buffalo Town) interacted. Minor shifts in town rolls between Buffalo Town, Welch's Town, and Hanging Dog support this idea: these communities were somewhat fluid, and they maintained regular intertown communication.

Through the remainder of December and well into January 1842, Hindman pressed through the mountains in a frustrated effort to recruit Cherokees for removal. His experience at Welch's Town gave him a taste of things to come. He spent weeks traveling on horseback through mountain passes in rain and snow, and, in the end, enlisted zero Cherokees for emigration. He returned to his native Alabama in late January 1842, his appointment as Cherokee agent ended.[18]

Although Hindman's failure might be partially explained by a lack of funding by federal agencies, the matter was extremely complicated. Cherokees east and west were divided into different political factions, each convinced that the financial settlements suggested by the government were inequitable.[19] The federal government, between 1836 and 1852, established four separate boards of commissioners to investigate the multitude of claims.[20] The boards, hobbled by infighting, corruption, and competing attorneys, failed to satisfy either the Cherokees' requests or the government's goal of settling the claims cheaply and quickly.[21] By 1850, the matter was becoming more urgent, because dispersal of funds, in the view of government officials, could be done only after equitable claims had been established for all Cherokees, east and west of the Mississippi River.

Commissioners of the various boards convened in Murphy, North Carolina, among other locations. The goal of the commissioners was as much to coerce the remaining Cherokees to leave as to pay their claims. The commissioners often set unreasonable standards of evidence to approve a claim. Further complications emerged from changing directives from the Indian Office, infighting among government officials, and the Cherokees' undefined status. The government wished to negotiate a new treaty to organize payments with all Cherokees, east and west. However, if the North Carolina Cherokees were US citizens, they could not be parties to a treaty.[22]

While the hearings attracted many Cherokees seeking money for their

losses, it also drew numerous lawyers and thieves, sometimes one and the
same, prepared to swindle the Cherokees out of their claim money.[23] In a letter to William Holland Thomas, his associate Felix Axley claimed "some men
have got a little taste of Cherokee money and it has created such a [illegible]
appetite that nothing will satisfy them but all or at least the control of it."[24]
Cherokee representatives, by acquiring power of attorney, stood to collect fees
in the range of 5 to 15 percent, a substantial income if a person could get the
signatures (or marks) of some of the hundreds of Cherokees who filed claims.
During the 1840s people who claimed power of attorney for various groups
of Cherokees (often whole towns would sign at once) included William Holland Thomas, Felix Axley, Preston Starrett, Johnson K. Rogers, and Duff and
Benjamin Green.[25] These and other men, some trained in law and some not,
competed with one another and sometimes worked together to entice, beg,
threaten, and plead with Cherokees to sign over power of attorney in the matter of claims. In 1844 J. W. King, another associate of Thomas, wrote a pleading
and fearful letter to him in Washington. In it he revealed his desperate financial
straits, the potential income from Cherokee claims, and some of the tactics he
was willing to use: "If we do not succeed in Realizing some means from the
Cherokee business I tell you I don't know what we are to do. . . . I want you
to inform me about Henry Smiths preemption claim whether or not in your
Judgment it will do to depend on or not as I have already got him in debt to our
House some 4 or 500$—and have opportunities that would suit our Interest to
get more debts on him provided that the debt is safe, and it would not be too
long before we could get the money."[26]

   Henry Smith was a Cherokee who lived on Peachtree Creek in a small
Cherokee community east of Murphy. He had served as an interpreter for the
army and later for Thomas and others. In the same letter King also discusses
an incident regarding Betty Welch and the Kilchuler family who resided in
Welch's Town:

> I succeeded for last court in getting appointed guardian for the Indian boy
> you mentioned in a former letter and now enclose you the power of attorney
> to act for me, in regards the dissatisfaction of Thompson Kilchuler and wife.
> I purchased their claim fairly and honorably. Henry Smith was present and
> interpreted they understood correctly the whole matter and was perfectly
> satisfied until that Demon in Human shape called Mrs Welch thought proper
> to interfere, and the Gnat John Timpson after a long time persuading them
> got them to agree to write the 2nd Auditer. So I was informed I think I shall

be able to fix all things wright [sic] with Thompson and his wife. It seems as if Mrs Welch & John Timpson make it their whole study to try to throw difficulties and frustrate our designs in Business and you should bear it in mind that either of them would do all they could to Injure us. I therefore would say to you as my friend to pay no more attention to their business whatever for I assure you they don't thank you for it. And I cannot help saying I would be Gratified if they never was to get one cent of their claims.[27]

Like Hindman, King seems to take particular offense that a woman had bested him. Certainly at the time, and perhaps especially in the South, women did not commonly serve in positions of political or economic power outside the household. This was even truer for married women, legally bound as their husband's property.[28] Hindman and King would have been aggravated by such hindrances instigated by anyone. However, it is probable that the mordant tone in their letters sprang from such treatment by a woman, and perhaps even more so by a white woman who ignored all social proscriptions and married a Cherokee. Betty served in some capacity as legal adviser or protector for at least some of the Welch's Town Cherokees, and it seems from King's account that she attempted to meet the best interests of the Cherokee community residing on her property. She advised Thompson Kilchuler to contact the board of commissioners. She did not ask him to transfer power of attorney to her. It is also clear that, like John Owl, Betty often served as a representative or spokesperson for the Welch plantation and for many of the affairs regarding Welch's Town. Absent from King's correspondence are John Welch, Ned Welch, and John Powell. Betty, with the assistance of John Timson, directed affairs regarding the claims of many of the Welch's Town Cherokees and their dealings with the boards of commissioners and with attorneys who tried to cheat them. This was in addition to attempting to settle her own family's claims against the government, which dated back to 1819. The voluminous Welch claims include preemptions, spoliation, and improvements, and encompass seven separate filings to the various boards of commissioners in Murphy. These documents were probably written for Betty (who could not write) by John Powell or Ned Welch and provide a remarkable amount of information regarding the Welch chattel and real property, their treatment by the army, and their affairs after the removal. Similar documents also describe the properties and holdings of all the families of Welch's Town, prior to their displacement in 1838.

The Welches and hundreds of other Cherokee families filed numerous claims to receive funds owed them through various articles in the Treaty of

New Echota. The most common were the spoliation and valuation claims. Valuations were records of real estate and improvements to the property, mainly structures. These records list the quality and quantity of land held by Cherokee families, as well as detailed descriptions of the house and other structures on the property. Spoliation claims recorded the chattel property owned by Cherokees—livestock, crops, tools, and, in a few cases, enslaved people. Another category was preemption claims. Only a small percentage of Cherokee families overall made these claims for lost property and improvements under the 1817 and 1819 treaties. However, the Welch family and many of the families in Welch's Town claimed compensation under preemption.

The failure to settle the claims of Cherokees east and west led to the Treaty of 1846, an attempt to finally settle all claims.[29] Although the treaty recognized the rights of Cherokees to funds stipulated in the Treaty of New Echota, the government still strongly supported emigration for the North Carolina Cherokees. In the words of Indian Commissioner William Medill: "Their natural and proper home is with their brethren in the west, where, when the present difficulties shall have been put to rest, it is believed they will be much more prosperous and happy than by residing where they now are. Every inducement should, therefore, be held out to them to remove, and none to remain."[30]

Following closely was the Indian Appropriations Act of 1848, another attempt to end the Cherokee claims. The act authorized a census of all Cherokees who had lived east of the Mississippi River since the passing of the Treaty of New Echota in May 1836.[31] Two rolls were taken of the Cherokees east of the Mississippi. John Mullay, an employee in the Indian Office, attempted the first. His first trip to the mountains of North Carolina began in August 1848, where he successfully enrolled most of the Cherokees in the region. However, he met with stubborn resistance from the Valley River Cherokees. John Owl, the Welch's Town spokesman, told him they suspected it was related to a second removal and therefore refused to be enrolled. Mullay, realizing the roll was incomplete, and while still on the Indian Office payroll, tried again in the mountains in the summer of 1850, where the hesitant Welch's Town Cherokees, realizing that they might actually be reimbursed for funds owed them for more than a decade, finally agreed to be included in the roll.[32]

The second roll was recorded by David Siler in the summer of 1851. Siler grew up in the area, lived in Franklin, and was a brother of William Siler, the patron of the Cherokee community of Sand Town, a few miles south. Siler visited all of the Cherokee settlements in North Carolina and had little difficulty in recording the census data.[33] While these efforts by the government—new treaties, acts, and rolls—did enable some Cherokees to receive some of the funds owed them, they did little to clarify the status of Cherokees in the Southern Appalachians regarding citizenship, land tenure, and their right to stay in their communities. Many people in every level of government continued to support removal for a variety of reasons: to make settlement of claims easier, out of a belief that it would be better for Cherokees, or out of a view that Indians were inferior. The one consistent factor, however, was a refusal to finance such a project. This fact, ultimately, was one of the key reasons the few Cherokees in the mountains were never forcibly moved to Indian Territory.

By the early 1850s, the social environment for the Cherokees in North Carolina had changed dramatically. Although their citizenship status remained undefined, their continued residence in North Carolina was largely unquestioned, if not yet legally sanctioned by the state. A few Cherokees had begun to acquire their own land. The first was Wachacha, who bought two tracts from Gideon Morris in the Cheoah River Valley in October 1845. In 1847 Wachacha's brother, Junaluska, purchased a tract in the same area. William Siler near Franklin sold two hundred acres along Cartoogechaye Creek to Chutasottee, the leader of Sand Town, in 1851. By 1855 several more Cherokees in the area owned their land, including John Axe, Joe Locust, and Nancy Hawkins. The number of landowning Cherokees remained low throughout the 1850s and 1860s, but they signaled a new era for those residing along the Valley and Cheoah River drainages. They felt more secure, and the need to be settled in compact communities was clearly subsiding.[34]

Another event in the 1850s helped spur the demise of Welch's Town. A marginal notation in a per capita claim handwritten by Ned Welch recorded, "John Welch the husband of Elizabeth died the 9th day of July 1852."[35] The cause of his death is unknown, but it almost certainly was associated with the illness and injuries incurred during his imprisonment at Fort Cass in the fall of 1838. His death would have elicited an emotional response not only from his family but from all the Cherokees of Welch's Town. His support for their community had been visible to all; his blindness and "wasted flesh" were the direct result of his resistance to forced emigration for the Cherokees in the surrounding communities. But his death, along with the awareness that threats of removal had ended, caused the Cherokees of Welch's Town to disperse to other nearby towns, most to Buffalo Town and the Qualla Towns. The last occupants of Welch's Town were gone by 1855, the cabins, townhouse, and other structures left to decay. Laurel and blackberry bushes grew over the remnants, along with the gardens and dance ground.

The abandonment of Welch's Town signaled the success of the Welch family and the members of Welch's Town to maintain local communities. These towns historically had been fluid, and the movement of individuals or families back and forth was common. Their achievement had begun more than fifteen years earlier as a concerted effort to hide from the US Army. Afterward they weathered an ambiguous status, greedy white individuals trying to wrest control of their funds, and the white supremacy of the antebellum South. The stability of these small communities, given the political, economic, and racial challenges they faced, is extraordinary.

Conclusions

The demise of Welch's Town in the mid-1850s was the choice of its members; they finally felt secure enough to relocate on their own terms, and most moved short distances to the Cheoah Valley or to the Qualla Towns. In July 1868 Congress passed an act that formally recognized, for the first time, the Cherokees in North Carolina as a tribal entity, separate from the Cherokees in the west. The first council meetings were held in the Cheoah townhouse in Buffalo Town in December 1868.[1] These early attempts at forming a central government for all Cherokees in North Carolina were characterized by intense factionalism. Lloyd Welch, Betty and John's youngest son, was from the beginning at the center of these struggles. Lloyd Welch became the second chief of the Eastern Band of Cherokee Indians (EBCI) in 1875. The "Lloyd Welch constitution," unquestioned for decades and still embraced by many in the tribe, established many of the precedents for governing that are still in place today. Lloyd Welch died in June 1880. He was replaced by Nimrod Jarrett Smith, whose father, Henry, had worked with the Welches for decades.[2] As the Cherokees in North Carolina began organizing and meeting as a corporate body in councils such as in Cheoah, the federal government began to recognize them as such. In the 1870 Indian Appropriations Act, they are, for the first time, described as the "Eastern Band of Cherokee Indians."[3]

In 1887 James Mooney, an anthropologist working for the Bureau of American Ethnology, first visited the EBCI, beginning several seasons of field work with the tribe.[4] By this time, John (Eteganah) and Annie (Sadayi) Axe, who had been members of Welch's Town, had moved to the Qualla Towns. John served as one of Mooney's main informants and provided him with numerous traditional stories of Cherokee history, lore, and mythology. Mooney photographed both of them for his major work *Myths of the Cherokee*, still considered a classic early publication on American Indian culture. In the photographs the Axes appear as elderly people, and the cares and concerns of the past half century are present on their faces. Mooney's interviews with the elders of the Eastern Band in the 1880s captured not only Cherokee myth, lore, and medical and magical practice but eyewitness accounts of the events of the removal.[5]

Confusion regarding citizenship continued well into the twentieth century. Dozens of Cherokee men were drafted to serve in World War I, although they were not US citizens. Roughly five years later, the Indian Citizenship Act declared that all Indians born in the United States were US citizens. Federal attempts at allotment of EBCI land during the same decade ultimately failed, and the tribally held land known as the Qualla Boundary remains intact.[6]

The Eastern Band of Cherokee Indians today is obviously not the tribe of 150 years ago. With the opening of a Harrah's Casino in 1997, they have achieved economic security, at least as a corporate body, if not for all individuals. The money from the casino is used to address some issues that Chief Smith would have addressed over a century ago—health care, education, and housing. Some of the funds go to per capita payments, which Lloyd Welch supported in the 1870s. It is also used for things that would have surprised those earlier chiefs, such as a language revitalization program. In 1880 the vast majority of Cherokees were fluent in their own language, and few spoke English. For those Cherokees who risked everything to stay in North Carolina during and after the removal, the current state of the tribe would signal a success: a continued presence in their homeland, and, just as significantly, intact local communities. Many of the descendants of those who struggled to stay in the mountains continue to live where their ancestors had lived prior to the removal; most people still identify with the town they are from, and some communities, such as Snowbird and Big Cove, are seen as particularly tight-knit. Until recently, some of the formal rules of the old towns were still in force. For example, Robert K. Thomas, a member of the Cherokee Nation of Oklahoma and an anthropology student at the University of Chicago, recorded the continued use of the gadugi, the communal work group, in these communities in the 1950s.[7]

Income from the casino has enabled the tribe to reclaim some of its old towns. In 1996 the EBCI purchased a 309-acre tract along the Tuckaseegee River between Cherokee and Bryson City. This tract contains the Kituwah mound and village sites and part of the 640-acre reservation of Yonaguska. The exchange represented the reacquisition of the mother town of Kituwah 175 years after it was taken from Yonaguska. The mound was plowed down in the early twentieth century and is only a few feet above ground surface now. However, its significance for the Cherokees has not diminished. An archaeological survey in the late 1990s, funded and directed by the tribe, revealed the remains of overlapping villages across the fields of Kituwah. Architectural remains and other archaeological features, including graves, dating from at least nine thousand years ago through the nineteenth century, were scattered across the entire property.[8] In 1998 the EBCI held the first mound-rebuilding ceremony at Kituwah. This ceremony, now an annual practice, represents not only the reclamation of these important sites but the symbolic and actual rebuilding of the mound. In 2007 the tribe purchased the site of Cowee, located on the Little Tennessee River about thirty miles southwest of Cherokee. This was also a significant event; Cowee was important throughout the eighteenth and early nineteenth centuries, and in 1819 reservees settled on the site. While Kituwah was one of the original mother towns, Cowee was an economic hub during the same era.

Reclamation of these old towns is part of the growing cultural heritage program initiated by the EBCI. Along with endeavors such as the language revitalization program, these actions realize a tribal goal to maintain those connections to the history of their own people. That history includes those Cherokees who, ironically, chose their local communities over the Cherokee Nation. It also reflects the continuation in modern Cherokee culture of the strength and importance of these local ties.

The eastern Cherokees of the 1840s were in a liminal state: they seemed to be neither citizens of the Cherokee Nation nor the United States. They were neither planning to move nor considered (at least by the US) to be permanent residents. My historical and archaeological research focuses on this period of being in-between. Primary documents set the context for the economic, political, and cultural relationships of the individuals and groups under investigation. The archaeological data provide another kind of evidence, the kind that no one in the 1840s bothered to write down or perhaps even consciously consider. People since the removal have been interpreting the motives of the Welch family: altruistic patrons or calculating capitalists? The archaeological remains of their lives, scattered throughout the buried soils of their old plantation, reveal something of their motives. The Welches found a niche by creating a hybrid space along the Valley River. Their closest social connections were to Cherokees who also adhered to the tenets of localism. Before and after removal, that connection was cemented by reciprocal exchanges and by the shared use of symbolic materials such as hand-carved pipes. The Welches also maintained connections outside of the Cherokee community. They built a plantation, hoarded substantial wealth, and enslaved people. They maintained relations with white elites and military officers; the architectural remains, as well as the description of the plantation by the army, show they lived in a substantial and comfortable house, an uncommon style in Cherokee society. The artifact assemblages show us that Betty could set a fashionable dining table. They practiced, under one roof, aspects of two very different cultural and economic systems. The assemblage of artifacts from the site shows that the Welch family actively participated in two worlds partly by establishing a hybrid material culture. They found that such a syncretic lifestyle enabled them to interact with numerous groups living in the region.

But their success and the associated success of Welch's Town depended upon the enslaved community on the plantation. The enslavement of African Americans was inseparable from their success in several ways. Primarily it reflected their financial achievement. It also promoted their ability to compete with a growing number of white families settling in the area. Like other Cherokee plantation owners, the Welches challenged the southern racial hierarchy of the antebellum era. They challenged gender roles as well. Betty's marriage to a Cherokee man itself contested the ideology of white womanhood. Slavery also enabled her to become the wealthy matriarch of the family. In this role she confronted the military, federal agents, and businessmen.

We know little about the enslaved people on the plantation. An isolated community, until the removal there were few free or enslaved African Americans in the region. The Trail also proved deadly for them. After the removal the number of enslaved people in the mountains grew dramatically, but most were scattered thinly throughout the region on small plantations. Life in bondage to Cherokees may have been a different experience than life under a white master, but it still demanded long hours of labor, physical and sexual abuse, and fears of family separation. Betty, like many plantation mistresses, performed her role forcefully. Since at least the early 1820s, the Welch family embraced large-scale agriculture and slavery.

The Welches and many members of Welch's Town shared a history spanning decades. This enabled a trust and dependency between the two groups during and after the military occupation. This mutual support was expressed after the removal through land provided by the Welches and goods and services by the Welch's Town inhabitants. This relationship served both patron and client, an exchange founded on solidarity. Although the family's world was very different from that of Welch's Town, they shared the ideology of localism. They held the common goal of maintaining their towns for over two decades. One group provided labor and the other a place to live, thereby strengthening the position of all in the community. After the removal, the Welches supported and even strengthened ties with the Cherokee communities around them.

The southern Indian removals were pivotal events during the early federal period of the United States. These large-scale deportations, based on racial hierarchy, attempted to create a society in which white people controlled land and labor across the South. The white supremacy of the antebellum South identified Indians as inferior to white people and prone to drunkenness and violence. Native people were also seen as suspect and perhaps as secretly supporting enslaved African Americans and fomenting rebellion. The small but growing planter class in Cherokee society even questioned the reign of white planters.[9]

However, by sidestepping the military occupation and white settlement of the region, the residents of Welch's Town broadened the range of possibilities, the breadth of dialogue for and about themselves and "others" in the region. The Welches consciously manipulated the marginalized world in which they lived. Standard definitions of race, gender, and class were, wherever possible, subverted. In the postremoval environment inhabited by the Welches, the "inferior race" of one was used to increase the power of another. The noncitizen status of her husband enabled Betty's power as a married woman; the deft timing of their legal transactions by her daughter's husband protected the family's holdings. At specific points in time, she became the owner of chattel property, then real property, and finally a representative for a whole community. Although suffering great losses, together they managed to conserve what held most importance for them: their plantation and local community.

Their success in the face of federal law, military occupation, and institutionalized racism reveals their extraordinary will and political intelligence. It also reveals the devastating realities of nineteenth-century white supremacy. Their success depended on Black enslavement. Their story, like the stories of James Vann and Shoeboots, exposes the heartbreaking choices made by Cherokees and the dramatic shift in racial perceptions during the era.[10]

The perseverance and strength of those people who lived on Welch land in the 1840s set the groundwork for a thriving EBCI today. Their descendants hold fast to tenets they fought for, a cultural identity based on small communities and corporate responsibility. The descendants of those families still live in these small communities: Yellow Hill, Big Cove, Bird Town, Paint Town, and Wolf Town around Cherokee, and Snowbird in Robbinsville, North Carolina. Although joined under the umbrella of a tribal government, these towns still maintain some autonomy. These communities are still discrete entities and remain a key aspect of identity for members of the EBCI. Their existence proves the lasting success of Cherokees' steadfast refusal to surrender to state violence.

NOTES

Introduction

1. Brett Riggs, "Removal Period Cherokee Households and Communities in Southwestern North Carolina (1835–1838)" (Final Report of the Cherokee Homestead Project, submitted to the North Carolina State Historic Preservation Office, Division of Archives and History, Department of Cultural Resources, Raleigh, North Carolina, 1996), 66–70; Gerald Schroedl, "Cherokee Ethnohistory and Archaeology from 1540 to 1838," in *Indians of the Greater Southeast: Historical Archaeology and Ethnohistory*, ed. Bonnie McEwan (Gainesville: University Press of Florida, 2000), 204–41; "Census Roll of the Cherokee Indians East of the Mississippi, 1835," Microcopy T-496, RG 75, NARA, Washington, DC, 1835.

2. In *Unworthy Republic: The Dispossession of Native Americans and the Road to Indian Territory*, Claudio Saunt discusses the terminology associated with the Indian removals of the 1830s. He argues that "removal" is a "soft word" because of its vagueness (who is doing the removing? what are the conditions?) and masks the violence of the event. Saunt explores the term "deportation," an expulsion carried out by a state on its own soil. The term is accurate in that it reflects the administrative and bureaucratic underpinning of the Cherokee removal and the US attack on Cherokee sovereignty. In this book I continue to use the term "removal" because it is most closely associated with the phenomenon. I also use phrases such as "forced emigration" in an attempt to identify violent or oppressive action.

3. William Holland Thomas, "Census of the North Carolina Cherokees, 1840," William Holland Thomas papers, David M. Rubenstein Rare Book and Manuscript Library, Duke University, Durham, North Carolina; William Holland Thomas, "Supplementary Report of Cherokee Indians Remaining in North Carolina, 1835–1840," manuscript copy in the William Holland Thomas papers, David M. Rubenstein Rare Book and Manuscript Library, Duke University, Durham, North Carolina.

4. Most of the histories written about resistance to removal focus on attempted political solutions by leaders of the Cherokee Nation, in particular John Ross. Brian Hicks, *Toward the Setting Sun: John Ross, the Cherokees, and the Trail of Tears* (New York: Grove Press, 2012); Jan Jordan, *Give Me the Wind: A Biographical Novel of John Ross, Chief of the Cherokee* (Englewood Cliffs, NJ: Prentice-Hall, 1973); Rachel Koestler-Grack, *Chief John Ross* (Chicago: Heinemann Library, 2004); Gary Moulton, *John Ross, Cherokee Chief* (Athens: University of Georgia Press, 1978); *The Papers of Chief John Ross*, Gary Moulton ed., (Norman: University of Oklahoma Press, 1985). Much has also been written about the members of the "Treaty Party" and their involvement in removal proceedings. Edward Dale and Gaston Litton, *Cherokee Cavaliers: Forty Years of Cherokee History as Told in the Correspondence of the Ridge-Watie-Boudinot Family* (Norman: University of Oklahoma Press, 1939); Thurman

Wilkins, *Cherokee Tragedy: The Ridge Family and the Decimation of a People* (Norman: University of Oklahoma Press, 1986). There are exceptions; research on Cherokees who resisted removal by fleeing the army includes John Finger, *The Eastern Band of Cherokees, 1819–1900* (Knoxville: University of Tennessee Press, 1984); Sarah Hill, *Weaving New Worlds: Southeastern Cherokee Women and Their Basketry* (Chapel Hill: University of North Carolina Press, 1997); James Mooney, *Myths of the Cherokee and Sacred Formulas of the Cherokees*; reproduction of 19th and 7th Annual Reports of the Bureau of American Ethnology (Nashville: Charles and Randy Elder Booksellers, 1982); Brett Riggs, "The Christie Cabin Site: Historical and Archaeological Evidence of the Life and Times of a Cherokee *Métis* Household (1835–1838)," in *May We All Remember Well: A Journal of History and Cultures of Western North Carolina, Volume 1*, ed. Robert Brunk (Asheville, NC: Robert S. Brunk Auction Services, 1997), 228–48.

5. Marisa Fuentes, *Dispossessed Lives: Enslaved Women, Violence, and the Archive* (Philadelphia: University of Pennsylvania Press, 2016), 5.

6. Lance Greene, "A Struggle for Cherokee Community: Excavating Identity in Post-Removal North Carolina" (PhD diss., University of North Carolina, Chapel Hill, 2009); Lance Greene, "Identity in a Post-Removal Cherokee Household, 1838–1850," in *American Indians and the Market Economy, 1775–1850*, eds. Lance Greene and Mark Plane (Tuscaloosa: University of Alabama Press, 2010), 53–66; Lance Greene, "Archaeology and Community Reconstruction of Mid-Nineteenth-Century Cherokee Farmsteads along Valley River, North Carolina," in *Archaeological Adaptation: Case Studies of Cultural Transformation from the Southeast and Caribbean*, ed. Clifford Boyd, Jr. (Knoxville: University of Tennessee Press, 2019), 193–222.

7. Wilma Dunaway, *Slavery in the American Mountain South* (Cambridge: Cambridge University Press, 2003); John Inscoe, *Mountain Masters: Slavery and the Sectional Crisis in Western North Carolina* (Knoxville: University of Tennessee Press, 1996); John Lewis, "Becoming Appalachia: The Emergence of an American Subculture, 1840–1860" (PhD diss., University of Kentucky, 2000).

8. Thavolia Glymph, *Out of the House of Bondage: The Transformation of the Plantation Household* (Cambridge: Cambridge University Press, 2008); Stephanie Jones-Rogers, *They Were Her Property: White Women as Slave Owners in the American South* (New Haven: Yale University Press, 2019).

9. Exceptions include R. Halliburton Jr., *Red over Black: Black Slavery among the Cherokee Indians*, Contributions in Afro-American and African Studies No. 27. (Westport, CT: Greenwood Press, 1977); and Theda Perdue, *Slavery and the Evolution of Cherokee Society, 1540–1866* (Knoxville: University of Tennessee Press, 1979).

10. Tiya Miles, *Ties That Bind: The Story of an Afro-Cherokee Family in Slavery and Freedom* (Berkeley: University of California Press, 2005); Tiya Miles, *The House on Diamond Hill: A Cherokee Plantation Story* (Durham: University of North Carolina Press, 2010); Fay Yarbrough, *Race and the Cherokee Nation: Sovereignty in the Nineteenth Century* (Philadelphia: University of Pennsylvania Press, 2008); Fay Yarbrough, "From Kin to Intruder: Cherokee Legal Attitudes toward People of African Descent in the Nineteenth Century," in *Race and Science: Scientific Challenges to Racism in Modern America*, ed. Paul Farber and Hamilton Cravens (Corvallis: Oregon State University Press, 2009), 32–57.

11. Miles, *The House on Diamond Hill*.

12. Cherokee women also were deprived of earlier sexual freedoms. Yarbrough writes extensively about the social and legal controls increasingly placed on Cherokee women during the nineteenth century and about changing views of interracial sex within the Cherokee Nation. Fay Yarbrough, "'Those Disgracefull and Unnatural Matches': Interracial Sex and Cherokee Society in the Nineteenth Century" (PhD diss., Emory University, 2003); Fay Yarbrough, "Legislating Women's Sexuality: Cherokee Marriage Laws in the Nineteenth Century," *Journal of Social History* 38, no. 2 (2004): 385–406; Yarbrough, "From Kin to Intruder."

13. Glymph, *Out of the House of Bondage*, 65; Miles, *Ties That Bind*; Yarbrough, "'Those Disgracefull and Unnatural Matches,'" 270–72.

14. As Miles found in the early nineteenth-century case of the Cherokee man Shoeboots marrying a white woman, Clarinda Allington, "by becoming the wives of Indian men and having sexual relations with them, white women forfeited their purity and honor in the eyes of white society" (Miles, *Ties That Bind*, 21). Although the white writer and traveler in the Cherokee Nation John Howard Payne thought that Clarinda had "civilized" Shoeboots, Clarinda's white family, upon her return, saw her as degraded by the relationship (Miles, *Ties That Bind*, 21–24). Although others (including Thomas Jefferson) held Payne's view of civilizing Indians through intermarriage with white people, the view of moral degradation, particularly of white women, through sexual interaction was a common theme in white society throughout this period.

15. Mooney, *Myths of the Cherokee*, 329–30, 405.

16. Mother towns, also referred to as beloved towns, were significant politically and historically. They were considered the original town of each region and were usually also the political hub of each region. Tyler Boulware, *Deconstructing the Cherokee Nation: Town, Region, and Nation among Eighteenth-Century Cherokees* (Gainesville: University Press of Florida, 2011), 24–27; Mooney, *Myths of the Cherokee*.

17. Boulware, *Deconstructing the Cherokee Nation*; Raymond Fogelson and Paul Kutsche, "Cherokee Economic Cooperatives: The Gadugi," in *Symposium on Cherokee and Iroquois Culture*, Bulletin 180, ed. William Fenton and John Gulick (Smithsonian Institution Bureau of American Ethnology, Washington, DC: US Government Printing Office, 1961), 88–98; Fred Gearing, *Priests and Warriors: Social Structures for Cherokee Politics in the Eighteenth Century*, American Anthropological Association, Memoir 93 (Menasha: American Anthropological Association, 1962); Hill, *Weaving New Worlds*, 107; Mooney, *Myths of the Cherokee*; Victor Persico, "Cherokee Social Structure in the Early Nineteenth Century" (MA thesis, University of Georgia, Athens, 1974), 34–38.

18. In *Deconstructing the Cherokee Nation*, Boulware provides a detailed discussion of the political and social significance of localism and community-based autonomy in eighteenth-century Cherokee life. The clan system is described in Gearing, *Priests and Warriors*; Hill, *Weaving New Worlds*, 27–31; William McLoughlin, *Cherokee Renascence in the New Republic* (Princeton: Princeton University Press, 1986).

19. McLoughlin, *Cherokee Renascence*.

20. Cherokees had been immigrating to Arkansas and other western regions as early as the 1790s and probably much earlier. This immigration increased during the first decade of the nineteenth century. McLoughlin, *Cherokee Renascence*, 56–57; James Mooney, *Historical Sketch of the Cherokee* (1900; rpt. Chicago: Aldine, 1975), 92–102; Mooney, *Myths of the Cherokee*, 77–105; Russell Thornton, *The Cherokees: A Population History* (Lincoln: University of Nebraska Press, 1990), 43–44.

21. William Jurgelski, "A New Plow in Old Ground: Cherokees, Whites, and Land in Western North Carolina, 1819–1829" (PhD diss., University of Georgia, Athens, 2004); Brett Riggs, "An Historical and Archaeological Reconnaissance of Citizen Cherokee Reservations in Macon, Swain, and Jackson Counties, North Carolina" (submitted to the North Carolina Division of Archives and History, Raleigh, Department of Anthropology, University of Tennessee, Knoxville, 1988); Charles Royce, *The Cherokee Nation of Indians* (Chicago: Aldine, 1975), 91–100.

22. Finger, *Eastern Band of Cherokees*; Gearing, *Priests and Warriors*; Mooney, *Myths of the Cherokee*; Robert Thomas, "Cherokee Values and World View," manuscript on file, North Carolina Collection, The Louis Round Wilson Special Collections Library, University of North Carolina at Chapel Hill, 1958.

23. Finger, *Eastern Band of Cherokees*; William McLoughlin and Walter Conser Jr., "The Cherokees in Transition: A Statistical Analysis of the Federal Cherokee Census of 1835," *Journal of American History* 64 (1977): 678–703; Theda Perdue, "Rising from the Ashes: The Cherokee Phoenix as an Ethnohistorical Source," *Ethnohistory* 24, no. 3 (1977): 214; Circe Sturm, *Blood Politics: Race, Culture, and Identity in the Cherokee Nation of Oklahoma* (Berkeley: University of California Press, 2002); Thomas, "Cherokee Values and World View."

24. Finger, *Eastern Band of Cherokees*; Perdue, "Rising from the Ashes."

25. McLoughlin and Conser Jr., "Cherokees in Transition."

26. Finger, *Eastern Band of Cherokees*, 60.

27. Roger Gould, "Patron-Client Ties, State Centralization, and the Whiskey Rebellion," *American Journal of Sociology* 102, no. 2 (1996): 400–429; Barry Mitchie, "The Transformation of Agrarian Patron-Client Relations: Illustrations from India," *American Ethnologist* 8, no. 1 (1981): 21–40; Frances Rothstein, "The Class Basis of Patron-Client Relations," *Latin American Perspectives* 6, no. 2 (1979): 25–35; James Scott, "Patron-Client Politics and Political Change in Southeast Asia," *American Political Science Review* 66, no. 1 (1972): 91–113; Howard Stein, "A Note on Patron-Client Theory," *Ethos* 12, no. 1 (1984): 30–36.

28. Jurgelski, "A New Plow in Old Ground"; John Welch, "Claim for spoliation of property, File 431," RFBCC, RG 75, NARA, Washington, DC, 1843; John Welch, "Claim for spoliation of property, File 418," RFBCC, RG 75, NARA, Washington, DC, 1846; John Welch, "Claim for spoliation of property, File 687," RFBCC, RG 75, NARA, Washington, DC, 1846.

29. For example, Miles documents that Cherokees and enslaved African Americans at the Diamond Hill plantation participated together in dances and ball play and shared medical care, *House on Diamond Hill*, 100–107.

30. "Census Roll of the Cherokee Indians East of the Mississippi, 1835," Microcopy T-496, RG 75, NARA, Washington, DC, 1835, quoted in Riggs, "Removal Period Cherokee Households and Communities in Southwestern North Carolina (1835–1838)," 22.

31. J. W. King, "Letter to William Holland Thomas, December 12, 1844," James Terrell papers, microfilm roll 1 (1813–1852), David M. Rubenstein Rare Book and Manuscript Library, Duke University, Durham, North Carolina.

32. Jeb Card, "Introduction," in *The Archaeology of Hybrid Material Culture*, ed. Jeb Card (Carbondale: Southern Illinois University Press, 2013), 2; Matthew Liebmann, "Parsing Hybridity: Archaeologies of Amalgamation in Seventeenth-Century New Mexico," in *The Archaeology of Hybrid Material Culture*, ed. Jeb Card.

33. Liebmann, "Parsing Hybridity," 27.

34. Liebmann, "Parsing Hybridity," 28–31.

35. Homi Bhabha, *The Location of Culture* (London: Routledge Press, 2004); John Hutnyk, "Hybridity," *Ethnic and Racial Studies* 28, no. 1 (2005): 79–102; Matthew Liebmann, "The Mickey Mouse Kachina and Other 'Double Objects': Hybridity in the Material Culture of Colonial Encounters," *Journal of Social Archaeology* 15, no. 3 (2015): 319–41; Philipp Stockhammer, ed., *Conceptualizing Cultural Hybridity: A Transdisciplinary Approach* (New York: Springer, 2012); Peter van Dommelen, "Colonial Interactions and Hybrid Practices: Phoenician and Carthaginian Settlement in the Ancient Mediterranean," in *The Archaeology of Colonial Encounters: Comparative Perspectives*, ed. Gil Stein (Santa Fe: School of American Research Press, 2005), 109–41.

36. Liebmann, "Parsing Hybridity," 30.

37. Liebmann, "Parsing Hybridity," 41.

38. Regarding how hybridity theory investigates how people challenge economic, political, or military power, see Bhabha, *Location of Culture*; Card, "Introduction"; John Hutnyk, "Hybridity"; Stephen Silliman, "What, Where, and When Is Hybridity?," in *The Archaeology of Hybrid Material Culture*, ed. Jeb Card, 486–500; Carlo Tronchetti and Peter van Dommelen, "Entangled Objects and Hybrid Practices: Colonial Contacts and Elite Connections at Monte Prama, Sardinia," *Journal of Mediterranean Archaeology* 18, no. 2 (2005): 183–208.

39. Liebmann, "Parsing Hybridity," 41.

40. Kathleen Deagan, "Hybridity, Identity, and Archaeological Practice," in *The Archaeology of Hybrid Material Culture*, ed. Jeb Card, 270–74.

41. Card, "Introduction," 6–8; Silliman, "What, Where, and When Is Hybridity?"; Laurie Wilkie, *Creating Freedom: Material Culture and African American Identity at Oakley Plantation, Louisiana, 1840–1950* (Baton Rouge: Louisiana State University Press, 2000).

42. Card, "Introduction"; Deagan, "Hybridity, Identity, and Archaeological Practice."

43. Ian Hodder and Scott Hutson, *Reading the Past: Current Approaches to Interpretation in Archaeology* (Cambridge: Cambridge University Press, 2003), 172.

44. For example, see Christopher Tilley and Kate Cameron-Daum, "An Anthropology of Landscape," in *The Anthropology of Landscape: The Extraordinary in the Ordinary*, ed. Christopher Tilley and Kate Cameron-Daum (London: UCL Press, 2017), 1–21; Barbara Voss and Eleanor Conlin Casella, eds., *The Archaeology of Colonialism: Intimate Encounters and Sexual Effects* (New York: Cambridge University Press, 2012); Mary Beaudry, "Stitching Women's Lives: Interpreting the Artifacts of Sewing and Needlework," in *Interpreting the Early Modern World: Transatlantic Perspectives*, ed. Mary Beaudry and James Symonds (New York: Springer, 2011), 143–58. Embodiment is also a theme in a special section of the *Cambridge Archeological Journal* 13, no. 2 (2003).

45. Sasha Turner, *Contested Bodies: Pregnancy, Childrearing, and Slavery in Jamaica* (Philadelphia: University of Pennsylvania Press, 2017), 5.

46. Stanly Godbold Jr., "William Holland Thomas: A Man for All Seasons," *Journal of Cherokee Studies* 24 (2005); Stanly Godbold Jr. and Mattie Russell, *Confederate Colonel and Cherokee Chief: The Life of William Holland Thomas* (Knoxville: University of Tennessee Press, 1990); Richard Iobst, "William Holland Thomas and the Cherokee Claims," in *The Cherokee Indian Nation: A Troubled History*, ed. Duane King, 181–201 (Knoxville: University of Tennessee Press, 1979); Mooney, *Myths of the Cherokee*; Mattie Russell, "William Holland Thomas, White Chief of the North Carolina Cherokees" (PhD diss., Duke

University, 1956). Thomas's life was fictionalized in the novel *Thirteen Moons* by Charles Frazier.

47. See Greene, "Struggle for Cherokee Community"; Greene, "Identity in a Post-Removal Cherokee Household"; Lance Greene, "Community Practice in a Post-Removal Cherokee Town," in *Investigating the Ordinary: Everyday Matters in Southeast Archaeology*, eds. Sarah Price and Philip Carr (Gainesville: University of Florida Press, 2018), 39–52; Greene, "Archaeology and Community Reconstruction."

48. Thomas, "Census of the North Carolina Cherokees, 1840"; Thomas, "Supplementary Report of Cherokee Indians Remaining in North Carolina, 1835–1840."

49. Many archaeologists have long seen the usefulness of fictional accounts, and many have written fiction based on sites they have worked on. The practice first came to the forefront in archaeology with James Deetz's very popular *In Small Things Forgotten: The Archaeology of Early American Life* (New York: Anchor Press/Doubleday, 1977), in which he provides brief fictional vignettes of people living in the past. Perhaps the most well-known example is Janet Spector's *What This Awl Means: Feminist Archaeology at a Wahpeton Dakota Village* (St. Paul: Minnesota Historical Society Press, 1993), in which she creates a fictional account of Mazaokiyewin, a young woman, based on excavations by Spector. Discussion about fictional writing in archaeology has appeared in two thematic journal issues: *Historical Archaeology* 32, no. 1 (1998) and 34, no. 2 (2000). A briefer version of the historical narrative in this book appears in Greene, "Community Practice."

50. Whitney Battle-Baptiste, *Black Feminist Archaeology* (Walnut Creek, CA: Left Coast Press, 2011), 46. The author makes a compelling argument that works such as Toni Morrison's *Beloved* provide significant insight into, for example, the "complexity of the captive family," 43. Battle-Baptiste writes that the Black literary tradition that helped enslaved people survive continues to help reclaim African and African American identities through the "shifting of literary authority," 44.

51. Marisa Fuentes's *Dispossessed Lives* recreates the world these enslaved women inhabited: foul-smelling waterfronts, caged runaways, and crowded, daily markets. Tiya Miles's *The Cherokee Rose: A Novel of Gardens and Ghosts* (Winston-Salem: John F. Blair, 2016) is based on the Vann family and their Diamond Hill plantation in northern Georgia.

52. Fuentes, *Dispossessed Lives*, 12. Fuentes's research looks at what she calls "vulnerable historical subjects": enslaved women in eighteenth-century Barbados.

WELCH PLANTATION, DECEMBER 1850

1. This narrative of a brief episode on the Welch plantation in the winter of 1850 is based on numerous kinds of evidence, including archaeology, documentary records, Cherokee history, and discussions with members of the Eastern Band of Cherokee Indians. Many of the details are well documented. The names of the Welches and the members of Welch's Town appear on rolls and censuses. The evidence used to create this brief narrative is presented in the following chapters. Although some of the details obviously cannot be proven, hopefully the evidence presented is strong enough that readers will agree that, although they may not be fact, they are truthful—they represent the underlying realities of the period regarding the interactions and relationships between the three communities.

2. The communal work party, called the gadugi, is well documented historically and was

a crucial part of the traditional Cherokee town structure. An integral part of the gadugi was often a feast, in which everyone supplied certain kinds of food. Raymond Fogelson and Paul Kutsche, "Cherokee Economic Cooperatives: The Gadugi," in *Symposium on Cherokee and Iroquois Culture*, Bulletin 180, ed. William Fenton and John Gulick (Smithsonian Institution Bureau of American Ethnology, Washington, DC: U.S. Government Printing Office, 1961); James Mooney, *Myths of the Cherokee and Sacred Formulas of the Cherokees*, reproduction of 19th and 7th Annual Reports of the Bureau of American Ethnology (Nashville: Charles and Randy Elder Booksellers, 1982), 519.

3. The dismantling of the kitchen on the Welch farm, the foods they were eating, and the items lost and discarded were defined archaeologically. For example, evidence for the corn being burned comes from the archaeological remains of several intensely burned ears of corn, which also was the reason for their good preservation in the soil for more than 150 years. Many of the mammal long bones had been cracked open with a hammer or other blunt object. This practice is usually associated with extraction of marrow. The presence of dogs and their scrambling to get food is also borne out by the archaeology; several animal bones show signs of canine chewing.

4. The story of Harry Morris's performance in the famous stickball game on Tallulah Creek is documented and still discussed. Raymond Fogelson, "The Cherokee Ballgame: A Study in Southeastern Ethnology" (PhD diss., University of Pennsylvania, 1962), 43; C. R. Harwood, "Lost Cherokee Towns of Graham County, North Carolina," *Tennessee Archaeologist* 15, no. 2 (1959): 111–12.

5. John Axe's preference for the wonder stories was documented by the anthropologist James Mooney in the 1880s, forty years after the Welch kitchen was torn down (Mooney, *Myths of the Cherokee*, 229–39). In *Myths of the Cherokee*, Mooney documented hundreds of these stories and, in many cases such as Tlanusiyi, connected them to locations on the landscape.

Some details in the narrative, such as activities in the evening and topics of conversation, are more tentative than those illustrated through archaeological excavations. However, they fall well within the realm of possibility and are based on specific historic evidence.

CHAPTER 1

1. For example, Tiya Miles, *Ties That Bind: The Story of an Afro-Cherokee Family in Slavery and Freedom* (Berkeley: University of California Press, 2005); Claudio Saunt, *Black, White, and Indian: Race and the Unmaking of an American Family* (Oxford: Oxford University Press, 2005); Claudio Saunt, *A New Order of Things: Property, Power, and the Transformation of the Creek Indians, 1733–1816* (Cambridge: Cambridge University Press, 1999); Circe Sturm, *Blood Politics: Race, Culture, and Identity in the Cherokee Nation of Oklahoma* (Berkeley: University of California Press, 2002); Fay Yarbrough, *Race and the Cherokee Nation: Sovereignty in the Nineteenth Century* (Philadelphia: University of Pennsylvania Press, 2008).

2. John Finger, *The Eastern Band of Cherokees, 1819–1900* (Knoxville: University of Tennessee Press, 1984); William McLoughlin, *Cherokee Renascence in the New Republic* (Princeton: Princeton University Press, 1986); James Mooney, *Myths of the Cherokee and Sacred Formulas of the Cherokees*, reproduction of 19th and 7th Annual Reports of the Bureau of American Ethnology (Nashville: Charles and Randy Elder Booksellers, 1982); Robert Thomas, "Cherokee Values and World View," manuscript on file, North Carolina Collection,

The Louis Round Wilson Special Collections Library, University of North Carolina at Chapel Hill, 1958; Yarbrough, *Race and the Cherokee Nation*.

3. Yarbrough, *Race and the Cherokee Nation*, 37–38.

4. Claudio Saunt, Barbara Krauthamer, Tiya Miles, Celia Naylor, and Circe Sturm, "Rethinking Race and Culture in the American South," *Ethnohistory* 53, no. 1 (2006): 399–405.

5. McLoughlin, *Cherokee Renascence*; Yarbrough, *Race and the Cherokee Nation*.

6. Yarbrough, *Race and the Cherokee Nation*, 38.

7. Gambold to Van Vleck, Dec. 28, 1814, Springplace Mission Letters, Cherokee Mission Papers, Moravian Archives, Winston-Salem, North Carolina, in *The Moravian Springplace Mission to the Cherokees*, 2 vols., ed. Rowena McClinton (Lincoln: University of Nebraska Press, 2007), and quoted in Tiya Miles, *The House on Diamond Hill: A Cherokee Plantation Story* (University of North Carolina Press, 2010), 106.

8. Miles, *House on Diamond Hill*, 104–7.

9. Miles, *House on Diamond Hill*, 167–70.

10. Fred Gearing, *Priests and Warriors: Social Structures for Cherokee Politics in the Eighteenth Century*, American Anthropological Association Memoir 93 (Menasha, WI: American Anthropological Association, 1962); Sarah Hill, *Weaving New Worlds: Southeastern Cherokee Women and Their Basketry* (Chapel Hill: University of North Carolina Press, 1997), 27–31; McLoughlin, *Cherokee Renascence*.

11. Theda Perdue, "Cherokee Women and the Trail of Tears," *Journal of Women's History* 1, no. 1 (1989): 135–58.

12. Mooney, *Myths of the Cherokee*, 88–89; James Mooney, *The Ghost-Dance Religion and the Sioux Outbreak of 1890*, Reproduction of 14th Annual Report of the Bureau of American Ethnology, Part 2, 1896 (Lincoln: University of Nebraska Press, 1991), 670–80; Saunt, *New Order of Things*, 233–36. Quotes from Mooney, *Ghost-Dance Religion and the Sioux Outbreak of 1890*, 676–77.

13. Charles Royce, *The Cherokee Nation of Indians* (Chicago: Aldine, 1975).

14. William McLoughlin, *Champions of the Cherokees: Evan and John B. Jones* (Princeton: Princeton University Press, 1990), 65–66.

15. Brett Riggs, "The Christie Cabin Site: Historical and Archaeological Evidence of the Life and Times of a Cherokee Métis Household (1835–1838)," in *May We All Remember Well: A Journal of History and Cultures of Western North Carolina, Volume 1*, ed. Robert Brunk, 228–48 (1997).

16. Riggs, "Removal Period Cherokee Households and Communities in Southwestern North Carolina (1835–1838)," Final Report of the Cherokee Homestead Project, submitted to the North Carolina State Historic Preservation Office, Division of Archives and History, Department of Cultural Resources, Raleigh, North Carolina, 1996, 34; Riggs, "Christie Cabin Site," 230.

17. Thomas, "Cherokee Values and World View"; McLoughlin, *Cherokee Renascence*.

18. Alexis, "A Visit to the Cartoogechaye Indians," *North Carolina University Magazine*, no. 1 (1851): 116–18.

19. Brett Riggs, "Removal Period Cherokee Households and Communities in Southwestern North Carolina (1835–1838)," 29.

20. Photograph by James Mooney, 1888, National Anthropological Archives, black and white gelatin glass negative, BAE GN 01000a 06212000.

21. Mooney, *Myths of the Cherokee*; Riggs, "Removal Period Cherokee Households and Communities in Southwestern North Carolina (1835–1838)," 29–34; William Welch and Nimrod Jarrett, "Valuations of Cherokee Property in North Carolina," Cherokee Property Valuations, 1835–1839, RG 75, NARA, Washington, DC, 1837.

22. Finger, *Eastern Band of Cherokees*.

23. For the use of blowguns, see Charles Hudson, *The Southeastern Indians* (Knoxville: University of Tennessee Press, 1976), 273. The chopping or fracturing of long bones has been documented in late prehistoric and historic Cherokee archaeological contexts: Arthur Bogan, Lori LaValley, and Gerald Schroedl, "Faunal Remains," in *Overhill Cherokee Archaeology at Chota-Tanasee*, ed. Gerald Schroedl, Report of Investigations 38 (Knoxville: University of Tennessee, Department of Anthropology, 1986), 482–84; Arthur Bogan and Richard Polhemus, "Faunal Analysis," in *The Toqua Site: A Late Mississippian Dallas Phase Town*, ed. Richard Polhemus, Report of Investigations, no. 41, vol. 2 (Knoxville: University of Tennessee, Department of Anthropology, 1987), 1089–92.

24. Bogan, LaValley, and Schroedl, "Faunal Remains," 481–82; Riggs, "Removal Period Cherokee Households and Communities in Southwestern North Carolina (1835–1838)," 111; John Lewis, "Becoming Appalachia: The Emergence of an American Subculture, 1840–1860" (PhD diss., University of Kentucky, 2000), 290.

25. James Adair, *Adair's History of the American Indians*, ed. Samuel Cole Williams (1775, rpt. Johnson City, TN: Watauga Press, 1930); Bogan, LaValley, and Schroedl, "Faunal Remains," 482–84; Roy Dickens, *Cherokee Prehistory: The Pisgah Phase in the Southern Appalachian Region* (Knoxville: University of Tennessee Press, 1976); Samuel Williams, ed., *Lieutenant Henry Timberlake's Memoirs, 1756–1765* (Johnson City, TN: Watauga Press, 1927).

26. Fishing methods discussed in Heidi Altman, *Eastern Cherokee Fishing* (Tuscaloosa: University of Alabama Press, 2006); Bogan, LaValley, and Schroedl, "Faunal Remains," 482–84; Hill, *Weaving New Worlds*; Brett Riggs, "Removal Period Cherokee Households in Southwestern North Carolina: Material Perspectives on Ethnicity and Cultural Differentiation" (PhD diss., University of Tennessee, Knoxville, 1999). Local availability of fishing supplies found in A. R. S. Hunter, "Cherokee Accounts Ledger of the Huntington Store," manuscript on file, Cherokee County Historical Museum, Murphy, North Carolina, 1836–1838. Uses of wild and domesticated faunal species are discussed in Riggs, "Removal Period Cherokee Households in Southwestern North Carolina: Material Perspectives on Ethnicity and Cultural Differentiation," 394. Robert Thomas, during his ethnographic research in the late 1950s on the Qualla Boundary around Cherokee, North Carolina, documented a pattern throughout the first half of the twentieth century of Cherokees continuing to hunt wild game and gather wild plant foods, although he stated these practices were diminishing. He writes that his informants "who were born before 1900 say they were raised on corn bread and wild meat." Robert Thomas, "Eastern Cherokee Acculturation." North Carolina Collection, The Louis Round Wilson Special Collections Library, University of North Carolina at Chapel Hill, 1958.

27. Hill, *Weaving New Worlds*, 10, 266.

28. Gary Goodwin, "Cherokees in Transition: A Study of Changing Culture and Environment prior to 1775." Department of Geography, University of Chicago, Research Paper 181, 1977, 59; Hill, *Weaving New Worlds*, 10.

29. Gerald Schroedl and Andrea Shea, "Plant Remains," in *Overhill Cherokee Archaeology*

at Chota-Tanasee, ed. Gerald Schroedl, Report of Investigations 38 (Knoxville: University of Tennessee, Department of Anthropology, 1986), 515–30; John Witthoft, "Cherokee Indian Use of Potherbs," *Journal of Cherokee Studies* 2, no. 2 (1977): 250.

30. Witthoft, "Cherokee Indian Use of Potherbs."

31. Hudson, *Southeastern Indians*; Mooney, *Myths of the Cherokee*.

32. Davis Barker and Teresita Majewski, "Ceramic Studies in Historical Archaeology," in *The Cambridge Companion to Historical Archaeology*, ed. Dan Hicks and Mary Beaudry, (Cambridge: Cambridge University Press, 2006), 205–34; James Deetz, *In Small Things Forgotten: The Archaeology of Early American Life* (New York: Anchor Press/Doubleday, 1977); Mary Douglas and Baron Isherwood, *The World of Goods: Towards an Anthropology of Consumerism* (New York: Basic Books, 1979); Mark Leone, Parker Potter, and Paul Shackel, "Toward a Critical Archaeology," *Current Anthropology* 28, no. 3 (1987): 287–89; Teresita Majewski and Michael O'Brien, "The Use and Misuse of Nineteenth-Century English and American Ceramics in Archaeological Analysis," in *Advances in Archaeological Method and Theory* 11, ed. Michael Schiffer (New York: Academic Press, 1987), 97–209; George Miller, "A Revised Set of CC Index Values for Classification and Economic Scaling of English Ceramics from 1787 to 1880," *Historical Archaeology* 25, no. 1 (1991): 1–25; Ivor Noël Hume, *Historical Archaeology* (New York: Alfred A. Knopf, 1969).

33. Riggs, "Removal Period Cherokee Households and Communities in Southwestern North Carolina (1835–1838)"; Riggs, "Removal Period Cherokee Households in Southwestern North Carolina: Material Perspectives on Ethnicity and Cultural Differentiation"; Welch and Jarrett, "Valuations of Cherokee Property in North Carolina"; "Census Roll of the Cherokee Indians East of the Mississippi, 1835," Microcopy T-496, RG 75, NARA, Washington, DC, 1835. The Welch and Jarrett valuations show the Chewkeeaskee holdings as "one cabin, 13 ft., part floored, joists and loft, wood chimney." In addition, the family had an eight-foot-square corncrib. These two buildings are the entirety of structural improvements by the family and are representative of the minimal nature of Cherokee architecture.

The Chewkeeaskee site was excavated during a project directed by Brett Riggs in 1990–91 as part of a Tennessee Valley Authority (TVA) archaeological survey of Hiwassee Lake (see Riggs, "Removal Period Cherokee Households and Communities in Southwestern North Carolina [1835–1838]").

34. Riggs, "Removal Period Cherokee Households and Communities in Southwestern North Carolina (1835–1838)," 394. The food remains from the Chewkeeaskee site reveal a family with a diverse diet that included domesticated animals and wild game. Not surprisingly, pig and chicken are both represented; by the 1830s both species were commonly raised and consumed by most Cherokee families.

35. Handmade Cherokee pottery was first classified as the Qualla series by Brian Egloff "An Analysis of Ceramics from Historic Cherokee Towns" (MA thesis, University of North Carolina, Chapel Hill, 1967). Ceramics of the Qualla series were produced from roughly AD 1400 into the early twentieth century. Styles of Qualla ceramics from the last half of the eighteenth century into the early twentieth century were usually check stamped. These vessels retained deep historical presence, symbolic and social meanings, and specific functional uses for the preparation and consumption of traditional Cherokee foods. During the nineteenth century (and earlier), wide-mouthed jars and bowls were common Qualla vessel forms. (Vladimir Fewkes, "Catawba Pottery-Making, with notes on Pamunkey Pottery-Making,

Cherokee Pottery-Making and Coiling," *Proceedings of the American Philosophical Society* 88, no. 2 (1944): 69–124; Mark Harrington, "The Last of the Iroquois Potters," in *New York State Museum Bulletin 133* (Albany: University of the State of New York, 1908), 222–27; Riggs, "Removal Period Cherokee Households and Communities in Southwestern North Carolina (1835–1838)," 103; Trawick Ward and R. P. Stephen Davis Jr., *Time before History: The Archaeology of North Carolina* (Chapel Hill: University of North Carolina Press, 1999). The Qualla vessel in Figure 1.3 was made in the 1880s. It is part of the Valentine Collection in the Research Laboratories of Archaeology, University of North Carolina at Chapel Hill.

36. Riggs, "Removal Period Cherokee Households and Communities in Southwestern North Carolina (1835–1838)," 87–115. Quote from Alexis, "Visit to the Cartoogechaye Indians."

37. Riggs, "Removal Period Cherokee Households and Communities in Southwestern North Carolina (1835–1838)," 380–92.

38. Riggs, "Christie Cabin Site," 243–44; Welch and Jarrett, "Valuations of Cherokee Property in North Carolina." The Welch and Jarrett valuations show that the Christie improvements included a sixteen-foot by seventeen-foot two-story log house, an external kitchen, over one hundred fruit trees, and a small log cabin across the river from the main house.

39. The Christie site was also excavated by Brett Riggs as part of the TVA archaeological project. In 1990–91 Riggs excavated a large cellar pit that would have been beneath the Christie cabin. The large amount of material recovered from the pit shows a very different cultural adaptation than the Chewkeeaskee family's.

40. Riggs, "Christie Cabin Site"; William Welch and Nimrod Jarrett, "Valuations of Cherokee Property in North Carolina." Their property valuation by Welch and Jarrett lists the family as owning eighteen acres of "bottomland in cultivation" and three acres of "upland in cultivation." While this is more than triple the regional average of 6.5 acres for Cherokee land use, it is still relatively low for a family involved in the market. The property valuation lists the Christie farm at just over $400, well above the average.

41. Riggs, "Christie Cabin Site," 246.

42. Riggs, "Christie Cabin Site."

43. Thurman Wilkins, *Cherokee Tragedy: The Ridge Family and the Decimation of a People* (Norman: University of Oklahoma Press, 1986), 7–19.

44. Wilkins, *Cherokee Tragedy*, 28–38.

45. Wilkins, *Cherokee Tragedy*; Saunt, *New Order of Things*.

46. Patrick Garrow, *The Chieftains Excavations, 1969–1971* (published with permission from the Chieftains Museum and the Trail of Tears Commission of the National Park Service, 2010), 16; Wilkins, *Cherokee Tragedy*, 186.

47. Wilkins, *Cherokee Tragedy*.

48. The Chieftains site was occupied after the Ridges left in 1837, and a number of these sherds date to later periods. However, the majority of the sherds date to when the Ridges lived at the site.

49. Garrow, *Chieftains Excavations*, 89. Excavations were performed both near the Ridge house and around Lavender's trading post.

50. Wilkins, *Cherokee Tragedy*.

51. Miles, *House on Diamond Hill*, 38–59.

52. Miles, *House on Diamond Hill*. Archaeological excavations were performed at Diamond Hill in the 1950s (Clemens de Baillou, "The Chief Vann House at Spring Place, Georgia," *Early Georgia* 2, no. 2 [1957]: 3–11). Unfortunately, little has been published on these excavations. Published findings state that the excavators uncovered a brick foundation of the external kitchen and found "early nineteenth century china and glass." Excavators also uncovered what they interpreted as Vann's tavern and found early nineteenth-century china and "Cherokee check-stamped" pottery. It is unclear whether the Cherokee ceramics are associated with the imported ceramics, and they might therefore predate the tavern. Most of what we currently know about the material culture of the Vann families comes from historical documents.

53. Miles, *House on Diamond Hill*, quote on page 114.

54. E.g. Marisa Fuentes, *Dispossessed Lives: Enslaved Women, Violence, and the Archive* (Philadelphia: University of Pennsylvania Press, 2016); Thavolia Glymph, *Out of the House of Bondage: The Transformation of the Plantation Household* (Cambridge: Cambridge University Press, 2008); Eugene Genovese, *Roll, Jordan, Roll: The World the Slaves Made* (New York: Vintage Books, 1976); Stephanie Jones-Rogers, *They Were Her Property: White Women as Slave Owners in the American South* (New Haven: Yale University Press, 2019); Deborah White, *Ar'n't I a Woman? Female Slaves in the Plantation South* (New York: W. W. Norton, 1999); Thomas Foster, "The Sexual Abuse of Black Men under American Slavery," in *Sexuality and Slavery: Reclaiming Intimate Histories in the Americas*, ed. Daina Berry and Leslie Harris, 124–44 (Athens: University of Georgia Press, 2018); Edward Baptist, "'Cuffy,' 'Fancy Maids,' and 'One-Eyed Men': Rape, Commodification, and the Domestic Slave Trade in the United States," *American Historical Review* 106, no. 5 (2001): 1619–50.

55. Miles, *House on Diamond Hill*, 91.

56. Miles, *House on Diamond Hill*, 29–30.

57. Miles, *House on Diamond Hill*, 164–65.

58. Miles, *House on Diamond Hill*, 167.

59. Miles, *House on Diamond Hill*, 167–70.

60. De Baillou, "Chief Vann House at Spring Place, Georgia"; McLoughlin, *Cherokee Renascence in the New Republic*, 174; Miles, *House on Diamond Hill*, 164. Unfortunately, faunal remains recovered during the excavations were poorly preserved and therefore tell us little about the foodways at the site.

61. Miles, *House on Diamond Hill*, 176–79.

62. Miles, *House on Diamond Hill*, 183–85.

63. McLoughlin, *Cherokee Renascence*, 34–40.

64. Carolyn Johnston, *Cherokee Women in Crisis: Trail of Tears, Civil War, and Allotment, 1838–1907* (Tuscaloosa: University of Alabama Press, 2003), 36–55; McLoughlin, *Cherokee Renascence*; Victor Persico, "Cherokee Social Structure in the Early Nineteenth Century" (MA thesis, University of Georgia, Athens, 1974), 28–29.

65. Johnston, *Cherokee Women in Crisis*, 11–13; McLoughlin, *Cherokee Renascence*, 139–40, 160–62; Persico, "Cherokee Social Structure in the Early Nineteenth Century," 99; John Reid, *A Law of Blood: The Primitive Law of the Cherokee Nation* (New York: New York University Press, 1970). Blood law, blood vengeance, or clan revenge was a clan-based practice of maintaining balance. If someone in a clan was killed (regardless of the motive), it was the

duty of members of that clan to kill the person responsible. If that person could not be killed, someone in the killer's clan would be murdered, thereby maintaining a proper balance. These practices, connected to maintaining social balance, were a central part of clan-based behavior as well as part of the adherence to local governance. Stripping local communities of these powers and placing them at the level of national government was central to the Cherokee leaders' plan for creating a tribe that conformed to a single governing body, as opposed to dozens of autonomous towns.

66. McLoughlin, *Cherokee Renascence*; Royce, *Cherokee Nation of Indians*.

67. McLoughlin, *Cherokee Renascence*, 389; Persico, "Cherokee Social Structure in the Early Nineteenth Century."

68. Yarbrough, *Race and the Cherokee Nation*, 35.

69. William Jurgelski, "A New Plow in Old Ground: Cherokees, Whites, and Land in Western North Carolina, 1819–1829" (PhD diss., University of Georgia, Athens, 2004); Mooney, *Myths of the Cherokee*, 102; Brett Riggs, "An Historical and Archaeological Reconnaissance of Citizen Cherokee Reservations in Macon, Swain, and Jackson Counties, North Carolina" (submitted to the North Carolina Division of Archives and History, Raleigh, Department of Anthropology, University of Tennessee, Knoxville, 1988).

70. McLoughlin, *Cherokee Renascence*, 80–81, 388–410.

71. Genovese, *Roll, Jordan, Roll*.

72. Finger, *Eastern Band of Cherokees*, 9.

73. Gearing, *Priests and Warriors*, 5.

74. Tyler Boulware, *Deconstructing the Cherokee Nation: Town, Region, and Nation among Eighteenth-Century Cherokees* (Gainesville: University Press of Florida, 2011); Gearing, *Priests and Warriors*; Persico, "Cherokee Social Structure in the Early Nineteenth Century."

75. Henry Malone, *Cherokees of the Old South: A People in Transition* (Athens: University of Georgia Press, 1956), 119.

76. Raymond Fogelson and Paul Kutsche, "Cherokee Economic Cooperatives: The Gadugi," in *Symposium on Cherokee and Iroquois Culture*, Smithsonian Institution Bureau of American Ethnology, Bulletin 180, ed. William Fenton and John Gulick (Washington, DC: US Government Printing Office, 1961), 88; Mooney, *Myths of the Cherokee*, 519.

77. Fogelson and Kutsche, "Cherokee Economic Cooperatives."

78. Ward (1817), quoted in Theda Perdue and Michael Green, *The Cherokee Removal: A Brief History with Documents* (Boston: Bedford/St. Martins, 2005), 131–32; partial quote in Johnston, *Cherokee Women in Crisis*, 58–59.

79. For discussion of Beloved Women and women's role in government in Cherokee society, see Virginia Carney, *Eastern Band Cherokee Women: Cultural Persistence in Their Letters and Speeches* (Knoxville: University of Tennessee Press, 2005); Johnston, *Cherokee Women in Crisis: Trail of Tears, Civil War, and Allotment, 1838–1907*, 13, 58–59; Mooney, *Myths of the Cherokee*, 203–4; Theda Perdue, *Cherokee Women: Gender and Culture Change, 1700–1835* (Lincoln: University of Nebraska Press, 1998); Perdue, "Cherokee Women and the Trail of Tears"; Reid, *Law of Blood*, 187–88.

80. Royce, *Cherokee Nation of Indians*, 256.

81. The Cherokees who accepted these 640-acre parcels were known as citizen reservees because they accepted US citizenship, and the parcels were considered by the US government to be reservations deeded to them. Although in most cases taken by white men within a few

years, these reservations were a necessary step for the continued presence of Cherokees in the region. Jurgelski, "New Plow in Old Ground."

82. Jurgelski, "New Plow in Old Ground," 153–54.

83. Jurgelski, "New Plow in Old Ground," 158; William McLoughlin, "Experiment in Cherokee Citizenship, 1817–1829," *American Quarterly* 33, no. 1 (1981): 5.

84. Jurgelski, "New Plow in Old Ground"; Brett Riggs, "An Historical and Archaeological Reconnaissance of Citizen Cherokee Reservations in Macon, Swain, and Jackson Counties, North Carolina," submitted to the North Carolina Division of Archives and History, Raleigh. Department of Anthropology, University of Tennessee, Knoxville, 1988.

85. Jurgelski, "New Plow in Old Ground," 71, 153.

86. Long Blanket, quoted in Jurgelski, "New Plow in Old Ground," 153. Morris's tract, which he lost in the early 1820s, encompasses what is currently the town of Franklin.

87. In 1819 Chief Yonaguska, like dozens of his kinsman, claimed a 640-acre reservation of land from the US government. He chose a tract along the Tuckaseegee River. Jurgelski "New Plow in Old Ground"; Riggs, "Historical and Archaeological Reconnaissance of Citizen Cherokee Reservations in Macon, Swain, and Jackson Counties, North Carolina," 89–91; Royce, *Cherokee Nation of Indians*, 256. Like most of the reservees, Yonaguska lost title to the land when white people refused to honor the deed awarded him by the state of North Carolina. Title to the tract was usurped in 1821, Jurgelski "New Plow in Old Ground," 201.

88. Jurgelski, "New Plow in Old Ground"; Riggs, "Removal Period Cherokee Households and Communities in Southwestern North Carolina (1835–1838)"; Riggs, "Historical and Archaeological Reconnaissance of Citizen Cherokee Reservations in Macon, Swain, and Jackson Counties, North Carolina."

89. Finger, *Eastern Band of Cherokees*, 11; Jurgelski, "New Plow in Old Ground."

90. Jurgelski, "New Plow in Old Ground," 222–23.

91. Mooney, *Myths of the Cherokee*, 506–48; Riggs, "Removal Period Cherokee Households and Communities in Southwestern North Carolina (1835–1838)"; Welch and Jarrett, "Valuations of Cherokee Property in North Carolina"; W. G. Williams, "Memoir Relative to the Cherokee Nation within the Limits of N. Carolina and Its Immediate Vicinity," February 8, 1838, *Journal of Cherokee Studies* 4, no. 4 (1979): 202–10.

92. Welch and Jarrett, "Valuations of Cherokee Property in North Carolina."

93. Matthew Rhea, "Map of the State of Tennessee," in *Tennessee Gazetteer*, ed. Robert McBride and Owen Meredith (1834; rpt. Nashville: Gazetteer Press, 1971).

94. "Census Roll of the Cherokee Indians East of the Mississippi, 1835"; John Welch, "Power of Attorney Contract, John Welch to Jonathon [*sic*] Blythe and Jonathon [*sic*] Parker," Macon County, North Carolina, Register of Deeds, deed book B, June 20, 1838.

95. Thomas, "Cherokee Values and World View," 7.

CHAPTER 2

1. John Finger, "The Impact of Removal on the North Carolina Cherokees," in *Cherokee Removal: Before and After*, ed. William Anderson (Athens: University of Georgia Press, 1991), 102.

2. What became known as the Qualla Towns was a cluster of small Cherokee communities settled by reservees of the 1819 treaty. The towns were settled in the 1820s, just outside

the boundary of the Cherokee Nation. At the time of removal, they argued that, since they were granted American citizenship as stipulated by the 1819 treaty and had lived outside the Cherokee Nation for over a decade, they were exempt from forced emigration. John Finger, *The Eastern Band of Cherokees, 1819–1900* (Knoxville: University of Tennessee Press, 1984), 11–17, 29; William Jurgelski, "A New Plow in Old Ground: Cherokees, Whites, and Land in Western North Carolina, 1819–1829" (PhD diss., University of Georgia, Athens, 2004).

    William Holland Thomas had operated a store in the Qualla Towns since 1822. He served as legal representative of the Qualla Town Cherokees beginning in 1831, after the passage of the Indian Removal Act, and also because of an influx of white people searching for gold on Cherokee land. In 1836 Thomas traveled to Washington, DC, to ensure the Qualla Town Cherokees would not be removed and to get the claim money owed them from the removal treaty. Stanly Godbold Jr. and Mattie Russell, *Confederate Colonel and Cherokee Chief: The Life of William Holland Thomas* (Knoxville: University of Tennessee Press, 1990), 12, 21–25. By the early 1830s, Thomas was buying tracts of land around the Qualla Towns, ostensibly to establish a large Cherokee reservation for these Cherokees who had chosen to live outside the boundaries of the Cherokee Nation. Finger, *Eastern Band of Cherokees, 1819–1900*, 21.

    3. Claudio Saunt, in *Unworthy Republic: The Dispossession of Native Americans and the Road to Indian Territory* (New York: W. W. Norton, 2020), argues that the Indian removals of the 1830s were the first state-organized mass deportations; unlike the mass migrations caused by earlier colonial wars, the removals were parts of a national project of forced expulsion founded in state bureaucracy—census data, landscape and cadastral surveys, and valuation data.

    4. John Swanton, *The Indians of the Southeastern United States* (Washington, DC: Smithsonian Institution Press, 1979), reprint of Bureau of American Ethology Bulletin 137 (1946), 79–80.

    5. William McLoughlin, *Champions of the Cherokees: Evan and John B. Jones* (Princeton: Princeton University Press, 1990), 138–39.

    6. Gaston Litton, "Enrollment Records of the Eastern Band of Cherokee Indians," *North Carolina Historical Review* 17 (1940): 191–231.

    7. McLoughlin, *Champions of the Cherokees*, 42; Brett Riggs, "Removal Period Cherokee Households and Communities in Southwestern North Carolina (1835–1838)," Final Report of the Cherokee Homestead Project, submitted to the North Carolina State Historic Preservation Office, Division of Archives and History, Department of Cultural Resources, Raleigh, North Carolina, 1996, 20–21.

    8. "Census Roll of the Cherokee Indians East of the Mississippi, 1835," Microcopy T-496, RG 75, NARA, Washington, DC, 1835; William McLoughlin, *Cherokee Renascence in the New Republic* (Princeton: Princeton University Press, 1986), 368.

    9. "Census Roll of the Cherokee Indians East of the Mississippi, 1835"; Riggs, "Removal Period Cherokee Households and Communities in Southwestern North Carolina (1835–1838)"; William Welch and Nimrod Jarrett, "Valuations of Cherokee Property in North Carolina," Cherokee Property Valuations, 1835–1839, RG 75, NARA, Washington, DC, 1837.

    10. The Treaty of New Echota has been widely written about. The treaty is infamous both for the underhanded, coercive, and corrupt methods for gathering signatures and for ratification, and for the aftermath—forced emigration, large numbers of deaths along the Trail of Tears, and decades of internal conflict. When federal agents began discussing a proposed

treaty, official government representatives would not meet with them, so they devised a plan to gather signatures of other leaders. A small, nonrepresentative group of Cherokee men, out of a population of roughly sixteen thousand, signed the treaty that gave the US the entire lands of the Cherokee Nation in the Southeast for land in "Indian Territory" (now Oklahoma). Finger, *Eastern Band of Cherokees, 1819–1900*, 16–19; James Mooney, *Myths of the Cherokee and Sacred Formulas of the Cherokees*, reproduction of 19th and 7th Annual Reports the Bureau of American Ethnology (Nashville: Charles and Randy Elder Booksellers, 1982), 123–26; Theda Perdue, *Cherokee Women: Gender and Culture Change, 1700–1835* (Lincoln: University of Nebraska Press, 1998), 157–58; Charles Royce, *The Cherokee Nation of Indians* (Chicago: Aldine, 1975), 125–76; Thurman Wilkins, *Cherokee Tragedy: The Ridge Family and the Decimation of a People* (Norman: University of Oklahoma Press, 1986), 177–91.

11. Finger, *Eastern Band of Cherokees, 1819–1900*, 17; Mooney, *Myths of the Cherokee*, 123; Royce, *Cherokee Nation of Indians*, 129, 160.

12. McLoughlin, *Champions of the Cherokees*, 139; Riggs, "Removal Period Cherokee Households and Communities in Southwestern North Carolina (1835–1838)," Final Report of the Cherokee Homestead Project, submitted to the North Carolina State Historic Preservation Office, Division of Archives and History, Department of Cultural Resources, Raleigh, North Carolina, 1996, 17.

13. McLoughlin, *Champions of the Cherokees*, 139–41.

14. General John Ellis Wool, "Letter to Brigadier General R. Jones, February 18, 1837." Report from the Secretary of War, January 12, 1838, United States Senate Document 120, 25th Congress, 2nd Session, United States Congressional Serial Set, Government Printing Office, Washington, DC, quoted in Brett Riggs, "Removal Period Cherokee Households and Communities in Southwestern North Carolina (1835–1838)," 17.

15. Royce, *Cherokee Nation of Indians*, 167.

16. Joseph Powell, "Proceedings of a court of Inquiry held on the 10th of November at Fort Butler N.C. at the request of Lieut. Col. Joseph Powell Tenn. Vol's," Court Martial Case Files, Records of the Office of the Judge Advocate General (Army), RG 153, NARA, Washington, DC, 1837.

17. Valuation claim 178, RFBCC, RG 75, NARA, Washington, DC, 1843.

18. Powell, "Proceedings of a court of Inquiry."

19. Powell, "Proceedings of a court of Inquiry." The court case is well documented in a set of papers sent to Secretary of War J. R. Poinsett; "unbound letters," Letters Received by the Office of the Adjutant General, Main Series, 1822–1860, M567, roll 173, RG 94, NARA, Washington, DC, 1838; Kennedy, Wilson, and Liddell, "Letter to Colonel William Lindsay, March 9, 1838," Letters received by the Office of Indian Affairs, 1824–1881, M-234, Roll 82, page 191, RG 75, NARA, Washington, DC, 1838; Kennedy, Wilson, and Liddell, "Letter to Colonel William Lindsay, March 13, 1838," Letters received by the Office of Indian Affairs, 1824–1881, M-234, Roll 82, pages 204–7, RG 75, NARA, Washington, DC, 1838; Lindsay, "Letter to Commissioners Kennedy, Wilson, and Liddell, March 10, 1838," Letters received by the Office of Indian Affairs, 1824–1881, M-234, Roll 82, pages 192–94, RG 75, NARA, Washington, DC, 1838.

20. "Census Roll of the Cherokee Indians East of the Mississippi, 1835"; Welch and Jarrett, "Valuations of Cherokee Property in North Carolina."

21. John Welch, "Power of Attorney Contract, John Welch to Jonathon [sic] Blythe and Jonathon [sic] Parker," Macon County, North Carolina, Register of Deeds, deed book B, June 20, 1838; Welch and Jarrett, "Valuations of Cherokee Property in North Carolina."

22. Riggs, "Removal Period Cherokee Households and Communities in Southwestern North Carolina (1835–1838)," 38.

23. W. G. Williams, "Memoir Relative to the Cherokee Nation within the Limits of N. Carolina and Its Immediate Vicinity," February 8, *Journal of Cherokee Studies* 4, no. 4 (1979): 202–10.

24. For survey methods, see Colonel John James Abert, "On the Use of the Common or Customary Instruments for the Making of Survey," RG 77, Folder E161, NARA, Washington, DC, 1850. For a composite map, see W. G. Williams, "Map of Part of the Cherokee Territory Situated among the Mountains of N. Carolina, Georgia, and Tennessee," United States National Archives Cartographic Division, Arlington, Virginia.

25. McLoughlin, *Champions of the Cherokees*, 65, 292; Brett Riggs, "Removal Period Cherokee Households in Southwestern North Carolina: Material Perspectives on Ethnicity and Cultural Differentiation" (PhD diss., University of Tennessee, Knoxville, 1999), 180–84.

26. Nathaniel Browder, *The Cherokee Indians and Those Who Came After: Notes for a History of Cherokee County, North Carolina, 1835–1860* (Hayesville, NC: self-published by Browder, 1973); Reuben Deaver, "Private Property Map of Cherokee County, North Carolina," copy on file, Cherokee County Court House, Murphy, North Carolina, 1837; Margaret Freel, *Our Heritage* (Asheville, NC: Miller, 1957); Riggs, "Removal Period Cherokee Households and Communities in Southwestern North Carolina (1835–1838)," 19.

27. John Kennedy, Thomas Wilson, and Nathaniel Smith, "Letter to the Cherokees, December 28, 1837," Report of Cherokee Commissioners, United States House Document 316, 25th Congress, 2nd Session, United States Congressional Serial Set, Government Printing Office, Washington, DC, quoted in John Ehle, *Trail of Tears: The Rise and Fall of the Cherokee Nation* (New York: Anchor Books, Doubleday, 1988), 319–20; John Ross, "Letter to Lewis Ross, April 5, 1838," in Gary Moulton, ed., *Papers of Chief John Ross* (Norman: University of Oklahoma Press, 1985), 622–24.

28. Grant Foreman, *Indian Removal: The Emigration of the Five Civilized Tribes of Indians* (Norman: University of Oklahoma Press, 1976), 286–93; Mooney, *Myths of the Cherokee*, 129–31; Royce, *Cherokee Nation of Indians*, 169.

29. Godbold and Russell, *Confederate Colonel and Cherokee Chief*, 36; Mooney, *Myths of the Cherokee*, 129.

30. General Winfield Scott, "Order 30, May 22, 1838," in Correspondence of the Eastern Division Pertaining to Cherokee Removal, April–December 1838, RG 393, M1475, NARA, Washington, DC, 1838; John Welch, Edward Welch, and Wachecher (Wachacha), "Letter to Commissioners, August 1843," Spoliation claim 458, RFBCC, RG 75, NARA, Washington, DC, 1843.

31. Ehle, *Trail of Tears*, 339; Riggs, "Removal Period Cherokee Households in Southwestern North Carolina: Material Perspectives on Ethnicity and Cultural Differentiation," 60.

32. Mooney, *Myths of the Cherokee*, 131–32; Moulton, *Papers of Chief John Ross*, 649–52; Russell Thornton, *The Cherokees: A Population History* (Lincoln: University of Nebraska Press, 1990), 68–72; Royce, *Cherokee Nation of Indians*, 169–70.

33. Mooney, *Myths of the Cherokee*, 131–32.

34. Daniel Butrick, "The Journal of Reverend Daniel S. Butrick," in the John Howard Payne papers, volume 9, pages 67–95, Newberry Library, Chicago, Illinois, 1838.

35. Russell Thornton, "The Demography of the Trail of Tears Period: A New Estimate of Cherokee Population Losses," in *Cherokee Removal: Before and After*, ed. William Anderson, (Athens: University of Georgia Press, 1991), 81.

36. John Gray Bynum, "Letter to General Winfield Scott, June 13, 1838," John Gray Bynum Papers, Southern Historical Collection, University of North Carolina, Chapel Hill.

37. Captain George Porter, "Letter to Major Kirby, June 18, 1838," Correspondence of the Eastern Division Pertaining to Cherokee Removal, April–December 1838, RG 393, M-1475, NARA, Washington, DC, 1838.

38. Welch, "Power of Attorney Contract, John Welch to Jonathon [*sic*] Blythe and Jonathon [*sic*] Parker."

39. John Powell, "Letter to Commissioners John Eaton and Edward Hubley, September 22, 1843." Valuation claim 178, RFBCC, RG 75, NARA, Washington, DC, 1843.

40. General Winfield Scott, "Order 30, May 22, 1838," in Correspondence of the Eastern Division Pertaining to Cherokee Removal, April–December 1838, RG 393, M1475, NARA, Washington, DC; General Winfield Scott, "Letter to H. R. Poinsett, September 4, 1838," M-234, Letters received by the Office of Indian Affairs, 1824–1881, RG 75, NARA, Washington, DC.

41. Scott, "Letter to H. R. Poinsett, September 4, 1838."

42. Scott, "Letter to H. R. Poinsett, September 4, 1838."

43. "Confessedly a Cherokee and alien by birth" quote in Scott, "Letter to Judge Keith, September 7, 1838," M-234, Letters received by the Office of Indian Affairs, 1824–1881, RG 75, NARA, Washington, DC, 1838. Scott's interpretation of the 1817 and 1819 treaty rights marked one of the first attempts to explain the status of Cherokees east during and after removal. Numerous contradicting interpretations have been presented to the present day. For example, see Royce, *Cherokee Nation of Indians*, 85; Jurgelski, "New Plow in Old Ground"; Ben Bridgers, "An Historical Analysis of the Legal Status of the North Carolina Cherokees," *North Carolina Law Review* 58 (1980): 1075–1131; John Finger, "The North Carolina Cherokees, 1838–1866: Traditionalism, Progressivism, and the Affirmation of State Citizenship," *Journal of Cherokee Studies* 5, no. 1 (1980): 41, 51–56; George Frizzell, "Legal Status of the Eastern Band of Cherokee Indians" (MA thesis, Western Carolina University, 1981).

44. The court case was followed closely in the regional press, e.g., *The Tennessean* (Nashville), September 12, 1838, accessed March 27, 2020, https://www.newspapers.com/image/118768318; *Daily Republican Banner* (Nashville), September 19, 1838, accessed March 27, 2020, https://www.newspapers.com/image/603781882. Barbara Duncan and Brett Riggs, *Cherokee Heritage Trails Guidebook* (Chapel Hill: University of North Carolina Press, 2003), 121, 209; Sarah Hill, *Weaving New Worlds: Southeastern Cherokee Women and Their Basketry* (Chapel Hill: University of North Carolina Press, 1997), 349, n. 67; Mooney, *Myths of the Cherokee*, 164.

45. H. L. Scott, "Letter to General Winfield Scott, August 22, 1838," M-234, Letters received by the Office of Indian Affairs, 1824–1881, RG 75, NARA, Washington, DC, 1838.

46. John Powell, "Letter to Commissioners, August 21, 1843," Spoliation claim 458, RFBCC, RG 75, NARA, Washington, DC, 1843. Other witnesses recounted the same event: see Drury Weeks, "Letter to Commissioners, August 19, 1843," Spoliation claim 458, RFBCC,

RG 75, NARA, Washington, DC, 1843; John Welch, Edward Welch, and Wachecher (Wacha-cha), "Letter to Commissioners, August 1843," Spoliation claim 458, RFBCC, RG 75, NARA, Washington, DC, 1843.

47. Welch, "Power of Attorney Contract, John Welch to Jonathon [sic] Blythe and Jon-athon [sic] Parker."

48. Powell, "Letter to Commissioners, August 21, 1843"; Weeks, "Letter to Commis-sioners, August 19, 1843"; Welch, Welch, and Wachecher (Wachacha), "Letter to Commis-sioners, August 1843."

49. Powell, "Letter to Commissioners, August 21, 1843."

50. Powell, "Letter to Commissioners John Eaton and Edward Hubley, September 22, 1843"; John Powell, "Letter to Commissioners, September 23, 1843," Spoliation claim 458, RFBCC, RG 75, NARA, Washington, DC, 1843; Johnson K. Rogers, "Letter to Commission-ers, August 1843," Spoliation claim 458, RFBCC, RG 75, NARA, Washington, DC, 1843; Weeks, "Letter to Commissioners, August 19, 1843."

51. Welch, Welch, and Wachacha, "Letter to Commissioners, August 1843."

52. Powell, "Letter to Commissioners, August 21, 1843."

53. Powell, "Letter to Commissioners, August 21, 1843."

54. John Welch, "Claim for spoliation of property." Spoliation claim 418, RFBCC, RG 75, NARA, Washington, DC, 1846.

55. Welch, Welch, and Wachecher (Wachacha), "Letter to Commissioners, August 1843."

56. *Stanmire vs. Powell*, 35 N.C. 312, Supreme Court of North Carolina, 1852.

57. Reuben Deaver, "Private property map of Cherokee County, North Carolina," copy on file, Cherokee County Court House, Murphy, North Carolina, 1837. The lands purchased by Powell at the state auction on November 2, 1838, included tracts 62, 68, 69, and 71 through 74 of District 6, part of the newly created property districting as surveyed in 1837.

58. Powell, "Letter to Commissioners, September 23, 1843"; Rogers, "Letter to Com-missioners, August 1843."

59. Preston Starrett, "Letter to commissioners, August 22, 1843. File 458," RFBCC, RG 75, NARA, Washington, DC, 1843.

60. John Welch, "Power of attorney contract, John Welch to Elizabeth Welch, December 24, 1838." RFBCC, RG 75, NARA, Washington, DC, 1838.

61. John Finger, "The Saga of Tsali: Legend versus Reality," *North Carolina Historical Review* 56, no. 1 (1979): 1–18; Finger, *Eastern Band of Cherokees, 1819–1900*; Finger, "Impact of Removal on the North Carolina Cherokees," 103–4; William Jurgelski, "New Light on the Tsali Affair," in *Light on the Path: The Anthropology and History of the Southeastern Indians*, ed. Thomas Pluckhahn and Robbie Ethridge (Tuscaloosa: University of Alabama Press, 2006), 133–64; Duane King, "The Origin of the Eastern Cherokees as a Social and Political Entity," in *The Cherokee Indian Nation: A Troubled History*, ed. Duane King (Knoxville: University of Tennessee Press, 1979), 175–76; Duane King and Raymond Evans, "Tsali: The Man behind the Legend," *Journal of Cherokee Studies* 4, no. 4 (1979): 194–201; Paul Kutsche, "The Tsali Legend: Culture Heroes and Historiography," *Ethnohistory* 10, no. 4 (1963): 329–57; Lan-man, *Letters from the Alleghany Mountains*; Mooney, *Myths of the Cherokee*. For Wachacha's involvement, see Finger, *Eastern Band of Cherokees, 1819–1900*, 27; King and Evans, "Tsali: The Man behind the Legend," 194–201. Much of the historical research on the "Tsali Affair" has attempted to dispel the mythic aspects and identify the facts of the event. Many authors

have observed that Tsali continues to serve as a founding father or martyr figure for the Eastern Band of Cherokee Indians.

62. Finger, *Eastern Band of Cherokees, 1819–1900*, 21–28; Jurgelski, "New Light on the Tsali Affair."

63. Riggs, "Removal Period Cherokee Households and Communities in Southwestern North Carolina (1835–1838)," 19; William Holland Thomas, "Census of the North Carolina Cherokees, 1840," William Holland Thomas papers, David M. Rubenstein Rare Book and Manuscript Library, Duke University, Durham, North Carolina; William Holland Thomas, "Supplementary Report of Cherokee Indians Remaining in North Carolina, 1835–1840," manuscript copy in the William Holland Thomas papers, David M. Rubenstein Rare Book and Manuscript Library, Duke University, Durham, North Carolina; William Welch and Nimrod Jarrett, "Valuations of Cherokee Property in North Carolina," Cherokee Property Valuations, 1835–1839, RG 75, NARA, Washington, DC.

64. Thomas, "Census of the North Carolina Cherokees, 1840"; Thomas, "Supplementary Report of Cherokee Indians Remaining in North Carolina, 1835–1840."

65. Weeks, "Letter to Commissioners, August 19, 1843"; Welch, Welch, and Wachecher (Wachacha), "Letter to Commissioners, August 1843"; Non-Population (Slave) Schedules of the Seventh Census, 1850, M-432, Roll 651, Records of the Bureau of the Census, RG 29, NARA, Washington, DC, 1850.

CHAPTER 3

1. Years of birth for members of the Welch family were calculated from the Thomas, Siler, and Mullay rolls and the 1850 census. William Holland Thomas, "Census of the North Carolina Cherokees, 1840," William Holland Thomas papers, David M. Rubenstein Rare Book and Manuscript Library, Duke University, Durham, North Carolina; William Holland Thomas, "Supplementary Report of Cherokee Indians Remaining in North Carolina, 1835–1840," manuscript copy in the William Holland Thomas papers, David M. Rubenstein Rare Book and Manuscript Library, Duke University, Durham, North Carolina; David Siler, "1851 Siler Roll," Eastern Cherokee Census Rolls, 1835–1884, M-1773, NARA, Atlanta, Georgia; John Mullay, "1848 Mullay Roll," Eastern Cherokee Census Rolls, 1835–1884, M-1773, NARA, Atlanta, Georgia; Population Schedules of the Seventh Census, 1850, M-432, Roll 625, Records of the Bureau of the Census, RG 29, NARA, Washington, DC, 1850.

2. Cherokee County Register of Deeds, Murphy, North Carolina.

3. Joseph Powell, "Proceedings of a court of Inquiry held on the 10th of November at Fort Butler N.C. at the request of Lieut. Col. Joseph Powell Tenn. Vol's," Court Martial Case Files, Records of the Office of the Judge Advocate General (Army), RG 153, NARA, Washington, DC, 1837.

4. Irish trader James Adair wrote in the mid-eighteenth century of the Cherokee "petticoat-government" in describing the lack of punishment in Cherokee society for women who had multiple sexual partners, including while married. James Adair, *Adair's History of the American Indians*, ed. Samuel Cole Williams (1775; rpt. Johnson City, TN: Watauga Press, 1930), 153. Numerous other eighteenth-century travelers described the sexual freedom as well as political and economic power of Cherokee women. See Virginia Carney, *Eastern Band Cherokee Women: Cultural Persistence in Their Letters and Speeches* (Knoxville: University of

Tennessee Press, 2005); Raymond Fogelson, "On the Petticoat Government of the Eighteenth-Century Cherokee," in *Personality and the Cultural Construction of Society*, ed. David Jordan and Marc Swartz, 161–81 (Tuscaloosa: University of Alabama Press, 1990); Carolyn Johnston, *Cherokee Women in Crisis: Trail of Tears, Civil War, and Allotment, 1838–1907* (Tuscaloosa: University of Alabama Press, 2003); Theda Perdue, *Cherokee Women: Gender and Culture Change, 1700–1835* (Lincoln: University of Nebraska Press, 1998).

5. Ellen Skinner, *Women and the National Experience: Primary Sources in American History* (New York: Addison-Wesley, 1996), 90–91. Gender roles were undergoing radical constructions. Betty maintained an unusual amount of power as a married woman in the antebellum South. Her ownership of the plantation occurred nine years before the Married Women's Property Act in New York. The act, the result of years of effort by reformers such as Susan B. Anthony and Elizabeth Cady Stanton, attempted to curb the complete loss of legal rights of married women under the common-law tradition of feme covert, or coverture. This tradition withheld the rights of married women to own property, acquire wealth, write a will or other contract, or sue, in their own name. Recent research has shown that, at least in the case of women who held captive laborers, they in some instances refused to surrender these workers into the care of their husband; they knew that this "property" was key to their own power. Stephanie Jones-Rogers, *They Were Her Property: White Women as Slave Owners in the American South* (New Haven: Yale University Press, 2019).

6. Jeanne Boydston, *Home and Work: Housework, Wages, and the Ideology of Labor in the Early Republic* (Oxford: Oxford University Press, 1990); Nancy Cott, *The Bonds of Womanhood: "Woman's Sphere" in New England, 1780–1835* (New Haven: Yale University Press, 1977).

7. Jones-Rogers, *They Were Her Property*, xvii.

8. Thavolia Glymph, *Out of the House of Bondage: The Transformation of the Plantation Household* (Cambridge: Cambridge University Press, 2008), 64.

9. Wilma Dunaway, *Slavery in the American Mountain South* (Cambridge: Cambridge University Press, 2003), 168; Jones-Rogers, *They Were Her Property*.

10. Brett Riggs, "Removal Period Cherokee Households and Communities in Southwestern North Carolina (1835–1838)," Final Report of the Cherokee Homestead Project, submitted to the North Carolina State Historic Preservation Office, Division of Archives and History, Department of Cultural Resources, Raleigh, North Carolina, 1996.

11. William Welch and Nimrod Jarrett, "Valuations of Cherokee Property in North Carolina," Cherokee Property Valuations, 1835–1839, RG 75, NARA, Washington, DC, 1837.

12. Lance Greene, "A Struggle for Cherokee Community: Excavating Identity in Post-Removal North Carolina" (PhD diss., University of North Carolina, Chapel Hill, 2009); Lance Greene, "Archaeology and Community Reconstruction of Mid-Nineteenth-Century Cherokee Farmsteads along Valley River, North Carolina," in *Archaeological Adaptation: Case Studies of Cultural Transformation from the Southeast and Caribbean*, ed. Clifford Boyd, Jr. (Knoxville: University of Tennessee Press, 2019), 193–222.

13. Welch and Jarrett, "Valuations of Cherokee Property in North Carolina."

14. Elliott Wigginton, *The Foxfire Book* (Garden City, NY: Anchor Press, 1972).

15. Non-Population (Agricultural) Schedules of the Seventh Census, 1850, M-432, Records of the Bureau of the Census, RG 29, NARA, Washington, DC, 1850.

16. Welch and Jarrett, "Valuations of Cherokee Property in North Carolina"; William

Reid, "Deposition in the Claim of Mary A. Powell," File 449, July 12, 1843, RFBCC, RG 75, NARA, Washington, DC, 1843.

17. Welch and Jarrett, "Valuations of Cherokee Property in North Carolina."

18. In *The House on Diamond Hill: A Cherokee Plantation Story* (Chapel Hill: University of North Carolina Press, 2010), 114, Tiya Miles refers to "white southern masculinity" in discussing James Vann's penchant for gambling, heavy drinking, and physically abusing his wife and enslaved people. She does not discuss any sexual assault perpetrated by Vann himself but does document a case in which another Cherokee owner sexually assaulted an enslaved woman, 90.

19. Cabins of enslaved African Americans in the Southern Appalachians (and in the lowcountry South) were usually built close to the plantation owner's house to monitor activities and hinder escape. Charles Orser, "Toward a Theory of Power for Historical Archaeology: Plantations and Space," in *The Recovery of Meaning: Historical Archaeology in the Eastern United States*, ed. Mark Leone and Parker Potter (Washington, DC: Smithsonian Institution Press, 1988), 313–44.

20. Margaret Smith and Emily Wilson, *North Carolina Women Making History* (Chapel Hill: University of North Carolina Press, 1999), 104.

21. Glymph, *Out of the House of Bondage*, 64–73; quote page 91.

22. Miles, *House on Diamond Hill*.

23. Miles, *House on Diamond Hill*, 104–7.

24. "Census Roll of the Cherokee Indians East of the Mississippi, 1835," Microcopy T-496, RG 75, NARA, Washington, DC, 1835; John Finger, *The Eastern Band of Cherokees, 1819–1900* (Knoxville: University of Tennessee Press, 1984), 16, 29.

25. Land tenure was a confusing issue for the Cherokees at the time. Indeed, it is still poorly understood. Most historians have claimed it was illegal for Cherokees to own land in North Carolina between 1838 and 1850. See Wilma Dunaway, *The First American Frontier: Transition to Capitalism in Southern Appalachia, 1700–1860*, Fred W. Morrison Series in Southern Studies (Chapel Hill: University of North Carolina Press, 1996), 256–57; Anna Kilpatrick and Jack Kilpatrick, "Chronicles of Wolftown: Social Documents of the North Carolina Cherokees, 1850–1862," Bureau of American Ethnology *Bulletin* 196 (Washington, DC, 1966), 31; James Mooney, *Myths of the Cherokee and Sacred Formulas of the Cherokees*, reproduction of 19th and 7th Annual Reports the Bureau of American Ethnology (Nashville: Charles and Randy Elder Booksellers, 1982), 159; Sharlotte Neeley, *Snowbird Cherokees: People of Persistence* (Athens: University of Georgia Press, 1991), 24; Henry Owl, "The Eastern Band of Cherokees before and after Removal" (MA thesis, University of North Carolina, Chapel Hill, 1929), 89–90. Historian John Finger claims that Cherokees could own land but that none could afford it or that most chose to live on communal lands ("The North Carolina Cherokees, 1838–1866"; Finger, *Eastern Band of Cherokees, 1819–1900*).

26. Stanly Godbold Jr. and Mattie Russell, *Confederate Colonel and Cherokee Chief: The Life of William Holland Thomas* (Knoxville: University of Tennessee Press, 1990); Mattie Russell, "William Holland Thomas, White Chief of the North Carolina Cherokees" (PhD diss., Duke University, 1956).

27. William Jurgelski, "A New Plow in Old Ground: Cherokees, Whites, and Land in Western North Carolina, 1819–1829" (PhD diss., University of Georgia, Athens, 2004);

Mooney, *Myths of the Cherokee*; Margaret Siler, *Cherokee Indian Lore and Smoky Mountain Stories* (Franklin, NC: Teresita Press, 2000).

28. Mooney, *Myths of the Cherokee*, 506–48; Riggs, "Removal Period Cherokee Households and Communities in Southwestern North Carolina (1835–1838)," 70–72; Welch and Jarrett, "Valuations of Cherokee Property in North Carolina"; W. G. Williams, "Memoir Relative to the Cherokee Nation within the Limits of N. Carolina and Its Immediate Vicinity," February 8, 1838, *Journal of Cherokee Studies* 4, no. 4 (1979): 202–10.

29. John Gray Bynum, "Letter to General Winfield Scott," June 19, 1838, John Gray Bynum Papers, Southern Historical Collection, University of North Carolina, Chapel Hill, 1838.

30. Neeley, *Snowbird Cherokees*; Riggs, "Removal Period Cherokee Households and Communities in Southwestern North Carolina (1835–1838)," 19; Thomas, "Census of the North Carolina Cherokees, 1840"; Thomas, "Supplementary Report of Cherokee Indians Remaining in North Carolina, 1835–1840."

31. Riggs, "Removal Period Cherokee Households and Communities in Southwestern North Carolina (1835–1838)," 19; Thomas, "Census of the North Carolina Cherokees, 1840"; Thomas, "Supplementary Report of Cherokee Indians Remaining in North Carolina, 1835–1840"; Welch and Jarrett, "Valuations of Cherokee Property in North Carolina."

32. Thomas Hindman, "Letter to Thomas Hartley Crawford, Commissioner of Indian Affairs, December 20, 1841," Letters received by the Office of Indian Affairs, 1824–1881, M-234, roll 86, pages 582–84, 1841; Chinoque Owl and Wa haw neet, "Letter to the Cherokee Commissioners, August 21, 1843," Unbound papers Box 2, William Holland Thomas papers, David M. Rubenstein Rare Book and Manuscript Library, Duke University, Durham, North Carolina; Thomas, "Census of the North Carolina Cherokees, 1840"; Thomas, "Supplementary Report of Cherokee Indians Remaining in North Carolina, 1835–1840."

33. Hindman, "Letter to Thomas Hartley Crawford, Commissioner of Indian Affairs, December 20, 1841."

34. For example, G. W. Gunter, "Claim for spoliation of property, File 766," RFBCC, RG 75, NARA, Washington, DC, 1843; A. R. S. Hunter, "Claim for spoliation of property, File 1134," RFBCC, RG 75, NARA, Washington, DC, 1843; Emanuel Shuler, "Claim for spoliation of property, File 400," RFBCC, RG 75, NARA, Washington, DC, 1843.

35. See Kilpatrick and Kilpatrick, "Chronicles of Wolftown: Social Documents of the North Carolina Cherokees, 1850–1862." Although little is known about these social structures for Welch's Town, some aspects are revealed for Wolf Town, one of the Qualla Town communities, in the 1850s. The Wolf Town chronicles are a body of documents collected in the late 1880s by anthropologist James Mooney. Most of the documents, written in Cherokee syllabary, pertain to the functioning of the Wolf Town council. The letters reveal a formal community-level government structure, and the continued functioning of the gadugi, or communal work party. Either the council or gadugi (or perhaps both) also maintained a fund from which community members could acquire loans, under strict conditions of repayment. The Wolf Town papers reveal that the council and the gadugi both maintained a formal structure with officers and rules of conduct.

36. These include Thomas, "Census of the North Carolina Cherokees, 1840"; Thomas, "Supplementary Report of Cherokee Indians Remaining in North Carolina, 1835–1840."

37. Thomas, "Census of the North Carolina Cherokees, 1840"; Thomas, "Supplementary Report of Cherokee Indians Remaining in North Carolina, 1835–1840."

38. Chinoque Owl and Wa haw neet, "Letter to the Cherokee Commissioners, August 21, 1843."

39. Thomas, "Census of the North Carolina Cherokees, 1840"; Thomas, "Supplementary Report of Cherokee Indians Remaining in North Carolina, 1835–1840"; "Census Roll of the Cherokee Indians East of the Mississippi, 1835."

40. Tiya Miles, *Ties That Bind: The Story of an Afro-Cherokee Family in Slavery and Freedom* (Berkeley: University of California Press, 2005), 83–84.

CHAPTER 4

1. John Finger, *The Eastern Band of Cherokees, 1819–1900* (Knoxville: University of Tennessee Press, 1984), 32; Thomas Hindman, "Letter to Thomas Hartley Crawford, Commissioner of Indian Affairs, December 20, 1841," Letters received by the Office of Indian Affairs, 1824–1881, M-234, roll 86, pages 582–84, 1841.

2. Historians have long examined these questions and come to many conclusions; e.g., see Finger, *Eastern Band of Cherokees, 1819–1900*; Stanly Godbold Jr. and Mattie Russell, *Confederate Colonel and Cherokee Chief: The Life of William Holland Thomas* (Knoxville: University of Tennessee Press, 1990); Mattie Russell, "William Holland Thomas, White Chief of the North Carolina Cherokees" (PhD diss., Duke University, 1956). Answering this question regarding the Welch family requires investigating the economic relationship between the family and the Cherokees of Welch's Town. Contemporary documents relating to the Cherokees on Valley River for this period are numerous and varied: censuses and rolls, government agent journals, business and personal correspondence, and travel writing. Archaeological data also help explain the Welches' methods and motives for providing a place for the creation of Welch's Town.

3. For example, Finger, *Eastern Band of Cherokees, 1819–1900*; Godbold and Russell, *Confederate Colonel and Cherokee Chief*; Russell, "William Holland Thomas, White Chief of the North Carolina Cherokees."

4. Godbold and Russell, *Confederate Colonel and Cherokee Chief*.

5. A broad body of literature on clientelism reveals a wide range of social and economic relationships within this phenomenon. Barry Mitchie, "The Transformation of Agrarian Patron-Client Relations: Illustrations from India," *American Ethnologist* 8, no. 1 (1981): 21–40; Frances Rothstein, "The Class Basis of Patron-Client Relations," *Latin American Perspectives* 6, no. 2 (1979): 25–35; James Scott, "Patron-Client Politics and Political Change in Southeast Asia," *American Political Science Review* 66, no. 1 (1972): 91–113.

6. Non-Population (Agricultural) Schedules of the Seventh Census, 1850, M-1805, Records of the Bureau of the Census, RG 29, NARA, Washington, DC, 1850; William Welch and Nimrod Jarrett, "Valuations of Cherokee Property in North Carolina," Cherokee Property Valuations, 1835–1839, RG 75, NARA, Washington, DC, 1837.

7. Population Schedules of the Sixth Census, 1840, M-704, Roll 357, Records of the Bureau of the Census, RG 29, NARA, Washington, DC, 1840.

8. John Inscoe, *Mountain Masters: Slavery and the Sectional Crisis in Western North Carolina* (Knoxville: University of Tennessee Press, 1996), 41–52.

9. Brett Riggs, "Removal Period Cherokee Households in Southwestern North Carolina: Material Perspectives on Ethnicity and Cultural Differentiation" (PhD diss., University of Tennessee, Knoxville, 1999), 223–24.

10. Non-Population (Agricultural) Schedules of the Seventh Census, 1850; Welch and Jarrett, "Valuations of Cherokee Property in North Carolina." After the Welch and Jarrett records created in 1837, the first detailed record of livestock in the area was created during the 1850 federal census. The 1850 agricultural census lists 102 head of cattle. By 1850 they had 109 head of hogs.

11. John Welch, "Claim for spoliation of property, File 687," RFBCC, RG 75, NARA, Washington, DC, 1846.

12. John C. Welch, "Letter to John Taylor, July 23, 1855," M-234, roll 97, pages 41–42, Letters received by the Office of Indian Affairs, 1824–1881, RG 75, NARA, Washington, DC, 1855.

13. William Baden, "A Dynamic Model of Stability and Change in Mississippian Agricultural Systems" (PhD diss., University of Tennessee, 1987); Riggs, "Removal Period Cherokee Households in Southwestern North Carolina: Material Perspectives on Ethnicity and Cultural Differentiation," 144–45.

14. Non-Population (Agricultural) Schedules of the Seventh Census, 1850. The phrase "Indian corn," used at the time in the federal census, encompassed several common varieties, including flint, dent, and sweet corn. These varieties were often planted sequentially, reducing the chances of crop failures through extremes in weather or pests.

15. Sarah Hill, *Weaving New Worlds: Southeastern Cherokee Women and Their Basketry* (Chapel Hill: University of North Carolina Press, 1997), 82–83; William Holland Thomas, "Murphy ledger F-3881," William Holland Thomas papers, David M. Rubenstein Rare Book and Manuscript Library, Duke University, Durham, North Carolina, 1841, 137.

16. Wilma Dunaway, *Slavery in the American Mountain South* (Cambridge: Cambridge University Press, 2003); John Lewis, "Becoming Appalachia: The Emergence of an American Subculture, 1840–1860" (PhD diss., University of Kentucky, 2000).

17. Welch and Jarrett, "Valuations of Cherokee Property in North Carolina."

18. Non-Population (Agricultural) Schedules of the Seventh Census, 1850.

19. Rob Cuthrell, "Mid-19th Century Cherokee Foodways and Identity in Western North Carolina" (MA thesis, University of North Carolina, Chapel Hill, 2005).

20. Non-Population (Agricultural) Schedules of the Seventh Census 1850.

21. Cuthrell, "Mid-19th Century Cherokee Foodways and Identity in Western North Carolina."

22. Cuthrell, "Mid-19th Century Cherokee Foodways and Identity in Western North Carolina," 40–45.

23. Arthur Bogan, Lori LaValley, and Gerald Schroedl, "Faunal Remains," in *Overhill Cherokee Archaeology at Chota-Tanasee*, ed. Gerald Schroedl, Report of Investigations 38 (University of Tennessee, Department of Anthropology 1986), 482–84; Arthur Bogan and Richard Polhemus, "Faunal Analysis," in *The Toqua Site: A Late Mississippian Dallas Phase Town*, ed. Richard Polhemus, Report of Investigations No. 41, Vol. 2 (University of Tennessee, Department of Anthropology, 1987), 1088–92. Livestock is also well represented by the abundance of faunal remains from the cellar pits. Cow, pig, and sheep are represented by fragments of ribs, mandibles and maxillae, vertebrae, and scapulae. The importance of cattle is also revealed in the numerous remains from the cellars. The vast bulk of cow bones are ribs, vertebrae, and mandible and maxilla fragments, while limbs are represented only by a single radius (exhibiting perimortem fractures) and two phalanges. What happened to the legs? The

answer is found in the collection of bones that could not be identified at the level of genus but were only identified as "large mammal." Within this category are numerous bones that have been fractured. It is probable that most of these bones are from butchered cattle (and perhaps pig as well), and the limbs have been chopped or fractured to access the marrow.

24. A. W. Coysh and R. K. Henrywood, *The Dictionary of Blue and White Printed Pottery, 1780–1880*, vol. I (Woodbridge, England: Antique Collectors' Club, 1982), 10; A. R. S. Hunter, "Cherokee accounts ledger of the Huntington store," manuscript on file, Cherokee County Historical Museum, Murphy, North Carolina, 1836–1838; William Holland Thomas, "Day Book F-3892, Quallatown, North Carolina," William Holland Thomas papers, David M. Rubenstein Rare Book and Manuscript Library, Duke University, Durham, North Carolina; Charles Zug, *Turners and Burners: The Folk Potters of North Carolina* (Chapel Hill: University of North Carolina Press, 1986), 70–104, 288–315.

25. See Lance Greene, "Archaeology and Community Reconstruction of Mid-Nineteenth-Century Cherokee Farmsteads along Valley River, North Carolina," in *Archaeological Adaptation: Case Studies of Cultural Transformation from the Southeast and Caribbean*, ed. Clifford Boyd, Jr. (Knoxville: University of Tennessee Press, 2019), 193–222. In contrast, William Holland Thomas and his wife were very careful about matching the dining sets they used for entertaining visitors. For example, on June 15, 1856, Thomas's wife purchased three sets of plates, three "dish plates" (large oval or rectangular platters), two sets of teacups and saucers, six mugs, four bowls, six glass tumblers, two pressed glass plates, and a pitcher from one of his stores. Thomas's wife purchased dishes in matched sets as well as expensive wares such as ceramic platters and pressed glass. Thomas, "Day Book F-3892, Quallatown, North Carolina."

26. The vast majority of ceramic sherds are whiteware, pearlware, redware, and stoneware. A single bone china sherd was part of a handleless teacup, the only expensive piece of pottery recovered from the site.

27. The Welch ceramic assemblage included about six hundred sherds representing just over one hundred individual vessels. Coffee consumption is documented in the historic record; John Powell purchased eight pounds of coffee for the Welches on January 24, 1837, at Hunter's store in Murphy. Numerous tin fragments from the site include a probable coffee pot, and some may have served as coffee cups. The ceramic assemblage includes eight alkaline-glazed stoneware vessels. Alkaline-glazed stoneware was produced throughout the nineteenth century in central and western North Carolina. This stoneware tradition was created through necessity, as early white settlers needed large vessels to store vegetables and other perishable food items. Common vessel forms included wide-mouthed jars, constricted-rim jugs, milk crocks or pans, and churns. Storage capacity for these vessels ranged from one pint to one gallon for storing jams, baking powder, sugar, tobacco, coffee, vinegar, cider, molasses, or whiskey, to one to five gallons (rarely ten- and fifteen-gallon vessels were produced) for storing fruit, butter, or salted meat.

28. The Welches had lived at the same location since 1822. If they had used Qualla ceramics to any degree during that period, some remnants would have made their way into the cellar-pit features. This suggests that the Welches had, long before removal, refused to have handmade pottery in their house.

29. In addition to handmade pipe fragments, excavations also recovered molded-clay pipes. These were available for sale at local stores for $0.10 and $0.25. Hunter, "Cherokee accounts ledger of the Huntington store." Tobacco seeds were also found. Cuthrell, "Mid-19th

Century Cherokee Foodways and Identity in Western North Carolina"; Lance Greene, "A Struggle for Cherokee Community: Excavating Identity in Post-Removal North Carolina" (PhD diss., University of North Carolina, Chapel Hill, 2009).

30. Dunaway, *Slavery in the American Mountain South*; Inscoe, *Mountain Masters*; Henry McKelway, "Slave and Master in the Upland South: Archaeological Investigations at the Mabry Site" (PhD diss., University of Tennessee, 1994); Frederick Law Olmsted, *A Journey in the Backcountry, 1853–1854* (New York: Schocken Books, 1860); Riggs, "Removal Period Cherokee Households in Southwestern North Carolina: Material Perspectives on Ethnicity and Cultural Differentiation"; William Trotter, *Bushwhackers: The Civil War in North Carolina*, vol. II: *The Mountains* (Winston-Salem, NC: John F. Blair, 1988), 28–29.

31. Dunaway, *Slavery in the American Mountain South*; Inscoe, *Mountain Masters*.

32. John C. Welch, "Letter to John Taylor, July 23, 1855," M-234, roll 97, pages 41–42, Letters Received by the Office of Indian Affairs, 1824–1881, RG 75, NARA, Washington, DC, 1855. Dunaway (*Slavery in the American Mountain South*, 55) documents that, on smaller plantations in the Appalachian South, there were not enough workers to maintain a strict division of labor, so free and enslaved people, both men and women, often performed agricultural labor together.

33. Dunaway, *Slavery in the American Mountain South*, 54–61.

34. Dunaway, *Slavery in the American Mountain South*, 165–68; Tiya Miles, *The House on Diamond Hill: A Cherokee Plantation Story* (Chapel Hill: University of North Carolina Press, 2010).

35. Blacksmith-related artifacts recovered during the Welch excavations include a fragment of iron tongs and a talc pencil fragment used for marking iron. Dunaway documents that enslaved men were often accomplished blacksmiths, *Slavery in the American Mountain South*, 108–9.

36. Welch and Jarrett, "Valuations of Cherokee Property in North Carolina."

37. Riggs, "Removal Period Cherokee Households in Southwestern North Carolina: Material Perspectives on Ethnicity and Cultural Differentiation," 238–39; "Census Roll of the Cherokee Indians East of the Mississippi, 1835," T-496, RG 75, NARA, Washington, DC, 1835.

38. William Blake, "Report upon the Property of the Valley River Gold Company," North Carolina Collection, The Louis Round Wilson Special Collections Library, University of North Carolina at Chapel Hill, 1860; George Featherstonaugh, *A Canoe Voyage up the Minnay Sotor* (London: R. Bentley, 1847).

39. Dunaway, *Slavery in the American Mountain South*, 119–25; Inscoe, *Mountain Masters*, 71–73.

40. Non-Population (Agricultural) Schedules of the Seventh Census, 1850.

41. Godbold and Russell, *Confederate Colonel and Cherokee Chief*; Hunter, "Cherokee accounts ledger of the Huntington store"; Riggs, "Removal Period Cherokee Households in Southwestern North Carolina: Material Perspectives on Ethnicity and Cultural Differentiation," 274; William Holland Thomas, "Murphy ledger F-3881," William Holland Thomas papers, David M. Rubenstein Rare Book and Manuscript Library, Duke University, Durham, North Carolina, 1841. As in most areas of the Southern Appalachians, storekeepers at A. R. S. Hunter's store in Murphy and William Holland Thomas's several stores in the region recorded regular sales of textile-related items such as pins, buttons, hooks and eyelets, and loom oil. In most cases these materials were sold in small quantities for production of clothing for home use. In other cases larger sales represented the production of clothing and/or cloth for sale or trade. Both Hunter

and Thomas purchased or traded goods for homemade cloth and clothing from local producers. As with livestock, many of these goods were shipped to the lowcountry South and purchased by plantation owners. Thomas sold a large quantity of handmade cloth, or homespun. Most homespun was produced locally and sold for $0.15 to $0.25 per yard. A wide variety of imported cloth was also available. In addition to homespun, Thomas offered over a dozen kinds of cloth, including flannel, calico, muslin, Irish linen, merino wool, cashmere, silk, and sailduck.

42. Marie Jenkins Schwartz, "'At Noon, Oh How I Ran': Breastfeeding and Weaning on Plantation and Farm in Antebellum Virginia and Alabama," in *Discovering the Women in Slavery: Emancipating Perspectives on the American Past*, ed. Patricia Morton (Athens: University of Georgia Press, 1996), 245.

43. Dunaway, *Slavery in the American Mountain South*; Inscoe, *Mountain Masters*, 59–86.

44. Riggs, "Removal Period Cherokee Households in Southwestern North Carolina: Material Perspectives on Ethnicity and Cultural Differentiation."

45. Paul Hamel and Mary Chiltoskey, *Cherokee Plants and Their Uses: A 400 Year History* (Sylva, NC: Herald, 1975); Hill, *Weaving New Worlds*, 80–82; Gerald Schroedl and Andrea Shea, "Plant Remains," in *Overhill Cherokee Archaeology at Chota-Tanasee*, ed. Schroedl, Report of Investigations 38 (University of Tennessee, Department of Anthropology, 1986), 515–30.

46. Heidi Altman, *Eastern Cherokee Fishing* (Tuscaloosa: University of Alabama Press, 2006); James Mooney, *Myths of the Cherokee and Sacred Formulas of the Cherokees*, reproduction of 19th and 7th Annual Reports the Bureau of American Ethnology (Nashville: Charles and Randy Elder Booksellers, 1982).

47. A deer femur provides important evidence for the season in which the cellar pits were filled. An eighteen-month-old deer was killed in November or December, revealed through seasonality studies of the femur and the associated distal and proximal epiphyses. Recovery of these bones from the same provenience shows the upper leg was articulated when deposited in the pit. Therefore, the deer was killed, and the remains deposited partly intact, in November or December. Faunal analysis of the Welch site assemblage was performed by Dr. Tom Whyte at Appalachian State University in Boone, North Carolina.

48. James Adair, *Adair's History of the American Indians*, ed. Samuel Cole Williams (1775; rpt. Johnson City, TN: Watauga Press, 1930), 242.

49. John Welch, "Claim for spoliation of property, File 687," RFBCC, RG 75, NARA, Washington, DC, 1846.

50. Adair, *Adair's History of the American Indians*, 242.

51. Cuthrell, "Mid-19th Century Cherokee Foodways and Identity in Western North Carolina."

52. Melanie Cabak and Mark Groover, "Bush Hill: Material Life at a Working Plantation," *Historical Archaeology* 40, no. 4 (2006): 51–83.

CHAPTER 5

1. John Finger, *The Eastern Band of Cherokees, 1819–1900* (Knoxville: University of Tennessee Press, 1984), 31–36.

2. John Finger, "The Abortive Second Cherokee Removal, 1841–1844," *Journal of Southern History* 47 (1981): 210.

3. Finger, *Eastern Band of Cherokees, 1819–1900*, 31.

4. Thomas Hindman, "Letter to Thomas Hartley Crawford, Commissioner of Indian Affairs, December 20, 1841," Letters received by the Office of Indian Affairs, 1824–1881, M-234, roll 86, pages 582–84, 1841.

5. Andrew Barnard, "Letter to Governor Edward Dudley," April 6, 1840, quoted in Finger, *Eastern Band of Cherokees, 1819–1900*, 68.

6. Quoted in Finger, *Eastern Band of Cherokees, 1819–1900*, 37–38.

7. Non-Population (Slave) Schedules of the Seventh Census, 1850, M-432, Roll 651, Records of the Bureau of the Census, RG 29, NARA, Washington, DC, 1850.

8. John Inscoe, *Mountain Masters: Slavery and the Sectional Crisis in Western North Carolina* (Knoxville: University of Tennessee Press, 1996), 60; Non-Population (Slave) Schedules of the Seventh Census, 1850.

9. Alfred Chapman, Chapman Roll of Eastern Cherokee, Roll 12, M-685, RG 75, NARA, Washington, DC, 1851.

10. Finger, *Eastern Band of Cherokees, 1819–1900*, 212. Disbursing agents were responsible for making payments to Cherokees who were owed funds as stipulated by the Treaty of New Echota. The government allowed these agents to collect a fee that could be drawn from the funds to be disbursed.

11. Charles Royce, *The Cherokee Nation of Indians* (Chicago: Aldine, 1975), 127.

12. Finger, "Abortive Second Cherokee Removal, 1841–1844," 213–14.

13. Hindman, "Letter to Thomas Hartley Crawford, Commissioner of Indian Affairs, December 20, 1841."

14. Finger, *Eastern Band of Cherokees, 1819–1900*, 33.

15. William Holland Thomas, "Census of the North Carolina Cherokees, 1840," William Holland Thomas papers, David M. Rubenstein Rare Book and Manuscript Library, Duke University, Durham, North Carolina; William Holland Thomas, "Supplementary Report of Cherokee Indians Remaining in North Carolina, 1835–1840," manuscript copy in the William Holland Thomas papers, David M. Rubenstein Rare Book and Manuscript Library, Duke University, Durham, North Carolina, 1840.

16. Hindman, "Letter to Thomas Hartley Crawford, Commissioner of Indian Affairs, December 20, 1841."

17. Hindman, "Letter to Thomas Hartley Crawford, Commissioner of Indian Affairs, December 20, 1841."

18. Finger, "Abortive Second Cherokee Removal, 1841–1844," 215.

19. Richard Iobst, "William Holland Thomas and the Cherokee Claims," in *The Cherokee Indian Nation: A Troubled History*, ed. Duane King (Knoxville: University of Tennessee Press, 1979), 181–201.

20. Finger, *Eastern Band of Cherokees, 1819–1900*; Iobst, "William Holland Thomas and the Cherokee Claims."

21. Finger, *Eastern Band of Cherokees, 1819–1900*, 46.

22. Finger, *Eastern Band of Cherokees, 1819–1900*, 34–37, 46.

23. Stanly Godbold Jr. and Mattie Russell, *Confederate Colonel and Cherokee Chief: The Life of William Holland Thomas* (Knoxville: University of Tennessee Press, 1990), 57.

24. Felix Axley, "Letter to William Holland Thomas, January 23, 1851," Unbound papers, William Holland Thomas papers, David M. Rubenstein Rare Book and Manuscript Library, Duke University, Durham, North Carolina, 1851.

25. Finger, *Eastern Band of Cherokees, 1819–1900*, 46.

26. J. W. King, "Letter to William Holland Thomas, December 12, 1844." James Terrell papers, microfilm roll 1 (1813–1852), David M. Rubenstein Rare Book and Manuscript Library, Duke University, Durham, North Carolina, 1844.

27. J. W. King, "Letter to William Holland Thomas, December 12, 1844."

28. Ellen Skinner, *Women and the National Experience: Primary Sources in American History* ([New York]: Addison-Wesley, 1996).

29. Finger, *Eastern Band of Cherokees, 1819–1900*, 46.

30. John Medill, "Report to Office of Indian Affairs," March 31, 1846, United States Senate Document 185, 18, 29th Congress, 1st Session, United States Congressional Serial Set, Government Printing Office, Washington, DC, 1846.

31. "Indian Appropriations Act of July 29, 1848," 30th Congress, 1st Session, U.S. Statutes at Large, Volume IX, Chapter 118, 252–65. United States Congressional Serial Set, Government Printing Office, Washington, DC, quoted in Finger, *Eastern Band of Cherokees, 1819–1900*, 37–38.

32. Finger, *Eastern Band of Cherokees, 1819–1900*, 48–49.

33. Finger, *Eastern Band of Cherokees, 1819–1900*, 52.

34. Wachacha, "Conveyance of title, Gideon Morris to Wachacha, February 17, 1845," manuscript on file, Cherokee County Register of Deeds, Book 2, page 493, 1845; Junaluska, "Conveyance of title, State of North Carolina to Junaluska, June 2, 1847," manuscript on file, Cherokee County Register of Deeds, Book 5, page 33, 1847; Chutasottee and his wife, Cunstagee, or Sally, are buried in the cemetery of St. John's Episcopal Church in Franklin. Local history states that Siler agreed to do this in response to Chutasottee's deathbed request. See William Jurgelski, "A New Plow in Old Ground: Cherokees, Whites, and Land in Western North Carolina, 1819–1829" (PhD diss., University of Georgia, Athens, 2004); James Mooney, *Myths of the Cherokee and Sacred Formulas of the Cherokees*, reproduction of 19th and 7th Annual Reports the Bureau of American Ethnology (Nashville: Charles and Randy Elder Booksellers, 1982); Margaret Siler, *Cherokee Indian Lore and Smoky Mountain Stories* (Franklin, NC: Teresita Press, 2000); John Axe, "Conveyance of title, State of North Carolina to John Axe, December 1, 1853," manuscript on file, Cherokee County Register of Deeds, Book 7, page 609, 1853; Nancy Hawkins, "Conveyance of title, State of North Carolina to Nancy Hawkins, May 8, 1852," manuscript on file, Cherokee County Register of Deeds, Book 6, pages 170–71, 1852; Joe Locust, "Conveyance of title, State of North Carolina to Joe Locust, March 24, 1852," manuscript on file, Cherokee County Register of Deeds, Book 5, page 381, 1852; Sapsucker, "Conveyance of title, State of North Carolina to Sapsucker, February 25, 1852," manuscript on file, Cherokee County Register of Deeds, Book 5, pages 363–64, 1852.

35. Elizabeth Welch, "Letter to the Commissioner of Indian Affairs, October 15, 1853," Letters Received by the Office of Indian Affairs, 1824–1881, M-234, roll 97, page 43, RG 75, NARA, Washington, DC, 1853.

CONCLUSIONS

1. John Finger, *The Eastern Band of Cherokees, 1819–1900* (Knoxville: University of Tennessee Press, 1984), 107.

2. Finger, *Eastern Band of Cherokees, 1819–1900*, 139.

3. Finger, *Eastern Band of Cherokees, 1819–1900*, 113–14.

4. Finger, *Eastern Band of Cherokees, 1819–1900*, 152–53.

5. James Mooney, *Myths of the Cherokee and Sacred Formulas of the Cherokees*, reproduction of 19th and 7th Annual Reports the Bureau of American Ethnology (Nashville: Charles and Randy Elder Booksellers, 1982).

6. John Finger, *Cherokee Americans: The Eastern Band of Cherokees in the Twentieth Century* (Lincoln: University of Nebraska Press, 1991), 44–51.

7. Robert Thomas, "Cherokee Values and World View," manuscript on file, North Carolina Collection, The Louis Round Wilson Special Collections Library, University of North Carolina at Chapel Hill, 1958.

8. Barbara Duncan and Brett Riggs, *Cherokee Heritage Trails Guidebook* (Chapel Hill: University of North Carolina Press, 2003), 73; Brett Riggs and Scott Shumate, "Archaeological Testing at Kituwah, 2001 Investigations at Sites 31SW1, 31SW2, 31SW287, 31SW316, 31SW317, 31SW318, and 31SW820," report prepared for the Eastern Band of Cherokee Indians Cultural Resources Program, manuscript on file, North Carolina Office of State Archaeology, Raleigh.

9. In *Unworthy Republic: The Dispossession of Native Americans and the Road to Indian Territory* (New York: W. W. Norton, 2020), Claudio Saunt convincingly documents that, while the discovery of gold and the value of Cherokee land motivated white usurpers, the ideology of white supremacy was at the root of the Indian removals.

10. Tiya Miles, *The House on Diamond Hill: A Cherokee Plantation Story* (Chapel Hill: University of North Carolina Press, 2010); Tiya Miles, *Ties That Bind: The Story of an Afro-Cherokee Family in Slavery and Freedom* (Berkeley: University of California Press, 2005); Fay Yarbrough, "From Kin to Intruder: Cherokee Legal Attitudes toward People of African Descent in the Nineteenth Century," in *Race and Science: Scientific Challenges to Racism in Modern America*, ed. Paul Farber and Hamilton Cravens, 32–57 (Corvallis: Oregon State University Press, 2009); Fay Yarbrough, *Race and the Cherokee Nation: Sovereignty in the Nineteenth Century* (Philadelphia: University of Pennsylvania Press, 2008); Fay Yarbrough, "'Those Disgracefull and Unnatural Matches': Interracial Sex and Cherokee Society in the Nineteenth Century" (PhD diss., Emory University, 2003).

Bibliography

Abbreviations

NARA   United States National Archives and Records Administration
RFBCC   Records of the Fourth Board of Cherokee Commissioners
RFRBCC   Records of the First Board of Cherokee Commissioners
RG   Record Group

Manuscript and Image Collections

Cherokee County Courthouse, Murphy, North Carolina
Cherokee County Historical Museum, Murphy, North Carolina
Cherokee County Register of Deeds, Murphy, North Carolina
David M. Rubenstein Rare Book and Manuscript Library, Duke University, Durham, North Carolina
Louis Round Wilson Special Collections Library, University of North Carolina at Chapel Hill
Macon County, North Carolina Register of Deeds, Franklin, North Carolina
National Anthropological Archives, Smithsonian Museum Support Center, Suitland, Maryland
North Carolina Office of State Archaeology, Raleigh
State Archives of North Carolina, Raleigh
United States National Archives at Atlanta
United States National Archives in College Park, Maryland
United States National Archives in Washington, DC

Published Primary Sources

Adair, James. *Adair's History of the American Indians*. 1775. Edited by Samuel Cole Williams. Reprint, Johnson City, TN: Watauga Press, 1930.
Alexis. "A Visit to the Cartoogechaye Indians." *North Carolina University Magazine*, no. 1 (1851): 116–18.
Featherstonaugh, George. *A Canoe Voyage up the Minnay Sotor*. London: R. Bentley, 1847.
Lanman, Charles. *Letters from the Alleghany Mountains*. New York: G. P. Putnam, 1849.
Moulton, Gary, ed. *The Papers of Chief John Ross*. Norman: University of Oklahoma Press, 1985.
Olmsted, Frederick Law. *A Journey in the Backcountry, 1853–1854*. New York: Schocken Books, 1860.
Rhea, Matthew. "Map of the State of Tennessee." In *Tennessee Gazetteer*. 1834. Edited by Robert McBride and Owen Meredith. Reprint, Nashville: Gazetteer Press, 1971.

Williams, Samuel, ed. *Lieutenant Henry Timberlake's Memoirs, 1756-1765.* Johnson City, TN: Watauga Press, 1927.

Williams, W. G. "Memoir Relative to the Cherokee Nation within the Limits of N. Carolina and Its Immediate Vicinity," February 8, 1838. *Journal of Cherokee Studies* 4, No. 4 (1979): 202-10.

Secondary Sources

Books

Altman, Heidi. *Eastern Cherokee Fishing.* Tuscaloosa: University of Alabama Press, 2006.

Anderson, William, ed. *Cherokee Removal: Before and After.* Athens: University of Georgia Press, 1991.

Battle-Baptiste, Whitney. *Black Feminist Archaeology.* Walnut Creek, CA: Left Coast Press, 2011.

Beaudry, Mary, and James Symonds, eds. *Interpreting the Early Modern World: Transatlantic Perspectives.* New York: Springer, 2011.

Berry, Daina, and Leslie Harris, eds. *Sexuality and Slavery: Reclaiming Intimate Histories in the Americas.* Athens: University of Georgia Press, 2018.

Bhabha, Homi. *The Location of Culture.* London: Routledge Press, 2004.

Block, Sharon. *Rape and Sexual Power in Early America.* Chapel Hill: University of North Carolina Press, 2006.

Boulware, Tyler. *Deconstructing the Cherokee Nation: Town, Region, and Nation among Eighteenth-Century Cherokees.* Gainesville: University Press of Florida, 2011.

Boyd, C. Clifford, Jr., ed. *Archaeological Adaptation: Case Studies of Cultural Transformation from the Southeast and Caribbean.* Knoxville: University of Tennessee Press, 2019.

Boydston, Jeanne. *Home and Work: Housework, Wages, and the Ideology of Labor in the Early Republic.* Oxford: Oxford University Press, 1990.

Browder, Nathaniel. *The Cherokee Indians and Those Who Came After: Notes for a History of Cherokee County, North Carolina, 1835-1860.* Hayesville, NC: self-published by Browder, 1973.

Brunk, Robert S., ed. *May We All Remember Well: A Journal of History and Cultures of Western North Carolina.* Vol. 1. Asheville, North Carolina: Robert S. Brunk Auction Services, 1997.

Card, Jeb, ed. *The Archaeology of Hybrid Material Culture.* Carbondale: Southern Illinois University Press, 2013.

Carney, Virginia. *Eastern Band Cherokee Women: Cultural Persistence in Their Letters and Speeches.* Knoxville: University of Tennessee Press, 2005.

Cott, Nancy. *The Bonds of Womanhood: "Woman's Sphere" in New England, 1780-1835.* New Haven: Yale University Press, 1977.

Coysh, A. W., and R. K. Henrywood. *The Dictionary of Blue and White Printed Pottery, 1780-1880.* Volume I. Woodbridge, England: Antique Collectors' Club, 1982.

Dale, Edward, and Gaston Litton. *Cherokee Cavaliers: Forty Years of Cherokee History as Told in the Correspondence of the Ridge-Watie-Boudinot Family.* Norman: University of Oklahoma Press, 1939.

Deetz, James. *In Small Things Forgotten: The Archaeology of Early American Life.* New York: Anchor Press/Doubleday, 1977.

Dickens, Roy. *Cherokee Prehistory: The Pisgah Phase in the Southern Appalachian Region*. Knoxville: University of Tennessee Press, 1976.

Douglas, Mary, and Baron Isherwood. *The World of Goods: Towards an Anthropology of Consumerism*. New York: Basic Books, 1979.

Dunaway, Wilma. *The First American Frontier: Transition to Capitalism in Southern Appalachia, 1700–1860*. Fred W. Morrison Series in Southern Studies. Chapel Hill: University of North Carolina Press, 1996.

———. *Slavery in the American Mountain South*. Cambridge: Cambridge University Press, 2003.

Duncan, Barbara, and Brett Riggs. *Cherokee Heritage Trails Guidebook*. Chapel Hill: University of North Carolina Press, 2003.

Ehle, John. *Trail of Tears: The Rise and Fall of the Cherokee Nation*. New York: Anchor Books, Doubleday, 1988.

Farber, Paul, and Hamilton Cravens, eds. *Race and Science: Scientific Challenges to Racism in Modern America*. Corvallis: Oregon State University Press, 2009.

Fenton, William, and John Gulick, eds. *Symposium on Cherokee and Iroquois Culture*. Smithsonian Institution Bureau of American Ethnology Bulletin 180. Washington, DC: US Government Printing Office, 1961.

Finger, John. *Cherokee Americans: The Eastern Band of Cherokees in the Twentieth Century*. Lincoln: University of Nebraska Press, 1991.

———. *The Eastern Band of Cherokees, 1819–1900*. Knoxville: University of Tennessee Press, 1984.

———. "The Impact of Removal on the North Carolina Cherokees." In *Cherokee Removal: Before and After*, edited by William Anderson, 96–111. Athens: University of Georgia Press, 1991.

Foreman, Grant. *Indian Removal: The Emigration of the Five Civilized Tribes of Indians*. Norman: University of Oklahoma Press, 1976.

Frazier, Charles. *Thirteen Moons*. New York: Random House, 2006.

Freel, Margaret. *Our Heritage*. Asheville, NC: Miller Printing Company, 1957.

Fuentes, Marisa. *Dispossessed Lives: Enslaved Women, Violence, and the Archive*. Philadelphia: University of Pennsylvania Press, 2016.

Garrow, Patrick. *The Chieftains Excavations, 1969–1971*. Published with permission from the Chieftains Museum and the Trail of Tears Commission of the National Park Service, 2010.

Gearing, Fred. *Priests and Warriors: Social Structures for Cherokee Politics in the Eighteenth Century*. American Anthropological Association Memoir 93. Menasha, WI: American Anthropological Association, 1962.

Genovese, Eugene. *Roll, Jordan, Roll: The World the Slaves Made*. New York: Vintage Books, 1976.

Glymph, Thavolia. *Out of the House of Bondage: The Transformation of the Plantation Household*. Cambridge: Cambridge University Press, 2008.

Godbold, Stanly Jr., and Mattie Russell. *Confederate Colonel and Cherokee Chief: The Life of William Holland Thomas*. Knoxville: University of Tennessee Press, 1990.

Goodwin, Gary. "Cherokees in Transition: A Study of Changing Culture and Environment prior to 1775." Department of Geography, University of Chicago, Research Paper 181, 1977.

Greene, Lance, and Mark R. Plane, eds. *American Indians and the Market Economy, 1775–1850*. Tuscaloosa: University of Alabama Press, 2010.

Halliburton, R. Jr. *Red over Black: Black Slavery among the Cherokee Indians*. Contributions in Afro-American and African Studies No. 27. Westport, CT: Greenwood Press, 1977.

Hamel, Paul, and Mary Chiltoskey. *Cherokee Plants and Their Uses: A 400 Year History*. Sylva, NC: Herald, 1975.

Harrington, Mark. "The Last of the Iroquois Potters." New York State Museum Bulletin 133. Albany: University of the State of New York, 1908.

Hicks, Brian. *Toward the Setting Sun: John Ross, the Cherokees, and the Trail of Tears*. New York: Grove Press, 2012.

Hicks, Dan, and Mary Beaudry, eds. *The Cambridge Companion to Historical Archaeology*. Cambridge: Cambridge University Press, 2006.

Hill, Sarah. *Weaving New Worlds: Southeastern Cherokee Women and Their Basketry*. Chapel Hill: University of North Carolina Press, 1997.

Hodder, Ian, and Scott Hutson. *Reading the Past: Current Approaches to Interpretation in Archaeology*. Cambridge: Cambridge University Press, 2003.

Hudson, Charles. *The Southeastern Indians*. Knoxville: University of Tennessee Press, 1976.

Inscoe, John. *Mountain Masters: Slavery and the Sectional Crisis in Western North Carolina*. Knoxville: University of Tennessee Press, 1996.

Johnston, Carolyn. *Cherokee Women in Crisis: Trail of Tears, Civil War, and Allotment, 1838–1907*. Tuscaloosa: University of Alabama Press, 2003.

Jones-Rogers, Stephanie. *They Were Her Property: White Women as Slave Owners in the American South*. New Haven: Yale University Press, 2019.

Jordan, David, and Marc Swartz, eds. *Personality and the Cultural Construction of Society*. Tuscaloosa: University of Alabama Press, 1990.

Jordan, Jan. *Give Me the Wind: A Biographical Novel of John Ross, Chief of the Cherokee*. Englewood Cliffs, NJ: Prentice-Hall, 1973.

Kilpatrick, Anna, and Jack Kilpatrick. "Chronicles of Wolftown: Social Documents of the North Carolina Cherokees, 1850–1862." Bureau of American Ethnology Bulletin 196, 1–112. Washington, DC: US Government Printing Office, 1966.

King, Duane, ed. *The Cherokee Indian Nation: A Troubled History*. Knoxville: University of Tennessee Press, 1979.

Koestler-Grack, Rachel. *Chief John Ross*. Chicago: Heinemann Library, 2004.

Leone, Mark, and Parker Potter, eds. *The Recovery of Meaning: Historical Archaeology in the Eastern United States*. Washington, DC: Smithsonian Institution Press, 1988.

Liebmann, Matthew. "Parsing Hybridity: Archaeologies of Amalgamation in Seventeenth-Century New Mexico." In *The Archaeology of Hybrid Material Culture*, edited by Jeb Card, 25–49. Carbondale: Southern Illinois University Press, 2013.

Malone, Henry. *Cherokees of the Old South: A People in Transition*. Athens: University of Georgia Press, 1956.

McClinton, Rowena, ed. *The Moravian Springplace Mission to the Cherokees*. 2 vols. Lincoln: University of Nebraska Press, 2007.

McEwan, Bonnie, ed. *Indians of the Greater Southeast: Historical Archaeology and Ethnohistory*. Gainesville: University Press of Florida, 2000.

McKenney, Thomas, and James Hall. *History of the Indian Tribes of North America with Biographical Sketches and Anecdotes of the Principal Chiefs*. Volume 1. 1836. Reproduction, Edinburgh: F. W. Hodge, 1933.

McLoughlin, William. *Champions of the Cherokees: Evan and John B. Jones.* Princeton: Princeton University Press, 1990.

———. *Cherokee Renascence in the New Republic.* Princeton: Princeton University Press, 1986.

Miles, Tiya. *The Cherokee Rose: A Novel of Gardens and Ghosts.* Winston-Salem, NC: John F. Blair, 2016.

———. *The House on Diamond Hill: A Cherokee Plantation Story.* Chapel Hill: University of North Carolina Press, 2010.

———. *Ties That Bind: The Story of an Afro-Cherokee Family in Slavery and Freedom.* Berkeley: University of California Press, 2005.

Mooney, James. *The Ghost-Dance Religion and the Sioux Outbreak of 1890.* Reproduction of 14th Annual Report of the Bureau of American Ethnology, Part 2 (1896). University of Nebraska Press, 1991.

———. *Historical Sketch of the Cherokee.* 1900. Reprint, Chicago: Aldine, 1975.

———. *Myths of the Cherokee and Sacred Formulas of the Cherokees.* Reproduction of 19th and 7th Annual Reports the Bureau of American Ethnology. Nashville: Charles and Randy Elder Booksellers, 1982.

Morton, Patricia, ed. *Discovering the Women in Slavery: Emancipating Perspectives on the American Past.* Athens: University of Georgia Press, 1996.

Moulton, Gary. *John Ross, Cherokee Chief.* Athens: University of Georgia Press, 1978.

Neeley, Sharlotte. *Snowbird Cherokees: People of Persistence.* Athens: University of Georgia Press, 1991.

Noël Hume, Ivor. *Historical Archaeology.* New York: Alfred A. Knopf, 1969.

Perdue, Theda. *Cherokee Women: Gender and Culture Change, 1700–1835.* Lincoln: University of Nebraska Press, 1998.

———. *Slavery and the Evolution of Cherokee Society, 1540–1866.* Knoxville: University of Tennessee Press, 1979.

Perdue, Theda, and Michael Green. *The Cherokee Removal: A Brief History with Documents.* Boston: Bedford/St. Martin's, 2005.

Pluckhahn, Thomas, and Robbie Ethridge, eds. *Light on the Path: The Anthropology and History of the Southeastern Indians.* Tuscaloosa: University of Alabama Press, 2006.

Polhemus, Richard, ed. *The Toqua Site: A Late Mississippian Dallas Phase Town.* Report of Investigations No. 41, Vol. 2. University of Tennessee, Department of Anthropology, 1987.

Price, Sarah, and Philip Carr, eds. *Investigating the Ordinary: Everyday Matters in Southeast Archaeology.* Gainesville: University of Florida Press, 2018.

Reid, John. *A Law of Blood: The Primitive Law of the Cherokee Nation.* New York: New York University Press, 1970.

Riggs, Brett. "An Historical and Archaeological Reconnaissance of Citizen Cherokee Reservations in Macon, Swain, and Jackson Counties, North Carolina." Submitted to the North Carolina Division of Archives and History, Raleigh. Department of Anthropology, University of Tennessee, Knoxville, 1988.

———. "Removal Period Cherokee Households and Communities in Southwestern North Carolina (1835–1838)." Final Report of the Cherokee Homestead Project, submitted to the North Carolina State Historic Preservation Office, Division of Archives and History, Department of Cultural Resources, Raleigh, North Carolina, 1996.

Riggs, Brett, and Scott Shumate. "Archaeological Testing at Kituwah. 2001 Investigations at Sites 31SW1, 31SW2, 31SW287, 31SW316, 31SW317, 31SW318, and 31SW820." Report prepared for the Eastern Band of Cherokee Indians Cultural Resources Program. Manuscript on file, North Carolina Office of State Archaeology, Raleigh.

Ross, John. *The Papers of Chief John Ross*. Edited by Gary Moulton. Norman: University of Oklahoma Press, 1985.

Royce, Charles. *The Cherokee Nation of Indians*. Chicago: Aldine, 1975.

Saunt, Claudio. *Black, White, and Indian: Race and the Unmaking of an American Family*. Oxford: Oxford University Press, 2005.

———. *A New Order of Things: Property, Power, and the Transformation of the Creek Indians, 1733–1816*. Cambridge: Cambridge University Press, 1999.

———. *Unworthy Republic: The Dispossession of Native Americans and the Road to Indian Territory*. New York: W. W. Norton, 2020.

Schiffer, Michael, ed. *Advances in Archaeological Method and Theory*, Vol. 11. New York: Academic Press, Inc., 1987.

Schroedl, Gerald, ed. "Overhill Cherokee Archaeology at Chota-Tanasee." Report of Investigations No. 38. University of Tennessee, Department of Anthropology, 1986.

Siler, Margaret. *Cherokee Indian Lore and Smoky Mountain Stories*. Franklin, NC: Teresita Press, 2000.

Skinner, Ellen. *Women and the National Experience: Primary Sources in American History*. New York: Addison-Wesley, 1996.

Smith, Margaret, and Emily Wilson. *North Carolina Women Making History*. Chapel Hill: University of North Carolina Press, 1999.

Sommerville, Diane. *Rape and Race in the Nineteenth-Century South*. Chapel Hill: University of North Carolina Press, 2004.

Spector, Janet. *What This Awl Means: Feminist Archaeology at a Wahpeton Dakota Village*. St. Paul: Minnesota Historical Society Press, 1993.

Stein, Gil, ed. *The Archaeology of Colonial Encounters: Comparative Perspectives*. Santa Fe: School of American Research Press, 2005.

Stockhammer, Philipp, ed. *Conceptualizing Cultural Hybridity: A Transdisciplinary Approach*. New York: Springer, 2012.

Sturm, Circe. *Blood Politics: Race, Culture, and Identity in the Cherokee Nation of Oklahoma*. Berkeley: University of California Press, 2002.

Swanton, John. *The Indians of the Southeastern United States*. Washington, DC: Smithsonian Institution Press, 1979. Reprint of Bureau of American Ethology Bulletin 137 (1946).

Thornton, Russell. *The Cherokees: A Population History*. Lincoln: University of Nebraska Press, 1990.

Tilley, Christopher, and Kate Cameron-Daum, eds. *The Anthropology of Landscape: The Extraordinary in the Ordinary*. London: UCL Press, 2017.

Trotter, William. *Bushwhackers: The Civil War in North Carolina*. Volume II: *The Mountains*. Winston-Salem, NC: John F. Blair, 1988.

Turner, Sasha. *Contested Bodies: Pregnancy, Childrearing, and Slavery in Jamaica*. Philadelphia: University of Pennsylvania Press, 2017.

Voss, Barbara, and Eleanor Conlin Casella, eds. *The Archaeology of Colonialism: Intimate Encounters and Sexual Effects*. New York: Cambridge University Press, 2012.

Ward, Trawick, and R. P. Stephen Davis Jr. *Time before History: The Archaeology of North Carolina*. Chapel Hill: University of North Carolina Press, 1999.

White, Deborah. *Ar'n't I a Woman? Female Slaves in the Plantation South*. New York: W. W. Norton, 1999.

Wigginton, Eliot. *The Foxfire Book*. Garden City, NY: Anchor Press, 1972.

Wilkie, Laurie. *Creating Freedom: Material Culture and African American Identity at Oakley Plantation, Louisiana, 1840–1950*. Baton Rouge: Louisiana State University Press, 2000.

Wilkins, Thurman. *Cherokee Tragedy: The Ridge Family and the Decimation of a People*. Norman: University of Oklahoma Press, 1986.

Woodward, Grace. *The Cherokees*. Norman: University of Oklahoma Press, 1963.

Yarbrough, Fay. *Race and the Cherokee Nation: Sovereignty in the Nineteenth Century*. Philadelphia: University of Pennsylvania Press, 2008.

Zug, Charles. *Turners and Burners: The Folk Potters of North Carolina*. Chapel Hill: University of North Carolina Press, 1986.

Articles

Baptist, Edward. "'Cuffy,' 'Fancy Maids,' and 'One-Eyed Men': Rape, Commodification, and the Domestic Slave Trade in the United States." *American Historical Review* 106, no. 5 (2001): 1619–50.

Bridgers, Ben. "An Historical Analysis of the Legal Status of the North Carolina Cherokees." *North Carolina Law Review* 58 (1980): 1075–31.

Cabak, Melanie, and Mark Groover. "Bush Hill: Material Life at a Working Plantation." *Historical Archaeology* 40, no. 4 (2006): 51–83.

De Baillou, Clemens. "The Chief Vann House at Spring Place, Georgia." *Early Georgia* 2, no. 2 (1957): 3–11.

Fewkes, Vladimir. "Catawba Pottery-Making, with notes on Pamunkey Pottery-Making, Cherokee Pottery-Making and Coiling." *Proceedings of the American Philosophical Society* 88, no. 2 (1944): 69–124.

Finger, John. "The Abortive Second Cherokee Removal, 1841–1844." *Journal of Southern History* 47 (1981): 207–26.

———. "The North Carolina Cherokees, 1838–1866: Traditionalism, Progressivism, and the Affirmation of State Citizenship." In *Journal of Cherokee Studies* 5, no. 1 (1980): 17–29.

———. "The Saga of Tsali: Legend versus Reality." In *North Carolina Historical Review* 56, no. 1 (1979):1–18.

Godbold, Stanly Jr. "William Holland Thomas: A Man for All Seasons." *Journal of Cherokee Studies* 24 (2005): 3–9.

Gould, Roger. "Patron-Client Ties, State Centralization, and the Whiskey Rebellion." *American Journal of Sociology* 102, no. 2 (1996): 400–429.

Harwood, C. R. "Lost Cherokee Towns of Graham County, North Carolina." *Tennessee Archaeologist* 15, no. 2 (1959): 111–12.

Hutnyk, John. "Hybridity." *Ethnic and Racial Studies* 28, no. 1 (2005): 79–102.

King, Duane, and Raymond Evans. "Tsali: The Man behind the Legend." *Journal of Cherokee Studies* 4, no. 4 (1979): 194–201.

Kutsche, Paul. "The Tsali Legend: Culture Heroes and Historiography." *Ethnohistory* 10, no. 4 (1963): 329–57.

Leone, Mark, Parker Potter, and Paul Shackel. "Toward a Critical Archaeology." *Current Anthropology* 28, no. 3 (1987): 283–302.

Liebmann, Matthew. "The Mickey Mouse Kachina and Other 'Double Objects': Hybridity in the Material Culture of Colonial Encounters." *Journal of Social Archaeology* 15, no. 3 (2015): 319–41.

Litton, Gaston. "Enrollment Records of the Eastern Band of Cherokee Indians." *North Carolina Historical Review* 17 (1940): 199–231.

McLoughlin, William. "Experiment in Cherokee Citizenship, 1817–1829." *American Quarterly* 33, no. 1 (1981): 3–25.

McLoughlin, William, and Walter Conser Jr. "The Cherokees in Transition: A Statistical Analysis of the Federal Cherokee Census of 1835." *Journal of American History* 64, no. 3 (1977): 678–703.

Miller, George. "A Revised Set of CC Index Values for Classification and Economic Scaling of English Ceramics from 1787 to 1880." *Historical Archaeology* 25, no. 1 (1991): 1–25.

Mitchie, Barry. "The Transformation of Agrarian Patron-Client Relations: Illustrations from India." *American Ethnologist* 8, no. 1 (1981): 21–40.

Perdue, Theda. "Cherokee Women and the Trail of Tears." *Journal of Women's History* 1, no. 1 (1989): 14–30.

———. "Rising from the Ashes: The Cherokee Phoenix as an Ethnohistorical Source." *Ethnohistory* 24, no. 3 (1977): 207–18.

Praetzellis, Adrian, and Mary Praetzellis, eds. "Archaeologists as Storytellers." Special issue, *Historical Archaeology* 32, no. 1 (1998).

Rothstein, Frances. "The Class Basis of Patron-Client Relations." *Latin American Perspectives* 6, no. 2 (1979): 25–35.

Saunt, Claudio, Barbara Krauthamer, Tiya Miles, Celia Naylor, and Circe Sturm. "Rethinking Race and Culture in the American South." *Ethnohistory* 53, no. 1 (2006): 399–405.

Scott, James. "Patron-Client Politics and Political Change in Southeast Asia." *American Political Science Review* 66, no. 1 (1972): 91–113.

Stein, Howard. "A Note on Patron-Client Theory." *Ethos* 12, no. 1 (1984): 30–36.

Tronchetti, Carlo, and Peter van Dommelen. "Entangled Objects and Hybrid Practices: Colonial Contacts and Elite Connections at Monte Prama, Sardinia." *Journal of Mediterranean Archaeology* 18, no. 2 (2005): 183–208.

Williams, W. G. "Memoir Relative to the Cherokee Nation within the Limits of N. Carolina and Its Immediate Vicinity." February 8, 1838, letter to Colonel T. T. Hubert, United States Topographical Engineers, Topographical Bureau, Washington. *Journal of Cherokee Studies* 4, no. 4 (1979): 202–10.

Witthoft, John. "Cherokee Indian Use of Potherbs." *Journal of Cherokee Studies* 2, no. 2 (1977): 250–55.

Yarbrough, Fay. "Legislating Women's Sexuality: Cherokee Marriage Laws in the Nineteenth Century." *Journal of Social History* 38, no. 2 (2004): 385–406.

Theses and Dissertations

Baden, William. "A Dynamic Model of Stability and Change in Mississippian Agricultural Systems." PhD diss., University of Tennessee, 1987.

Cuthrell, Rob. "Mid-19th Century Cherokee Foodways and Identity in Western North Carolina." MA thesis, University of North Carolina, Chapel Hill, 2005.

Egloff, Brian. "An Analysis of Ceramics from Historic Cherokee Towns." MA thesis, University of North Carolina, Chapel Hill, 1967.

Fogelson, Raymond. "The Cherokee Ballgame: A Study in Southeastern Ethnology." PhD diss., University of Pennsylvania, 1962.

Frizzell, George. "Legal Status of the Eastern Band of Cherokee Indians." MA thesis, Western Carolina University, 1981.

Greene, Lance. "A Struggle for Cherokee Community: Excavating Identity in Post-Removal North Carolina." PhD diss., University of North Carolina, Chapel Hill, 2009.

Jurgelski, William. "A New Plow in Old Ground: Cherokees, Whites, and Land in Western North Carolina, 1819–1829." PhD diss., University of Georgia, Athens, 2004.

Lewis, John. "Becoming Appalachia: The Emergence of an American Subculture, 1840–1860." PhD diss., University of Kentucky, 2000.

McKelway, Henry. "Slave and Master in the Upland South: Archaeological Investigations at the Mabry Site." PhD diss., University of Tennessee, 1994.

Owl, Henry. "The Eastern Band of Cherokees before and after Removal." MA thesis, University of North Carolina, Chapel Hill, 1929.

Persico, Victor. "Cherokee Social Structure in the Early Nineteenth Century." MA thesis, University of Georgia, Athens, 1974.

Riggs, Brett. "Removal Period Cherokee Households in Southwestern North Carolina: Material Perspectives on Ethnicity and Cultural Differentiation." PhD diss., University of Tennessee, Knoxville, 1999.

Russell, Mattie. "William Holland Thomas, White Chief of the North Carolina Cherokees." PhD diss., Duke University, 1956.

Yarbrough, Fay. "'Those Disgracefull and Unnatural Matches': Interracial Sex and Cherokee Society in the Nineteenth Century." PhD diss., Emory University, 2003.

Index